Better Homes and Gardens®

Sewing
for Your
Home

Contents

BETTER HOMES AND GARDENS BOOKS

Editorial Director: Don Dooley
Managing Editor: Malcolm E. Robinson   Art Director: John Berg
Asst. Managing Editor: Lawrence D. Clayton   Asst. Art Director: Randall Yontz
Senior Editor: Marie Schulz
Designers: Tonya Rodriguez, Harijs Priekulis

Introduction

Today, sewing is more than a hobby; it's a practical
and easy way to save money and perk up your home's
decor. With minimal sewing skill, you can make a few
accent pillows, recycle an old chair with a new
slipcover, or change the decor of an entire room.
And, you will be able to match your needs exactly,
because *you* choose the fabric in the color, texture,
and style you want.

Sewing for Your Home covers all areas of home
sewing. If you're a beginning seamstress, start with
one of the more simple projects: cafe curtains, shower
curtains, throw-style bedspreads, knife-edge pillows,
wall hangings, table linens, and sun mats. Try something
a little more challenging—lined draperies, a fitted
bedspread, or slipcovers—if you're experienced
at home sewing.

And, if you have lots of spare time, and enjoy
detailed work, make a traditional pieced quilt;
or if your time is limited, machine-sew a colorful
comforter in a couple of hours.

Whatever your level of sewing knowledge, you'll
find projects you can enjoy in *Sewing for Your Home.*

You really can't lose when you sew for your home.
With careful planning and selection of fabrics,
you'll get the results that you desire—
and at a price that won't strain your budget.

We are indebted to Joy Gerard, noted sewing
authority, who wrote this book and to Mary Roby who
produced the illustrations.

If you look closely, you'll find that the elegant room pictured
at the left owes much of its charm to the home sewing
projects that are included—a stunning wall hanging, table cover,
decorative pillows, and snow-white sheer draperies.

Chapter 1

Colors and Fabrics

Of all the creative projects you can explore, what is more rewarding than sewing for your home. Each project you make decorates your home with items that you want. Just think of the array of items you can make—pillows and slipcovers, bedspreads and quilts, window shades and draperies, and many more, in every imaginable style. Make them with your total decorating scheme in mind and you'll enhance the attractiveness and function of your home.

There's a wide range of fabrics to work with— smooth or textured, solid colors or patterned, in every color of the rainbow. This is your opportunity to inject individual preferences into every room in your home.

Also, there's the practical aspect. Sewing for your home not only allows you the freedom to select and create the items you want, but it also enables you to stretch your home furnishings budget to the utmost. A vast number of home furnishings fabrics are available now, as well as the ever-increasing supply of fashion fabrics and designer bed sheets in every price range. You can make curtains, a tablecloth, or window shades just by using the fabric of your choice, a little sewing know-how, and your imagination.

If you're a beginner, start by making a decorative pillow or a simple cafe curtain, then advance to more difficult projects as you develop the necessary confidence and sewing skills. Sewing is a wonderful way to add beauty to your home.

In the room at the left, a host of sewing possibilities have been explored in order to achieve a total decorating scheme. Plaid roller shades and knife-edge pillows coordinate with the contemporary chairs and with the earthtone draperies and table cover.

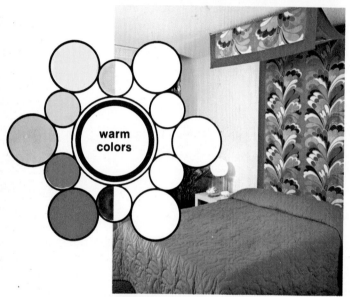

Color Basics

Color is the most vital element in home decorating. When used well, it can be the magic key that unlocks the treasure chest of exciting decorating plans. Now that you've decided to sew for your home, one of the first things you should learn is how to use color wisely. For example, you may decide to feature a delicate pastel tint in a guest bedroom. But in a family room that receives more than normal wear, select a bold color or a deep shade of durable, soil-resistant fabric.

First, you need to establish the needs of the area you wish to redecorate; do you want the room to look vibrant or serene, formal or casual, busy or simple? Next, become familiar with color terminology and its use. Remember that color can work magic in any room. Light colors will make a small room appear larger, while deeper shades will make a large, high-ceilinged room seem warm and friendly. Colors that get tiresome in rooms where you spend a lot of time will work well in rooms that you use only for short periods.

Color Terminology

Understanding these terms will help you to use color effectively.

Primary colors occur naturally and cannot be produced by combining other colors. They are red, blue, and yellow. These colors are mixed to form all other colors.

Secondary colors are made by mixing equal parts of any two primary colors. There are three secondary colors: green, made by mixing yellow and blue; orange, made by mixing red and yellow; and violet, made by mixing red with blue.

Tertiary colors are those colors made by mixing equal parts of adjacent primary and secondary colors. If you mix blue and green in equal parts you will get blue green. There are six tertiary colors: blue green, blue violet, red violet, red orange, yellow orange, and yellow green.

The neutral color is gray. It is made by combining the primaries. Equal parts of red, blue, and yellow make a medium value gray. White is added to lighten and black to darken gray.

Color Vocabulary

This is a universal language used to identify other color qualities and make the world of color easier to understand.

Hue is another word for the name of a color —such as yellow, orange, or purple.

Value is the lightness or darkness of a color. If you add a lot of white to a color, you get a *tint* of the color; a lot of black added to a color results in a *shade*.

Intensity is how bright or dull a color appears. A color is dulled by adding gray; as a result, the less gray you add, the brighter the color will be.

Warm or cool is the psychological feeling conveyed by colors. All the colors around you are either warm or cool. One-half of the color wheel is considered warm (the reds, oranges, and yellows). These colors are vibrant, reflecting sun and fire. The other half of the wheel is considered cool (the blues, greens, and violets). These reflect other colors in nature—sky, ice, water, and night. These qualities are very important when planning a color scheme, or in creating a particular feeling in your room.

A room with a northern or eastern exposure will not get a great deal of sunlight, which results in an impression of coolness. To overcome this and create a warm room, choose from the warm range of colors for the main colors. Rooms with southern and western exposures are sunny and bright. If you feel this exposure overpowers your room, counteract it with cool colors, which will soften its overall effect. But do not mute the brightness completely. Add small accents of warm colors.

Use these color tips to achieve the effect you want in a room. Brighter colors on the walls cause a room to appear smaller because the colors seem to advance. A tint can make a room appear to grow in size. If your ceiling is low, a tint will create an open effect.

Use contrast to achieve your decorating goals. Colors are always affected by their neighboring colors. If you wish to highlight a design feature of a room or a particular piece of furniture, use strong contrasting colors. To draw attention away from a badly shaped room, you must keep your background colors light and dulled. Add splashes of color with your accessories. The walls will seem to fade into the background, creating the illusion you want.

mono-chromatic scheme

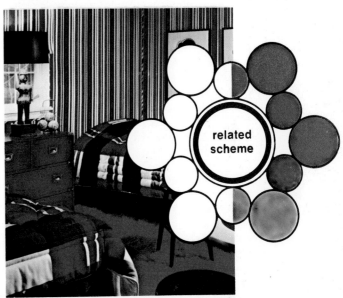

related scheme

contrasting scheme

Planning a Color Scheme

When planning a color scheme or assembling colors to achieve the look you desire, select dominant and accenting hues for a particular area. With all the colors available, this seems like quite a job. However, with a few basic guides anyone can develop exciting, soothing, vibrant, or restful color schemes. Selecting colors is not a mysterious business; all you have to do is to learn how to see color and understand a few key methods of combining colors. With this knowledge you can take any room—oblong, square, L-shaped, with large windows, small windows, high ceilings, low ceilings, much sunlight, little sunlight—and design and sew projects to create a decorating effect that will enhance the beauty of your home.

Monochromatic describes a color scheme planned around one color, usually containing several values and intensities. This scheme is restful and creates a pleasant background. Neutrals are added here for a little contrast; black, white, brown, or beige will help to add another dimension but will not interfere with the scheme. Accessories and accents are important in heightening the overall effect of a monochromatic room, but they should not interfere with the subtle tones. Monochromatic color schemes are easy to achieve and are easy to live with.

Analogous or related is the term used to identify a color scheme using neighboring colors on the color wheel such as yellow, yellow orange, and orange. This type of color scheme always includes at least one primary color in a three-color scheme, and two in a four-color scheme. Since these colors have something in common, the resulting effect is an interesting combination of blends and soft contrasts, which can be heightened by varying the values and intensities. This is a good scheme for the person who likes to change the look of a room frequently.

With sewing for the home, you can simply change the look of any room by making curtains or draperies in a brighter shade, by adding pillows, by appliqueing a few items, or simply by giving a new look to a favorite chair or sofa with a slipcover. Because of this, a related color scheme is an easy type to work with.

Complementary or contrasting colors are those directly opposite on the color wheel, such as violet and yellow or blue and orange, including all their tints and shades. One will always be cool, the other warm. This type of scheme is stronger and more vibrant than the others because of the nature of opposites. When using complementary colors, you create more division in the room, highlighting more of its features. If you wish to accent individual areas and furnishings in a room, choose a complementary scheme. These schemes result in a dramatic effect and will give any room a personality of its own.

Triad color schemes are developed by combining three hues that are equally spaced around the color wheel. Two examples of triad color schemes are red, yellow, and blue, and yellow green, blue violet, and red orange. Although these sound like rather violent schemes, they are quite pleasant when the values and intensities are varied.

To begin your plan, select the dominant color for the room. Remember that unequal areas of color are more interesting than equal areas. Plan to use your dominant color for a major element of the room—walls or floors. If your dominant color is to be a strong or intense color, you may wish to use a tint or shade for other large areas in the room.

Planning a total color scheme will be easier if you select a fabric with a pleasing pattern and color assortment and use it as the basis for the room. This simplifies your choices by limiting the scheme to the colors in the fabric design. It also allows you to see how the colors will work together in your room. Use the fabric for an important part of the room—draperies, slipcovers, or bedspread—and pick up the other colors in the design for the walls, floor coverings, and decorative accessories. The result will be an attractive, well-coordinated room.

You may wish to make some changes in a room without changing the entire color scheme. In such cases, start by evaluating the colors that will remain. For instance, if you plan to sew new draperies for a room with a monochromatic scheme in shades of blue and you wish to achieve an entirely new look, choose a fabric with bold splashes of red and white for the draperies. Add matching red and white accents throughout the room. This will enable you not only to brighten the room, but to bring a warm tone into a previously cool-hued room. The result is a completely new look with only a few simple changes.

The color wheel spins to give you a wonderful array of decorating fabrics just waiting to be sewn into a million-and-one exciting and useful furnishings. When you sew for your home, you have the opportunity of making it more expressive of your personality and your tastes.

In the color wheel above, you can see colors with their complements and their related colors, how each looks with another, and which colors can be mixed in order to make new ones. The color wheel above, surrounded by an assortment of fabric swatches, could well be the starting point in planning a room's decorating scheme. It's easy to learn the basic color facts; and once you have learned them, you can apply them to decorating your own home and to selecting the best fabrics for your home sewing projects.

And remember that color has no price tag. It costs no more to have vibrant and stimulating shades than it does to have dull and dreary ones.

Fabrics, Fibers, and Finishes

As color provides the general mood in a room, fabrics introduce the texture and pattern. When selecting fabrics, consider appearance and ease of maintenance.

Weight and Texture

Lightweight fabrics are supple and shapable, so use them in projects such as curtains, pillows, quilts, and dust ruffles.

Medium-weight fabrics are firmer and more durable; use them for draperies, slipcovers, bedspreads, and window shades.

Heavyweight fabrics are strong, durable, and possess a great deal of body. Use them for slipcovers and upholstery.

Also consider surface characteristics or **texture** of the fabric. Texture is created by the weave and by the type of yarns used. Simple weaves result in smooth fabrics; more intricate weaves produce more surface texture. The tighter the weave, the more durable a fabric will be. In selecting fabrics for draperies, look at the weave aesthetically.

Fiber Content

The fiber content of the fabric you choose is important because it affects the wear and care of the finished item.

Acetate, a man-made fiber, is soft to the touch and drapes well, giving an elegant look. Draperies and curtains are often made from acetate fabrics or blends. It's best to dry clean acetate fabrics.

Acrylic is a man-made fiber with qualities similar to wool—soft, sometimes fluffy, warm, and lightweight. Acrylic fabrics are strong and resistant to wrinkles, sunlight, fire, and chemicals. They are often used in drapery, slipcover, and bedspread fabrics.

Cotton, the most widely used of the natural fibers, drapes fairly well, takes dye well, and can be washed or dry-cleaned.

Glass fibers are fire resistant, flexible, and strong. Available in many colors, they are washable and are best suited for draperies.

Linen, a natural fiber, has long been a favorite in decorator fabrics. It drapes well and

The sampler of fabrics shown here is only a random offering of the many fine materials that are available to the homemaker. Not too long ago, one might have had to sacrifice functional aspects for beauty or vice versa. Now, due to modern manufacturing processes, fabrics can be beautiful and still have the practical qualities such as durability, cleanability, and colorfastness.

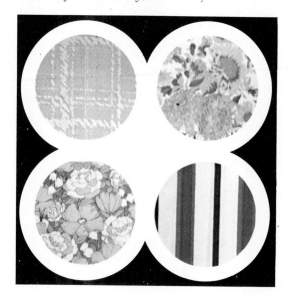

has an interesting surface texture, but it must be treated with special finishes to prevent wrinkles and retard soil.

Nylon, one of the oldest man-made fibers, has found wide use in decorating because of its strength and its easy-care qualities. It washes easily and requires little or no ironing. It is favored for curtains, draperies, bedspreads, comforters, and other items.

Polyester is one of the highest quality synthetic fabrics. It is durable, resists fading, has high crease retention, is machine washable and wrinkle resistant. It is used for curtains, draperies, bedspreads, quilts, and as fiber filling in quilts and comforters.

Rayon is the most widely used synthetic fiber. Its soft, drapable quality makes it ideal for curtains and draperies. It is also used for slipcovers, bedspreads, and pillow covers. Rayon is strong, fairly resistant to fading, and can be washed or dry-cleaned.

Silk, a natural protein fiber, is naturally lustrous and drapes beautifully. Silk fibers are easily damaged by the sun, so silk must be lined when it is used for draperies.

Vinyl, a plastic derivative, is extremely durable and resists abrasion. Use it for upholstery, shower curtains, and covers for pillows and outdoor furniture.

Wool, a natural protein fiber, drapes well, resists wrinkles, and is very soft and warm. Wool is often combined with other natural and synthetic fibers for home decorating fabrics. Wool and wool blends are used for slipcovers, cushion covers, and comforters.

Special Finishes

When you are purchasing fabrics for home furnishing, be sure to ask about finishes.

Colorfast fabrics are able to retain color without noticeable change.

Crease-resistant finishes help fabrics to resist and shed wrinkles. They also help the fabric to drape nicely.

Fire-retardant or fire-resistant fabrics have the ability to resist fire after being chemically treated. This does not mean the fabric is fireproof.

Permanent-press fabrics resist wrinkles and retain their shape.

Soil release finishes are used on permanent-press fabrics to ease the removal of soil and to provide some resistance to soil.

Stain-resistant fabrics are chemically treated to eliminate spots and stains.

Water repellent fabrics have the ability to resist the penetration of water.

Fabrics that you might use for sewing for your home can begin with sheer, filmy fabrics that you would use for ruffled, glass, or casement curtains, or ruffled bed canopies; they range to *firmly woven and/or heavyweight fabrics for draperies, slipcovers, bedspreads, bolsters, and pillows. With such a wide selection, you'll have no trouble finding the right fabric.*

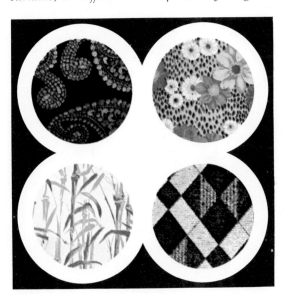
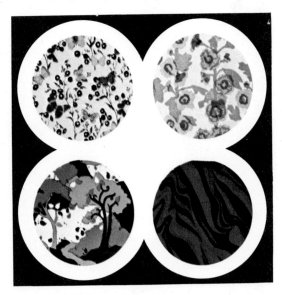

Home Decorating Fabrics

These are many and varied. The following list will help you choose the right fabric for your next project.

Brocade is a jacquard-weave fabric that has an allover interwoven design. The intricate weaving produces an embossed or embroidered effect. Woven from a number of different fibers, brocade varies in weight, price, and quality. Its primary use is for draperies and upholstery.

Burlap is a plain-weave fabric made from hemp, jute, or cotton. Finished burlap often is used to make durable curtains, wall hangings, and dividers.

Calico is a lightweight cotton fabric printed with a small allover design, and is used for curtains, bedspreads, and quilts.

Casement cloth is a general term applied to lightweight, sheer, or semi-sheer fabrics used for curtains and for screening purposes.

Chintz is a glazed, plain-weave cotton fabric usually printed with bright colors in gay patterns. It is used most often for slipcovers, draperies, and bedspreads.

Corduroy is a durable, cut-pile fabric usually made from cotton or synthetic fibers. The pile forms ribs that can be either wide or narrow. It is used most often for bedspreads, slipcovers, and cushion covers.

Crash refers to a rugged, coarsely woven, durable fabric. Cotton and linen blends are used for towels; linen and jute for curtains.

Damask is a jacquard-weave fabric with a reversible design. Made from a variety of fibers, it can be inexpensive or costly. The quality depends on the construction; tightly woven, small designs are usually strong and long wearing. Damask is used for table linens, draperies, and bedspreads.

Denim is a sturdy cotton fabric with a firm twill weave. The lengthwise yarns are colored, while crosswise yarns are white. Denim is used for slipcovers and curtains.

Double-knit fabrics are knitted on special machines that give the fabric the ability to give or stretch. Special weights are made for slipcovers and cushion covers.

Duck is an extremely durable, closely woven fabric, usually made from cotton. Often used for slipcovers and outdoor furniture.

Felt is a nonwoven fabric made by matting fibers together. Usually made from wool or combinations of wool and cotton or rayon.

Gingham is a firmly woven, light- to medium-weight fabric with woven checks or plaids. It is used for curtains and quilts.

Fabrics today are available in a wide range of colors, patterns, textures, weaves, and weights. Patterns can be simple sprigs of garden flowers scattered on a plain background or grandiose artwork reproduced on textiles in threads that resemble fine, spun gold. It's up to you to decide what type of fabrics suit your furnishings and your lifestyle.

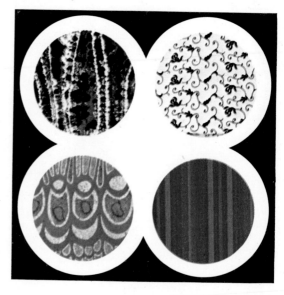

Homespun refers to a plain-weave fabric having a tweedy appearance, which results from coarse, uneven yarns. It is used for slipcovers, curtains, and draperies.

Hopsacking is a loosely woven fabric often used for draperies in informal settings. It usually is made from coarse cotton or linen in an open basket weave.

Marquisette is a sheer fabric with an open-mesh construction made from cotton, silk, or synthetic fibers; it is used for curtains.

Monk's cloth is a loosely woven, heavy cotton fabric. It is used primarily for draperies and couch throws.

Muslin is a plain-weave cotton fabric in weights from sheer to coarse. It can be unbleached, bleached, dyed, or printed. Fine grades are used for bed linens and curtains.

Ninon is a sheer, filmy fabric used for curtains. It usually is made of synthetic fibers.

Percale is a fine, lightweight, plain-weave fabric made from cotton or synthetic fibers. Made in several weights, it can be printed or plain. It is used for bed linens, bedspreads, table linens, curtains, and quilts.

Sailcloth is a strong, firmly woven fabric usually made from cotton, linen, or jute. It is a plain-weave fabric and is used for slipcovers, draperies, and cushion covers.

Satin is a smooth, lustrous fabric. Antique satin is woven with a crosswise slub yarn, which produces ridges or slubs on the surface. Satin is woven from silk, acetate, or a number of fiber blends. It is used for draperies, slipcovers, bedspreads, bed linens, pillows, and bolsters.

Scrim is a coarse, lightweight fabric with an open weave. It usually comes in white, cream, or ecru and is used for curtains.

Ticking is a term that applies to many tightly woven cotton fabrics. The familiar striped ticking was used originally as a featherproof covering for pillows and mattresses. Today, it is a popular choice used for slipcovers, bedspreads, draperies, and curtains as well as window shades.

Velour is a smooth, soft, closely woven fabric made from cotton, wool, or synthetics. It is heavier than velvet and often is used for draperies and upholstery.

Velvet can be made from cotton, silk, rayon, or synthetic fibers. It has a short, soft, thick, cut-pile surface. Heavy velvets are used for draperies and pillow covers.

Velveteen is a strong, durable cotton fabric with a short, cut-pile surface. It is used for draperies, bedspreads, cushion covers, and decorative pillow covers.

Take a good look at all the fabric samples shown on these pages and the suggestions on what weaves and weights are best for your home sewing projects; then start shopping for fabric.

You can use denim, gingham, sailcloth, striped mattress ticking, or corduroy with a flair and achieve dramatic results as if you had chosen velvet, damask, or fine handblocked linen.

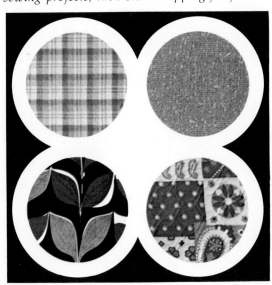

Chapter 2

Start with Sewing Basics

All you need to create imaginative fashions for your home is a place to work, the basic equipment, and an acquaintance with the fundamental sewing skills.

First, find a special spot for your sewing nook— an area near a window is best. Stake your claim in a bedroom alcove, or a corner of the den or family room— any place with enough room to work will do. When planning, remember to allow enough space for laying out patterns, opening your machine, and pressing.

Next, consider the equipment you'll need. Shears, scissors, pins, needles, thread, measuring tools, chalk, and an iron and ironing board are essential for most sewing. If you plan on doing a lot of sewing, you'll want a sewing machine and attachments. For comfortable sewing, your worktable should be the proper height—about 30 inches.

Good lighting is important for good sewing, too. Be sure that there is enough artificial light for sewing at night and on dark or rainy days. You can use a high-intensity lamp for brighter light on detail work.

Cabinets, shelves, and plastic or cardboard storage boxes will keep patterns, projects, and bolts of fabric clean and out of the way until you need them. And, you'll be better organized the next time you sew—no more hunting for "lost" patterns or projects.

Lively colors spark this special sewing center. Adjustable shelves and sliding door cabinets provide plenty of storage space for bolts of fabric, sewing projects, and other equipment. The wide sewing table folds up into the wall when not in use.

Basic Equipment for Sewing

With just a few pieces of basic equipment, you can start sewing for your home. Besides the all-important sewing machine, shears and scissors, pins, needles, thread, measuring equipment, tailor's chalk or chalk pencils, and an iron and ironing board are essential.

Hand Equipment

While it's easy to get by with inexpensive equipment, the wise seamstress invests in quality merchandise.

Shears and scissors: Good cutting tools are essential to any sewing project. For cutting

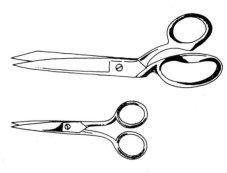

fabrics, buy a pair of bent-handled shears, seven or eight inches long. With this type of shears, the blades will rest flat on the work surface so that you won't have to lift the fabric while you are cutting.

For cutting threads, clipping seams, slashing, and trimming, buy a pair of five- or six-inch scissors—you'll find that the type with sharp points is the best and easiest to handle.

Nonrusting pins: The two most common types are straight pins, which are used for most sewing projects, and T-pins, commonly used when making slipcovers. As a rule, also have a pincushion on hand. Pincushions come in many different sizes and shapes.

Hand sewing needles: These come in sizes 1 (very coarse) to 10 (very fine). The most commonly used needle—sharp—is medium length. 'Betweens' are shorter and are used for fine stitching on heavier fabrics. Embroidery needles are like sharps but have a larger eye, making them easier to thread. In fact, many people prefer these embroidery needles for general sewing.

Thread: There are two basic rules to follow when selecting thread. **(1)** Select thread to match the weight of the fabric. For light- and medium-weight fabrics, use mercerized cotton thread or an all-purpose synthetic thread. On heavier fabrics, use a heavy-duty thread. **(2)** For the best possible color match, select a thread that is one shade darker than the fabric you are using.

Measuring equipment: You'll need these items for any project you choose: A metal tape measure or a carpenter's folding ruler is the best for taking measurements for curtains and draperies. You'll need a flexible tape measure for slipcovers and pillows in order to measure around curves and odd shapes. Be sure to use one that is strong and will not stretch. A yardstick is best for

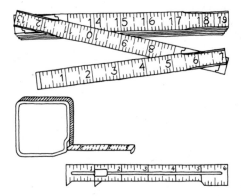

checking grain lines and for marking long straight lines. A seam gauge or hem gauge (a 6-inch metal ruler with an adjustable slide) is particularly convenient for measuring hems because you can be assured of uniformity. If you plan to sew draperies for tall windows, you'll also need a stepladder.

Iron and ironing board: In both cases, good equipment is a must. For a professional-looking, speedy job, use a steam iron. Also purchase an ironing board that adjusts to various heights. This makes it possible for you to work at the height that is best for you.

Tailor's chalk or chalk pencils: The tailor's chalk rubs off easily, so you can use it on the right side of the fabric. Chalk pencils are more accurate because you can sharpen them to a fine point.

Sewing Machine

The two major types are the straight stitch and the zigzag. The sewing machine is your most important piece of sewing equipment. Maintaining it can be costly if you don't care for it properly. However, regular maintenance can eliminate many service calls. Keep the machine free of lint and dust, and oil and lubricate it regularly. Remove the lint and fluff from exposed parts with a lint brush every time you sew. Clean around the feed dog, under the throat plate and side plate, and around the sewing hook or shuttle. (If your machine has a removable bobbin case, remove the bobbin before cleaning.)

Before purchasing a sewing machine, carefully analyze your sewing needs. Do you sew occasionally or often? Are your projects generally small, such as pillows, place mats, or napkins or do you plan to do big projects, such as draperies, slipcovers, shower curtains, or bedspreads? Do you have room for a console model that will do double duty as an occasional table, or must the machine be small and portable so that you can store it easily? Most machines come with a selection of basic attachments. You can add other more specialized attachments when you need them.

Acquaint yourself with the attachments that come with your sewing machine and practice using them before you start sewing for your home. All of them are time-savers. For instructions on attaching these aids to your machine, refer to the machine manual.

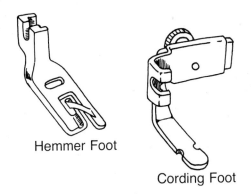

Hemmer Foot

Cording Foot

An **adjustable zipper** or **cording foot** makes it possible to stitch along a raised edge such as a zipper, welting, or cording.

A timesaving accessory for ruffles or any long edge along which you need a narrow hem, a **hemmer foot** allows you to turn and stitch a narrow hem without basting or pressing. You also can use the hemmer foot to make a French seam in sheer fabrics.

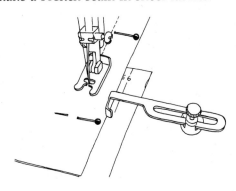

Attached to the bed of the sewing machine, the **seam guide** aids in sewing straight, even seams. It can be adjusted to various widths, depending on your requirements.

There are other attachments you can add that will be useful for your home decorating projects. Although these attachments are for specific projects and may have limited use, it is worth your time to learn to use them. Remember, in home sewing projects you are often working with large yardages. These attachments can help cut your sewing time.

Gathering foot. This automatically gathers or shirrs the fabric as you stitch.

Binder foot. Without the aid of pinning or basting the binding to the fabric, the foot attaches bias binding to an unfinished edge.

Roller foot. It controls fabrics that are hard to handle, such as delicate nylon, which tends to slide, or vinyl, which tends to stick to the bed of the machine.

Quilter attachment. The quilter not only guides the placement of the stitches, it also keeps the rows of stitches even.

Ruffler. This makes uniformly gathered ruffles on light- to medium-weight fabrics.

Machine needles. These are available in sizes 9 (fine) to 18 (coarse). Select needles to correspond with the weight of your fabric; the heavier the fabric, the coarser the needle. Sewing machines vary, so be sure to ask for needles according to the make and model number of your machine. Change your machine needle frequently because bent, rough, or dull needles will decrease your sewing efficiency. Special "ball point" needles are designed for sewing on knit fabrics. The rounded point pushes between threads and reduces the possibility of snagging the fabric.

Basic Sewing Techniques

A foundation of basic sewing knowledge is necessary to be successful in any sewing project, whether you are making a dress for yourself or cafe curtains for the kitchen. If you have had experience sewing clothing, you will find that many of the same techniques are used in sewing projects for your home. And, you will learn many new techniques as you go along.

Fabric Preparation

In all sewing for your home projects, from simple patchwork pillows to elegant, formal draperies, you must consider the grain lines—the direction of the threads in woven fabrics.

Threads that are parallel to the selvage form the *lengthwise grain* of a fabric. This is usually the most stable grain in a fabric because there is little give. The *crosswise grain* runs at right angles to the lengthwise grain. These threads run from selvage to selvage. There is usually more give in the crosswise grain. The *true bias* is the diagonal line formed by folding the lengthwise grain parallel to the crosswise grain. The greatest amount of give in any type of woven fabric is along the true bias.

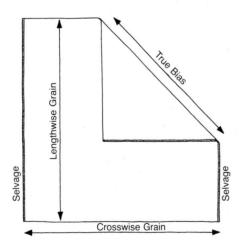

Fabrics often are pulled off-grain in the manufacturing process. If this has happened, you will need to prepare the fabric by straightening the grain. If you fail to do this, you won't get the best results when you sew.

First, straighten the fabric's ends. Make a small cut through the selvage near the ends of the fabric. Grasp one thread that runs across the fabric and pull it gently, allowing the fabric to gather on the thread. Cut along this pulled thread as far as you can. Pull the thread (or the one next to it) again, then cut. Repeat these two steps until you have cut through the other selvage.

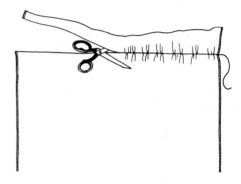

Next, determine the fabric's grain. To do this, place the fabric on a flat surface and fold it in the center with the selvages together. Pin the edges together along a straightened end. If the fabric lies flat when the selvages are held together, you can be sure that the grain is straight. If it does not lie flat, the fabric needs to be straightened.

To straighten the fabric, gently pull the fabric on the true bias, working down the full length of the fabric as you do so.

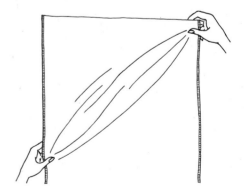

Some fabrics—chintz, polished cotton, and those treated with permanent-press finishes—cannot be straightened. Their permanent finish prevents them from stretching. To straighten the ends on these fabrics, square off the ends with a ruler before cutting.

Cutting Special Fabrics

These fabrics often require special care in cutting. Study the fabrics before cutting into them because most cutting errors cannot be corrected. Although you probably won't choose one of these for your first project, you will use some of them eventually.

Fabrics with a pile or nap have a surface texture that must be cut in one direction. Pile fabrics include velvet, corduroy, and some fake furs. Nap fabrics are suede cloth, flannelette, and fur fabrics. Textured fabrics such as brocade and satin also should be cut with nap running in one direction.

To find out which way the nap runs, brush your hand along the surface of the fabric. If it ruffles up like an animal's fur, then the nap runs in that direction.

Double-knit fabrics also should be cut like nap fabrics, with all of the pieces cut in the same direction.

One-directional designs (below) may be prints, plaids, stripes, or checks and must be cut with all the pieces in one direction, too. Always examine a printed fabric carefully to see how the motif is repeated. If there is a definite pattern, such as a sprig of flowers with the design all pointing the same way, cut as you would a nap fabric.

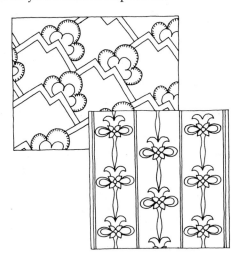

Prints with an allover effect, those with no specific motif, are cut in the same way as a plain fabric. The same rule applies to prints that have a definite design, but with the motif repeated in either direction. The print that is illustrated below (top left) is an all-over print.

Prints with a broken effect (above, bottom right) don't have a definite design. In cutting these fabrics, it isn't necessary to match the design exactly, but do cut it so that the design has continuity. Many contemporary and abstract designs are this type.

Plaids may be balanced (matching on both lengthwise and crosswise plaid) or one-directional. Cut the latter the same way as a one-directional print fabric.

When using fabrics that have a definite design repeat that must be matched, be sure to allow adequate fabric for matching. On projects such as curtains, draperies, and bedspreads, the designs must be matched horizontally, so allow one design repeat for each length of fabric that you will be using. Add this to your fabric measurements.

To measure the length of the design repeat, place a pin at a specific point in the pattern—a color change, the top of a flower, or the top of a pictorial design. Then, let your eye run down the fabric until that exact point is reached again and mark it with another pin. Measure the distance between the two pins to find the length of one repeat. For projects such as slipcovers and pillows, the placement of the design is also important, although you will not be matching the design at the seam lines. For slipcovers, allow enough fabric so that you can center a design on each pillow or seat cushion, as well as on the back sections of the chairs or sofa you are covering.

Hand Stitching

In all probability, you'll do most of the sewing for your home with a sewing machine, but there are almost always some details that are best done with hand stitching. Choose the size of needle and weight of thread according to the weight of the fabric you are using. Select the hand stitch that best fits your sewing needs.

Running Stitch. Use this simplest of all hand stitches for seams that receive less than a normal amount of strain. You also can use a running stitch for gathering, mending, and tucking, as well as for sewing together patchwork quilt pieces. Take several small stitches in succession, draw the thread through the fabric, and repeat the procedure.

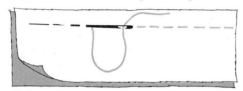

Backstitch. This is the strongest of the hand stitches. Bring the needle through the fabric and take a small backstitch, bringing the needle out ahead of the preceding stitch. Take another backstitch, putting the needle in at the end of the preceding stitch. (The stitches on the underside will be twice as long as those that are on the top.)

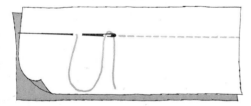

Even basting. You can make this stitch any length you want, depending on your needs. This is a temporary stitch and is easily removed. Use this stitch to hold drapery hems in place while you check the length, and wherever you want to check the fit of an item before sewing it permanently.

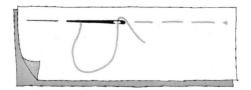

Overcasting. Use on raw edges to prevent raveling. Use deeper stitches on loosely woven fabrics. Make evenly spaced, slanted stitches over the edge, making stitches a uniform depth. Where seams are to be pressed open, overcast each allowance separately.

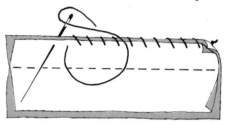

Slip stitch. Bring the needle through the fold of the hem and pick up one thread of the fabric at the same point. Make stitches about ½ inch apart and fairly loose. Use this stitch for hems and hand appliqueing.

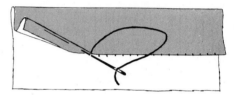

Catch stitch. Use this stitch to finish hems and on areas where the edges need to be held flat. Work from left to right, taking tiny stitches on the hem, and then on the article. Keep your stitches loose and even.

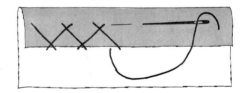

Hemming stitch. Anchor the thread to the underside of the hem edge. First, take a small stitch (one or two threads) in the fabric under the fold of the hem, then bring the needle up through the edge of the hem. Draw up the thread and repeat the operation.

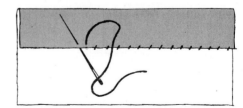

Machine Stitching

A sewing machine—whether it is an out-moded treadle, a dependable straight stitch, or the latest zigzag model—is your single most important aid to quick and easy stitching. Most of your sewing probably will be plain straight stitching, which you can do equally well on Grandma's treadle or a brand-new machine. Regardless of the type machine you have, you will need to understand stitch length, tension, and pressure. Your sewing machine manual will explain in detail exactly how to make these adjustments.

The basic stitch length is regulated according to the type of stitching you are doing and the weight of the fabric you are using.

The regulation stitch is the one you will use most often. Use 12 to 16 stitches per inch, depending on the weight of the fabric.

Machine basting is the longest stitch on your machine (six to eight stitches per inch). Use this for temporary stitching.

Ease stitching is used for easing in fullness, about 10 stitches per inch.

Reinforcement stitching is used for strengthening the stitching at points of strain.

The tension on the thread must be adjusted properly to produce a balanced stitch. A balanced stitch is one that looks exactly the same on both sides. To test your machine tension, place a row of stitches in a double layer of your fabric. Then, examine the stitches carefully and compare them to the illustrations below. The bottom row is correct.

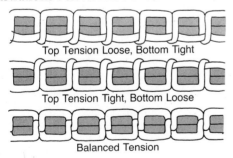

Top Tension Loose, Bottom Tight

Top Tension Tight, Bottom Loose

Balanced Tension

If stitches are unbalanced, adjust tension as instructed in your machine manual.

The pressure on the presser foot must be correctly adjusted to hold the fabric firmly in place while the machine is stitching. The amount of pressure required depends on the fabric's weight, texture, fibers, and finish. With properly adjusted pressure, two or more layers of fabric should move together.

Types of Seams

There are four basic seams—plain, French, flat-fell, and self-bound.

Plain. To ensure accurate widths use the seam guide on the throat plate or an attached seam guide.

French are best for sheer fabrics. Place the *wrong* sides together and stitch ¼ inch from the raw edges. Press the seam allowance to one side, then trim to ⅛ inch. Place the right sides together, folding along stitching line. Enclose the raw edges by stitching along the seam line.

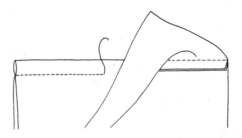

Or, use the narrow hemmer foot attachment. With the right sides together, ease the two raw edges into the scroll of the foot.

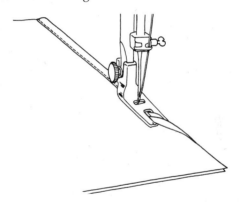

Flat-fell seams are preferred on heavier fabrics. Stitch a plain seam on right side and press to one side. Trim underseam allowance to ⅛ inch. Turn under raw edge of top seam allowance and topstitch near fold.

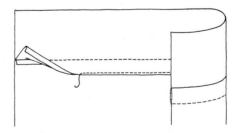

Self-bound seams are another way of encasing the raw edges. Make a plain seam and press it as stitched. Trim one seam allowance to ⅛ inch. Turn under the raw edge of the remaining seam allowance and pin to the seam along stitching line. Stitch close to the folded edge, encasing all raw edges.

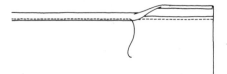

Slip basting is used to ensure a perfect match along the seam lines of plaids, stripes, and prints. With the fabric right side up, fold under one seam allowance and lap it over the right side of the adjoining seam allowance; match each plaid or stripe and pin. Slip needle into fold and out ⅜ inch to the left. Insert needle into lower layer. Take a ⅜-inch stitch, then take a stitch back into the fold and repeat alternating stitches in fold and below fold. Machine-stitch the seam on the wrong side, using the basting as a guide.

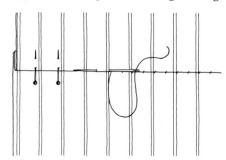

Bonding webs are made of a heat-sensitive, nonwoven material that will bond one layer of fabric to another when heat is applied. Using bonding webs is an easy way to finish hems or facings or to do applique. To bond a hem, cut the fusible web to the desired

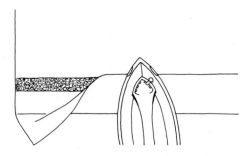

length and place it between the hem and the fabric. Then apply heat, following the package instructions. Bonding webs are available in a variety of weights; use the one that is suitable for your fabric.

Bias Binding

Learning to make bias binding is a valuable sewing technique to master because it has so many applications in sewing for your home. You will find that slipcovers, pillows, cushions, bolsters, and bedspreads all require bias binding if they are to have that truly professional custom appearance.

Cutting and joining bias strips. Remember that a true bias is the diagonal of a square. To determine this, fold the straight grain of the material parallel to the cross grain; the folded edge will be the true bias. Measure from the folded edge, and mark the cutting lines for the width of bias strip you need. Be accurate about locating the true bias; otherwise, the binding will not go around curves and corners smoothly.

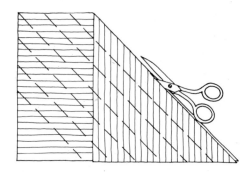

Join the bias strips by placing the right sides together and lapping the ends so that the strips form a right angle. Stitch on the straight grain; press the seams open.

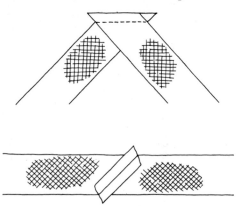

Continuous bias is the best method to use when you need several yards of bias strips. It will take 10 to 12 yards of bias to cover the cord for a slipcover of an average-size chair with a cushion. A sofa slipcover will require approximately 25 yards of bias.

To cut continuous bias strips, prepare a rectangle of fabric on the straight grain. Lay it on a flat surface, wrong side up, and mark the true bias on the wrong side, starting at the top left-hand corner. Measuring from this starting line, mark the width of the bias strips. Continue to measure and mark until you have marked sufficient length.

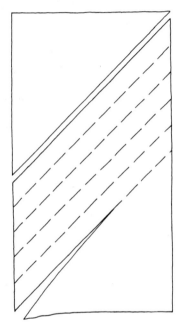

Next, cut off the excess fabric. Form a tube by bringing the lengthwise edges together, matching the lines. The first line extends above the others. Pin and stitch a ¼-inch seam. Press open the seam. Start cutting on the first line and continue cutting around the tube on the marked lines.

Make cording or welting by enclosing cord in bias strips. First, fold the bias strip around the cord, right side out, encasing it completely. Then, using an adjustable cording or zipper foot, stitch close to the cord, without crowding it. Stretch the bias slightly as you are stitching it over the cord.

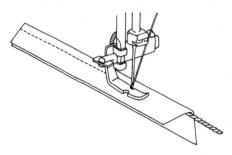

To insert cording in a seam, first pin the cording to the right side of one seam allowance, placing the cording's stitching along the seam line. Stitch, using a cording foot. Then pin the corded edge right side down, over the other seam allowance. Stitch between the first row of stitching and cord.

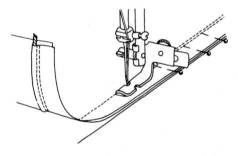

To fit cording around a square corner, pin cording to seam allowance. At corner, clip bias strip to, but not through, the stitching.

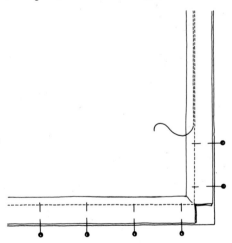

When cording a curved seam, you must fit the cording to the shape of the curve. To ensure a smooth fit around outside curves, as on round or oval cushions and pillows, pin the cording in place, stretching the seam allowance around the outside curve and easing the cord. For inside curves, stretch the cord and slightly ease the seam allowance. Pin the cording to the right side of one seam allowance. Clip the seam allowances where necessary to keep the seams lying flat. Using a cording foot, stitch along the seam line.

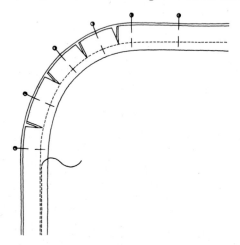

Next, pin over other seam allowance with right sides together. Carefully match seams at the curves. Stitch between cord and previous stitching, crowding foot against cord. To reduce the bulk in the seam, trim the seam allowances of the cording to ⅛ inch. Trim remaining seam allowances to ¼ inch.

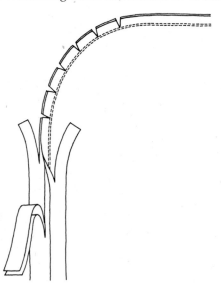

Binding raw edges—on place mats, wall hangings, quilts, bedspreads, and other items—is another function of bias strips. Cut strips from a matching fabric, or select a contrasting color for accent. Checked gingham or calico print bindings add charm to patchwork or appliqued quilts.

Bias strips easily conform to circles and curves. However, you must give special attention to square corners. With right sides together, stitch the binding along one edge to the corner. Raise the needle from the fabric, but do not cut the thread. Fold the binding at a right angle to the stitching line, forming a diagonal fold at the corner.

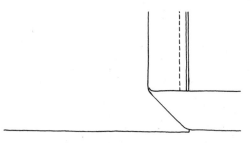

Now, fold the binding back on itself, forming a small triangular pleat. Lower the needle into the binding at the corner, and stitch the binding to the next edge.

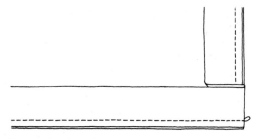

Press the binding over the stitching line. (The binding will extend beyond the edge of the fabric.) Form a miter at the corner, then pin in place. Fold the binding to the underside and miter the corner. Turn under the raw edge and hem to the stitching line. Slipstitch the mitered corners.

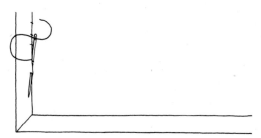

Special Finishes

To add that decorative touch to your project, use a braid or ribbon edging, or gathers or ruffles.

Bands of braid or ribbon often are used to trim various household items. You can attach rows of decorative braid or ribbon to ready-made curtains, draperies, towels, sheets, place mats, slipcovers, and pillow covers to give them a custom-made look.

Attach the trim along the edge or, if you wish, several inches in from the edge. With chalk, mark the exact position of the trim. Pin it in place along one side, then edgestitch the inner edge by machine or by hand. Fold the band back on itself, then diagonally to the side, making a right angle in line with the corner. Press along the fold. Open the fold and stitch on the diagonal crease, stitching through both trim and fabric.

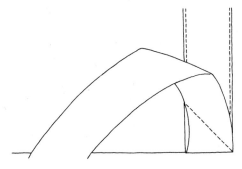

Backstitch to prevent the ends from working out. If the trim is bulky, cut out excess close to the corner. Press miter and stitch along next inner edge. After all corners and inner edges are completed, stitch the outer edge in a continuous motion.

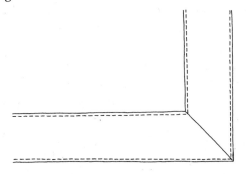

Gathers are formed by drawing fabric up on a line of stitching. Length of stitch used depends on weight of fabric—the heavier the fabric, the longer the stitch needed. A heavy-duty bobbin thread makes it easier to pull up gathers without breaking the thread. Also, loosening top tension will make gathering easier. Stitch one row on the seam line and a second row ¼ inch away, but still within the seam allowance. To form the gathers, pin the piece to be gathered to the corresponding edge, with the right sides together. Pin at both ends and the center. Draw up the bobbin thread until the gathered edge fits the straight edge. Adjust the gathers evenly, and then pin in place. Stitch on the seam line, with the gathered side up.

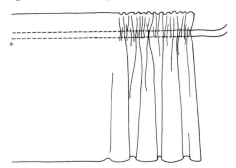

Ruffles add a soft, feminine touch to curtains and bedspreads. You can either gather them as illustrated above or make them with a ruffler. Ruffles are usually double or triple fullness. The weight of the fabric and the width of the ruffle will determine the amount of the fullness needed. Wide ruffles require more fullness than narrow ruffles.

Cut the fabric for the ruffle two to three times the length of the finished ruffle. Seam the sections together, if necessary, and press the seams open. Finish the outer edge either by hemming by hand or with a hemmer foot attachment. In the latter case, adjust the ruffler attachment for the amount of fullness you desire. Test the fullness on a scrap of your fabric. Thread the fabric to be gathered into the ruffler by following the attachment instructions.

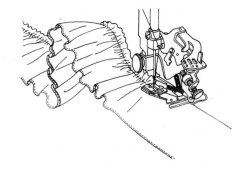

Chapter 3

Window Fashions– A Decorating Asset

With a little imagination and ingenuity, you can create exciting fashions for all your windows—even those odd-shaped 'problem' windows. Starting with draperies or curtains will give you the opportunity to dress up your home and practice your sewing skills. Most window fashions require only careful measuring and straight seams, so don't be overwhelmed by the physical size of most of these projects. And, while you're personalizing your home, you'll be saving dollars that can be used for other decorating projects.

If you are a novice at sewing, start with a simple-to-make item such as cafe curtains for your kitchen windows. Soon, you'll move on to more sophisticated projects, such as lined draperies, Austrian or Roman shades, cornices, and valances.

You need to consider several things when planning window fashions. First, decide what you want to do with the window. Do you want to frame a beautiful view or conceal a nonview? Will the window become the center of interest, or would you rather minimize its size? Determine what types of fabric and hardware will work best in each situation—and how they will add to your overall decorating plan. Above all, remember that the ideal window fashion should provide privacy and complement your furnishings.

Draperies, cafe curtains, and a valance all join together to give this living room bay window maximum versatility and decorative impact. Here, the use of a single pattern, tastefully balanced by solid colors on walls and carpet, gives the room a sense of unity.

Basic Information for Windows

Before you can sew new curtains or draperies for your home, consider the basics of window fashions: types of windows, the various treatments, rods and fixtures, and fabrics.

Window Types

Familiarize yourself with the windows in your home or apartment. You may find several different shapes and sizes if you live in a large house, but in an apartment every window possibly is the same type. Below are a few of the more common types used by architects and builders in houses and apartments.

Double-hung sash windows are the most common. Opened from either the top or bottom, some have two large panes, while on others, each half has several smaller panes.

French windows or doors can open inward or outward. Curtains and draperies may become tangled with the windows as they are opened or closed, so inward-opening windows or doors pose decorating problems.

Picture windows have one large fixed pane, framing a beautiful view. They are often combined with double-hung sash or casement windows for ventilation.

Casement windows open outward. Most are opened and closed by hand or crank.

Sliding glass doors and windows, which are set into tracks, open by sliding one in front of the other. They often come in pairs — one stationary pane and one sliding pane.

Bay windows (three or more windows set at angles to each other) can be combinations of sash windows, picture windows, casements, or louvered windows. Special rods and fixtures fit all shapes of bay windows.

Strip or ranch windows (wide windows set high in the wall) are most often found in ranch-style and contemporary houses. Sill- or apron-length curtains usually look best.

Louvered windows have horizontal panes that open outward to any desired angle. They are usually opened and closed with a crank.

In addition to knowing the type of window you are dealing with, you should also know the parts of the window. The casing is the part of the window that fits into the wall structure. It usually is covered by a wide molding. The sill is the narrow horizontal shelf at the bottom of the window. The part of the casing below the sill is called the apron. The sash supports the glass.

Identifying your basic window type will help you to select an attractive window fashion. These eight drawings show the most common *types. Your windows may be variations or combinations of these types. Each of your windows can be decorated attractively.*

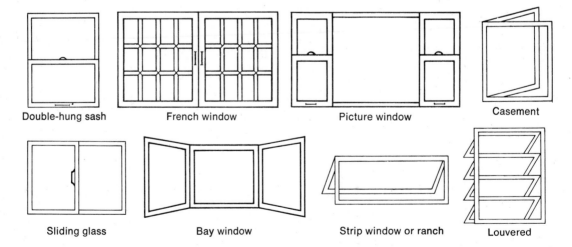

Double-hung sash   French window   Picture window   Casement

Sliding glass   Bay window   Strip window or ranch   Louvered

Window Fashions

Given a well-styled decorative treatment, a window can become one of the most eye-appealing features of your home. When you design and sew your own window fashions, let your imagination go — you have an almost unlimited selection of styles and fabrics from which to choose. As you start to plan your window fashion, consider the number, size, and placement of windows; the style of your furniture; the color scheme; and the mood of the room. Also keep your budget in mind.

Remember that curtains and draperies should never be skimpy. If your budget is limited, it is better to buy a bolt of inexpensive fabric rather than a few yards of costly fabric. For example, muslin cafe curtains with ample fullness will be more attractive than skimpy draperies made from elegant (and expensive) fabric.

Draperies offer a wide variety of possibilities and can be used with most types of windows. They can complement any room — from the most formal to the very casual. Opaque draw draperies of heavy fabric or lined draperies provide complete privacy when they are closed. Besides being decorative, these draperies also act as insulation from heat and cold. Panel draperies are for decoration only and cannot be drawn together. They are often combined with glass curtains.

Glass curtains are used primarily to diffuse light and to provide a measure of privacy during the daytime hours. Made from sheer fabrics, they hang directly in front of the glass and add elegance to any room.

Cafe curtains are straight curtains hung from rings that slide along a brass or wooden rod. True cafe curtains cover only the lower half of the window, allowing light to enter at the top of the window. Cafe curtains may have scalloped tops, looped tops, or pinch-pleated headings. They may be lined or unlined.

Ruffled tieback or priscilla curtains are gathered directly onto the curtain rod. They are usually short, just covering the apron, but they can also extend to the floor. They may meet at the center or they may cross over on the upper half of the window.

Cornices and valances are stationary trimmings across the top of the window. They often are used to tie two or more windows together as a unit. If hung high above the window frame, they can add height to windows. Use them to conceal the rods, fixtures, and window moldings.

Shades and shutters offer additional variety to window fashions. The feminine, graceful Austrian shade and the tailored Roman shade can also function as a total window treatment. Use plain roller shades if you coordinate them with your existing furnishings.

The most widely used types of window treatments are illustrated below. Use them as a guide to create decorative and functional treatments for your windows. The degree of privacy and light control will determine, in part, the style you select; leave the rest to your imagination.

Two-way traverse

One-way draw traverse

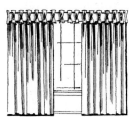
Draw draperies, valance

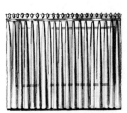
Shirred glass curtains

Double-hung traverse

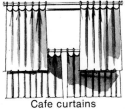
Cafe curtains

Decorative traverse, w/cafe

Ruffled tiebacks

Rods and Fixtures

Curtain and drapery hardware plays an important role in window dressing. It adds decorative value to a room and contributes greatly to the appearance of the curtains or draperies. To suit your needs, a wide variety of curtain and drapery hardware is available.

With traverse rods, you open or close draperies with a cord. Draperies are attached to slides on the inside of the rod. Hooks that are pinned, sewn, or slipped into the drapery heading fit into the slides. Pulling the cord causes the slides to move. Traverse rods usually are used with pleated draperies. These rods are designed for windows covered by draperies that are opened and closed frequently.

Traverse rods come in a variety of weights, styles, and price ranges. Most of the cords are located at the right side of the window, but you can hang the cord on the left side by following the manufacturer's instructions. Most traverse rods are center-opening, so the draperies will draw back evenly on both sides. However, there are also one-way rods that permit draperies to be pulled to one side. Double traverse rods are used where you want two pairs of draw draperies—one of sheer fabric that is hung next to the glass and one of heavier fabric that is used as over-draperies. Traverse rods are also available in combination with a curtain or valance rod. They can be mounted on the ceiling.

Cafe rods are designed to be seen. They come in either a beautiful shiny brass or wood finish that will last for years. The metal rods are adjustable; the wood ones are not. The rods may be plain or fluted, with finials that are fluted, rosette-style, or acorn design to dress up the brackets. As a rule, cafe rods are used for stationary curtains, although the curtains can be opened or closed easily. Some cafe rods are available with plain ends for installing inside casement windows or wherever decorative finials are not desirable.

In deciding on the rod length, be sure to allow for extension of the decorative end-pieces (the finials) beyond the window frame. Cafe rod brackets are mounted several inches in from the end of the rod. A complete range of fittings is available to allow mounting on any type of window.

Cafe rods are suited to hanging either pleated or straight panels.

Flat curtain rods have a multitude of uses. For stationary curtains or draperies these hidden rods are practical and economical. For heavy fabrics, use heavy-duty rods. Standard rods support only lightweight fabrics. Both weights are available as single or double rods, used for crisscross curtains or curtains-with-valance. Use flat curtain rods with glass curtains, ruffled priscillas and tie-backs, and shirred tiers.

Sash rods permit hanging lightweight curtain panels over doors or windows where the rod must be flat against the surface. Swinging extension rods, because they will swing clear, are ideal for French doors, inswinging casement windows, or narrow windows where there isn't space to draw the curtains back far enough to let in light.

Window-widener rods permit curtains to extend beyond the frame without mounting the rods on plaster walls.

Special rods have been designed to solve common window problems. Corner window rods permit smooth curtaining of both halves of twin corner windows—without having extra brackets getting in the way. Valance rods have a greater projection, allowing the valance to be hung over curtains. Canopy rods project a full eight inches to permit a canopy treatment over a window, door, or bed. All-curve curtain rods have the outward curve popular for certain window fashions. Spring-tension rods hold firmly where brackets cannot be used.

Installing hardware is an important step in beautifying your windows. Use plastic anchors when attaching hardware for lightweight draperies to plaster or wallboard. Drill a hole smaller than the screw and insert a plastic plug. Tap the plug into the wall and insert the screw. As the screw is driven into the wall, the plug expands and provides a firmer grip. Toggle bolts are pushed through a drilled hole, arms folded; when tightened, the arms open and hold bolt securely. An anchor screw—similar to a plug—will hold heavier draperies.

From top to bottom: **(1)** *flat rod,* **(2)** *double rod,* **(3)** *cafe rod,* **(4)** *sash rod,* **(5)** *spring-tension rod,* **(6)** *swinging extension rods,* **(7)** *center-draw traverse rod,* **(8)** *traverse-curtain rod,* **(9)** *double traverse rod, and* **(10)** *decorative traverse rod.*

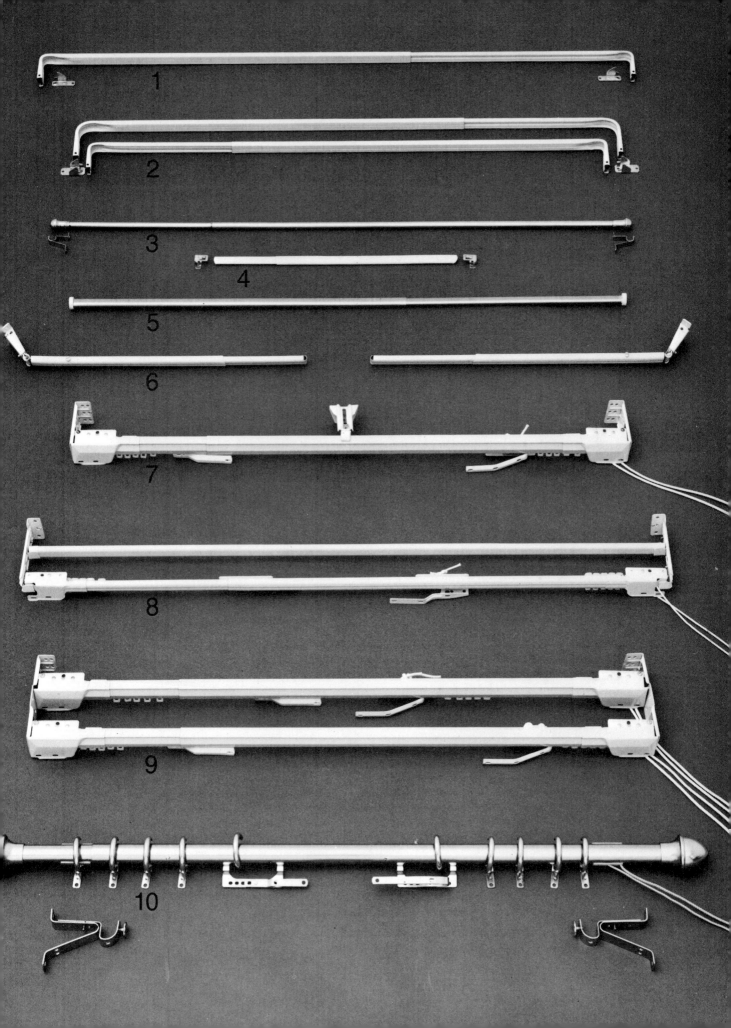

1

2

3

4

5

6

7

8

9

10

34

Fabrics Amplify the Mood

The combination of fabric and drapery or curtain style sets the mood of the room. The most formal floor-length draperies call for a formal fabric such as a silk brocade, cut velvet, or damask. The most casual curtains are made of unbleached muslin, burlap, or ticking. Between these two extremes lies a range of fabric choices that lets you create the exact mood you want—at a cost you can afford.

Color, texture, and design of your fabric should harmonize naturally with other features of the room. When using color on windows, remember: a strong color contrasting with the walls emphasizes the windows and makes the room appear smaller; a color matching the walls gives an unbroken effect, making the room appear larger.

A print that repeats the colors of upholstery, carpet, and walls can help to unify a room. However, in choosing a print, be sure the design is in proportion to the size of the room—as well as to the size of the window. Reserve large, bold designs for very large rooms. Remember that fabrics with small designs will repeat more often—and require less yardage—than those with large designs. You'll also find that colors and patterns have a way of changing character when they are taken from the fabric department to your home. There are times when what appeared to be apple red in the store may take on an orange hue in your family room, or the print that seemed just the right size in the store may be too large and overpowering when you transfer it to your quiet bedroom. Small swatches can be equally deceiving, so be sure to buy a yard or two of the fabric you are considering before making a large purchase. Hang it in the room for a few days to make sure it has the effect you had hoped for.

Your curtain's or drapery's purpose will help to determine the weight and texture of your fabric. When you wish to provide daytime privacy, soften the interior, or diffuse sunlight, select a sheer or open-weave fabric. To ensure privacy at night, select a tightly woven opaque fabric. For maximum light control, you may wish to combine sheer draperies and overdraperies. Don't be inhibited by the idea that certain fabrics can only be used at certain windows. Today's free spirit in decorating lets you draw from the entire range of fabrics for every room in your house.

Fabrics for windows are now more beautiful and practical than ever. Before you buy, check the tags and labels on fabrics for special finishes and easy-care features. Look for permanent-press fabrics, which can be machine washed and tumble dried. Soil-resistant finishes will reduce the need for dry-cleaning draperies. Most fabrics are treated during the manufacturing process; if you should select a fabric that has not been treated, you can treat it yourself with one of the soil-resistant aerosol sprays.

Fabrics for curtains and draperies also should be preshrunk and colorfast. And check the grain of the fabric you're considering. Is the fabric printed off-grain? Check the cut end of the bolt to see that a straight thread runs through the design. This is particularly important with printed designs, printed plaids, and stripes. Be very sure to check the grain of sale fabric—it could be the reason why it's on the bargain table. This distortion can never be remedied, so don't buy off-grain fabric.

To line or not to line? Linings are necessary for fragile or loosely woven fabrics. They protect against "hanging wear" and sun fading. Linings are also needed for fabrics with prints that are lost when backlighted. To determine which prints require linings, hold a sample up to a sunlit window. In addition, linings give richer, more formal folds because they add weight to the draperies, make draperies opaque to ensure privacy, give continuity to the outside appearance of your home, and provide insulation from heat and cold.

Generally, linings are made of white, soft gray, or cream-colored sateen. For a special effect, use a brightly colored or printed fabric.

Unlined draperies are generally less formal, less expensive, and less work to make than lined draperies. They often are used in combination with glass curtains. Many drapery fabrics look best without a lining because light filtering through a coarse, heavy weave fabric enhances the beauty of the fabric.

Your personal styling can combine a bit of the formal with a casual mood. Using companion prints for matching cafe curtains and ceiling-to-floor tieback draperies is a distinctive decorator touch you can easily sew for yourself.

Measure Accurately

Follow these basic rules to ensure accurate measuring for window treatments:

● Be sure to mount the rods before taking any window measurements.

● Measure with a steel tape measure or a carpenter's rule—cloth tapes can stretch.

● To avoid costly errors, write down all of the measurements as you take them.

● Measure every window, even if some of them appear to be the same size.

The type of rod you use and the effects you want to achieve determine the necessary measurements.

The basic measurements (the length and the width) should be taken in the following manner:

● Length—Measure from the top of the rod to the desired finished length: sill **(A)**, apron **(B)**, or floor **(C)**. Full-length curtains and draperies should barely clear the floor or carpeting. For rooms with baseboard heating, choose a style and length that will not interfere with the airflow of the heating unit.

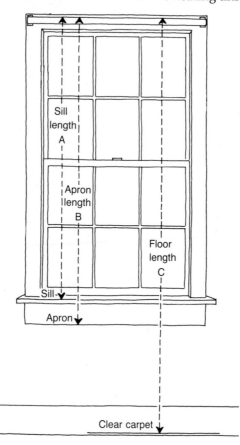

● Width—Measure the width of the rod **(D)**. Measure the returns **(E)** at both ends and add to the width measurement.

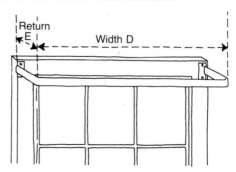

Additional measurements are required for a perfect fit on the specific rod that you have chosen for your window:

● Traverse rods—Draperies should extend ½ inch or more above the rod, depending on the hooks you select. Check the hooks and add the correct amount to the length measurement. Measure the length, width, and returns as illustrated above. To the width measurement, add the overlap at the center of the rod and the returns. If you use a one-way traverse rod, you will have no overlap.

● Decorative rods—Measure the length from the lower part of the clip or ring. Measure width of the rod (between the finials), and add the returns and overlap, if any exist. Measure the return on a decorative rod from the end ring to the wall—usually 3 inches.

● Recessed windows—Measure the length from the top of the rod to the length you plan. Then, measure the width of the rod.

● Casement curtains or French doors—Measure the length from the top of the upper rod to the bottom of the lower rod. Measure the width of the rod inside the brackets.

● Cafe curtains—Measure the length of each tier from the lower part of the clip or ring on the upper rod to 3 inches below the clip or ring on the lower rod. This is the finished length with a 3-inch overlap. If you wish to leave rods and rings exposed, measure from the lowest part of the ring to the top of the lower rod. For the lower tier, measure from the bottom of the ring on the lower rod to the planned finished length (sill, apron, or floor). Measure the width of the rods between the finials.

● Adjustable curtain rods—Measure length from the top of the rod to the planned length, and the width of the rod and the returns.

Estimate Yardage

After you have taken all the necessary measurements, add sufficient length and width to allow for headings, the fullness required, and seam allowances. Because fabric widths vary, you cannot estimate yardage until you have selected the fabric.

Determine the length required, then add the amount needed for hems and headings.
• Sheer fabrics require double hems. For example, add 6 inches for a 3-inch double hem.
• Unlined curtains (nonsheer fabrics) need a single hem; for a 3-inch hem allow 3½ inches of fabric.
• Drapery hems usually require 3-inch double hems, so allow 6 inches. You may wish to use wider hems (up to 5 inches) on very long draperies.

Next, add the amounts needed for finishing the top:
• Curtains shirred on a rod—Add 5 inches for a 1½-inch heading with 1½-inch casing. To make a 2-inch heading, add 6 inches.
• Casement curtains or French doors—Add 2¾ inches at the top and 2¾ inches at the bottom for ¾-inch headings and casings at both top and bottom.
• Cafe curtains—For a plain top, allow 3 inches for a single hem and 5 inches for a double hem; a pleated heading using pleater tape, allow 1 inch; a regular scalloped heading, allow 4½ inches; a scalloped heading with pleater tape, allow ½ inch.
• Draperies—Lined draperies require ½ inch for the top seam; for unlined draperies with handsewn pleats, allow 5½ inches; unlined draperies with pleater tape, allow 1 inch.
• Pattern repeat—Fabrics with designs or patterns must be matched, and additional fabric must be allowed for matching the design. To determine the length of the repeat, place a pin at the top of the design, then pin when that exact point is reached again. Measure the distance between the two pins, and add that amount to the length of each panel.

Now, determine the width required. After you have determined the exact length needed, you must figure how many lengths you need to make the curtains the correct width. Curtains and draperies should always be full enough to hang gracefully. Inadequate fullness will make them look skimpy and unattractive. For sheer curtains, be sure to allow 2½ to 3 times the width of the window to be covered. For heavier fabrics, allow 2 to 2½ times the area to be covered. Fabrics for curtains and draperies are generally 48 inches wide. But width can vary from 36 to 60 inches, so check the width of the fabric before figuring the exact yardage.

When you are planning multiwidth panels, allow 1 inch for each seam (½-inch seam allowances on each panel). One and a half widths are usually sufficient for one panel. The seam should be near the outside of the window rather than at the center. Don't forget to make a right and left panel for each window when split widths are used.

To the width measurements, add the allowances for side hems. Allow 1½ inches for each double hem. Each window will have four side hems—a total of 6 inches for single hems or 8 inches for double hems. For lined draperies, allow 2½ inches for each side hem—a total of 10 inches for side hems for each pair of draperies. Casement curtains should have very narrow double hems. Allow 2 inches per panel.

If you plan to use pleater tape for the heading, purchase the tape and hooks before cutting your fabric. For curtains of double fullness, buy regular pleater tape twice the width of the rod plus ½ yard for each window to take care of returns, overlap, and any necessary adjustments in fitting the tape to the width of the panel. For cafe curtains and other rods without returns and overlap, an excess of 6 inches is ample. For curtains with extra fullness, buy multipocket tape 2½ to 3 times the rod length plus ½ yard for each window. Pleat tape to desired fullness for half the window, including the return and overlap. Cut the tape, allowing ½ inch at each end. Remove pleater hooks and measure tape's length to find finished panel width.

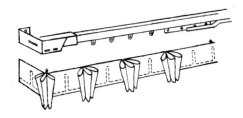

Make sure to take all of the window measurements with you when you are buying fabric because fabric widths and the lengths of pattern repeats will vary.

Yardage Work Chart

To determine drapery or curtain length add the following:
 1. Finished length   _____
 2. Bottom hem   _____
 3. Top: hem, heading,
       casing, or seam   _____
 4. Length of repeat   +_____
 5. Total length for a panel _____
To determine width:
   Note: When using pleater tape, width and fullness are determined by tape. Refer to specific type of curtain for measuring instructions. Determine the width of tape for ½ window, multiply by 2, and write the answer on line 11.
 6. Width of rod   _____
 7. Returns   _____
 8. Overlaps   +_____
 9. Total width to cover   _____
10. Fullness (multiply)   ×_____
11. Curtain width
      (before pleating)   _____
12. Side hems   +_____
13. Total (without
      seam allowances)   _____
Determine number of panels per window by dividing total width (13) by the width of your fabric minus selvages. If your answer is not a whole number, increase to the next high number.
14. _____ _____ = _____
     width   fabric   number
      (13)   width   of widths
One-half of this width will be used for each curtain. For multiwidth curtains, remember that you need to adjust width measurement to include 1 inch for each seam where the panels are joined.

_____ × _____ = _____
length (5) widths (14) total fabric
Your answer will be in inches, so divide this number by 36 to determine the exact number of yards that you'll need for the project. It is always a good idea to purchase an extra 9 inches of fabric to allow for straightening the fabric.

How to Make Curtains

On the following pages you will find detailed instructions for making cafe curtains, glass curtains, and casement curtains.

Cafe Curtains

There's no better way to start sewing for your home than by making cafe curtains. They're easy to handle during construction because they're made of lightweight fabrics and because each section is short. Also, cafe curtains usually are not lined, so they are easier to make than most curtains. To line your curtains, refer to the directions for lining draperies on page 46.

Technically, a cafe curtain is one that leaves some part of the window exposed. But don't let this stop you from covering the entire window with more than one tier if you wish to do so. Cafe curtains often are used with overcurtains or draperies, or are combined with shutters or shades, allowing maximum flexibility for light or privacy. One, two, three, or even four tiers may be used as long as each tier overlaps the one below it by the same amount. However, tiers can end at the top of the lower rod if you wish to expose the rods.

Select cafe rods and rings to complement your choice of window treatment. You can select from two basic kinds of rings for cafe rods: clip-on rings, which grip the fabric with tiny teeth; or sew-on rings, which have a built-in eye to sew to curtain headings. Select a ring with an inside diameter of at least ⅛ to ¼ inch larger than the rod diameter. Find out whether the rings you choose are washable. If they're not washable, be sure to remove them before laundering your curtains.

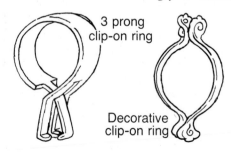

Clip-on rings, either the three-prong type or the decorative claw-tooth, are easily removed and are ideal for use with curtains that are finished with a plain hem or a scalloped edge. Choose decorative endpieces and brackets to finish your window's new look.

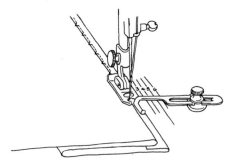

Pleater hook with separate ring

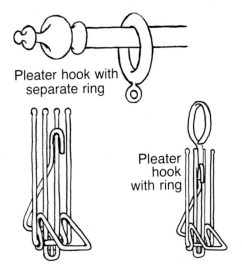

Pleater hook with ring

When using pleater tape, select either pleater hooks, which attach to separate rings, or pleater hooks with rings attached.

The procedure for making all cafe curtains is similar. Read the following general directions, then select the specific directions for the type of curtain you choose—plain, pleated, or scalloped (with or without pleats).

Once you've decided on the style of cafe curtain, select and install the rods and hardware. Mount the rods so that the curtains will cover the window frame, unless the window is recessed and curtains are to be hung within the recess. Hardware is best mounted over the horizontal structures of a window. Measure and figure the amount of fabric needed.

First, straighten the fabric. Measure and cut the lengths of fabric for each panel, matching the designs if necessary. To prevent curtain seams from puckering, cut off the selvages. Press fabrics so all panels are flat and ready for sewing. If seams are necessary to join sections, use a French seam.

To finish the side and bottom hems, use single or double hems. For a single side hem, turn under ½ inch and press. Then turn a 1-inch hem. Pin and press, then stitch close to the hem edge. For a double hem, turn under a scant 1 inch and press. Turn a second 1-inch fold. Pin and press. Stitch by hand or blind-stitch, using a zigzag sewing machine or a zigzag attachment.

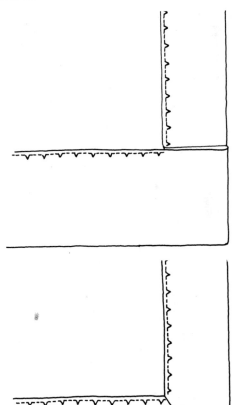

Hem lower edge. For a single hem, turn under ½ inch and press. Then turn a 3-inch hem, pin, and press. For a double hem, turn under a scant 3 inches and press. Turn fabric again the same amount. Pin, press, and stitch. Fold corner into hem, forming a miter, and hand stitch as shown.

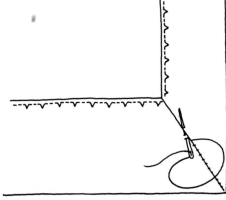

40

The simplest cafe curtain of all can be made with absolutely no sewing. Secure all hems with a fusible web strip. (Be sure to test the webbing on a scrap of your curtain fabric first to make sure it does not show through.) Fold and press hems and heading in place. Then place a strip of the fusible web between the curtain and hem, and press, following package directions carefully. Use either pre-cut narrow strips or cut strips the width of the hems. Wider strips will add body to hems.

Another quick and easy cafe curtain can be made from terry cloth towels. Ideal for bathrooms, they're easy to care for and no sewing is needed. Purchase bright cheery towels in lengths to fit your windows. You may wish to use two or three tiers of hand towels or a combination of bath towels hung

from the top rod and pulled back to expose color-coordinated hand towels on a lower rod. Simply select the towels, clip on the hooks, and hang the curtains.

The plain cafe curtain is another easy-to-make curtain. Simply a panel hemmed on all four sides, it is hung with clip-on or sew-on rings. Fullness falls in soft folds from the rod.

Begin by finishing side hems, then the top and bottom. For the top hem, allow 3 inches for a single, and 5 inches for a double hem. Attach sew-on or clip-on rings 3 to 4 inches apart along the top of the curtain. Use an uneven number of rings for each section.

The plain cafe curtain will look pleated if you use a three-prong clip-on ring. Each pressed pleat will be 2 inches wide with a 3-inch space between.

One of the reasons for the popularity of cafe curtains is their ability to combine with other window fashions. In the picture below, cafe curtains plus coordinated roller shades and fabric-coordinated lambrequins join forces to create an appealing "sun porch" mood.

To make pleats, finish plain cafe curtains as above, except do not attach rings. Then mark the center of each pleat. The first and last pleat should be 3 inches from either edge. Divide the remaining width into equal parts (approximately 5 inches each), and mark. Fold at each mark, wrong sides together, and press a 4- to 6-inch crease down the center of each pleat. Be sure all creases are parallel to the side hem.

Insert the pleat between two prongs of a three-prong cafe curtain clip. Two prongs fasten to the front side of the curtain; the third-and-middle-prong fastens to the back. Attach one hook at each end. Hang the curtains and adjust the pleats, if necessary.

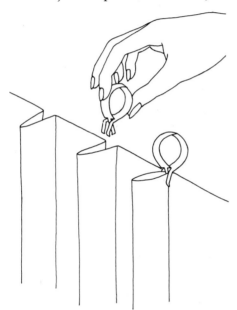

Pleated cafe curtains are today's most popular cafes. Pleater tape is another shortcut to success: it's a quick and easy way to stitch perfect pinch pleats, and the tape automatically measures and spaces the pleats.

Purchase pleater tape and pleater hooks before figuring yardage. Measure width of the rod or rods; for curtains of double fullness buy regular pleater tape twice the width of the rod (plus 6 inches per curtain) to allow for adjustments in fitting tape to panel width.

For curtains with extra fullness, buy tape that is two-and-one-half to three times the rod width—plus 6 inches per curtain. Buy the special four-prong hooks to fit your pleater tape. For curtains of double fullness buy 10 pleater hooks for each 48 inches

of window width plus end-pin hooks for the ends of each of the curtains.

Before attaching the tape to the curtain, pleat the tape to the desired fullness for half the window, beginning and ending with an end-pin hook or a clip-on ring. Cut the tape, allowing ½ inch at each end for hemming. Remove the pleater hooks, and measure the length of the tape—minus the half-inch at each end—to find the finished width of one curtain. Add allowances for side hems and seams to this measurement. To determine the cut length of each panel, add the bottom hem allowance and 1 inch for top finish to finished length measurement.

Follow general directions for cutting, seaming, and hemming the sides and bottom. Press under 1 inch along top. Pin tape to the wrong side of the curtain—¼ inch from fold at top of curtain—with the ends of tape extending ½ inch at each end of the tape. Fold the tape ends under. Stitch close to the edge along top, bottom, and ends of the pleater tape.

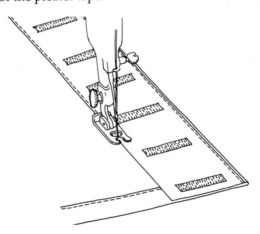

Insert pleater hooks with rings; use clip-on rings or end pins with rings at ends to hang.

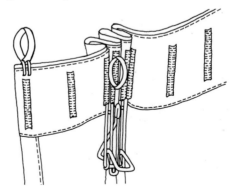

Scalloped top cafe curtains are versatile. You can design your own scallops as deep or as wide as you desire. Scalloped-top curtains are casual and easy to make. You can use a scalloped heading on plain cafes or in combination with pinch pleats.

To make a scalloped heading without pleats, use stiffening in the heading. This maintains the scallop shape. When measuring for cafes with scalloped tops, add 4½ inches for the top hem. Cut 4-inch-wide strips of stiffening the width of the finished curtain. Any size scallop is acceptable, but plan an even number of scallops for each curtain width. Plan your scallop pattern on a piece of paper, and then transfer the outline to the stiffening. Start and end scallops 2 inches from either end. Vary the space between the scallops from ½ inch to 1 inch, but make sure that you space them evenly. Pin the stiffening strip to the *wrong* side of the curtain, 4½ inches below the top. Fold and pin the side hems over the stiffening.

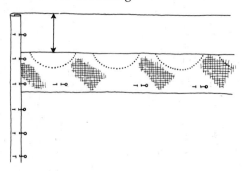

Stitch the side hems. Fold, pin, and stitch the bottom hems. Turn the 4½-inch heading to the right side, along the top of the stiffening. With the stiffening on top where you can see the pattern, stitch along the outline of the scallops. Cut around the scallops ¼ inch from stitching. Clip seam allowances every ½ inch so scallops are eased and smooth when curtain is turned right side out.

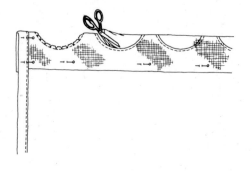

Turn the hem right side out. Carefully pull out the corners and ease the scallop seams until they are smooth. Press carefully, letting the curtain fabric roll slightly to the back so that no pleater tape can be seen at the top of the curtain. Along the raw edge, turn under a narrow hem. Stitch by hand or machine. Then, attach the rings and hang.

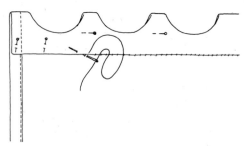

To make a scalloped heading with pleats, purchase scalloped pleater tape and pleater hooks before figuring yardage. You'll need a length of pleater tape twice the width of the rod plus 6 inches. Using pleater hooks, pleat the tape to the desired fullness for half the curtain rod. Arrange the pleats so that you have a single pocket and then a scallop at each end. Allow an additional inch at each end, and cut the tape. This is the finished width of the panel. To the length measurement, add ½ inch for the top seam and 3½ inches for a single hem (or 6 inches for a double hem). Follow the general directions for cutting and seaming. Center the tape on the right side of the curtain. With the scallops at the top, pleat spaces even with the edge. The pocket openings should be against the right side of the curtain. Stitch ¼ inch from the edge along the scallops and pleat spaces. Backstitch at beginning and end.

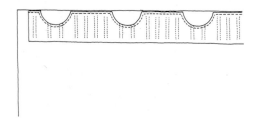

Cut out the scallops, clip the seam allowances, and turn tape to the wrong side. Press the heading down, and be sure no heading shows on the front of the curtains. Stitch the tape to the curtain along its lower edge. Then hem the sides and bottom of the curtains.

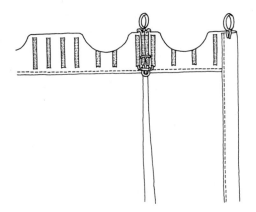 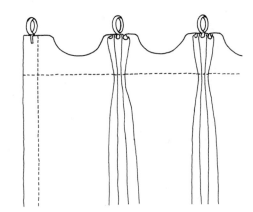

Insert prongs of pleater pins into pockets of tape to form pleats between scallops. Finger press to straighten pleats. Then slip end pins with rings into pockets at each end.

Hang scalloped and pleated cafe curtains and arrange the pleats. To ensure total window coverage, place the first ring on each curtain on the rod outside of the brackets.

Scalloped-top cafe curtains—made from sheets —help to coordinate this bedroom. Don't be afraid to experiment; here, the top rod is hung at the level of the first row of panes—rather than mounting it at top of window frame. The second rod is hung at third row of panes.

Glass Curtains

Glass curtains are made of sheer fabric and hang straight from the rod to the floor or sill. Usually they are cut to triple fullness and are shirred on an adjustable rod. Use them alone or in combination with side draperies or overdraperies. They diffuse light, provide privacy, and soften mood of a room.

Select lightweight fabrics such as sheer polyester or nylon, theatrical gauze, marquisette, ninon, batiste, or pongee; Dotted Swiss, organdy, lawn, and unbleached muslin for special effects. Glass curtains usually are neutral in color—beige, white, or ecru. However, don't feel limited to the neutrals if brightly colored curtains fit into your decorating plan. When selecting fabrics for sheer curtains, always hold a sample of material up to the sunlight to test its light filtering property.

In the photo below glass curtains combine with a shaped cornice to turn a problem glass wall into a decorative advantage.

First, select and mount the rods. Mount adjustable rods on the window frame so the curtains will cover only the glass portion of the window. If curtains hang inside the window frame, use spring-tension rods or rods with brackets for inside mounting. Measure, following the directions on page 38. Determine the yardage needed, including the following: 6 inches for a double bottom hem,

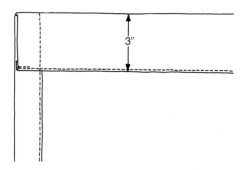

1½ inches for casing, 3 inches for heading, and ½ inch for turning under (a total of 11 inches per panel). This creates a heading and casing of 1½ inches each; for a wider heading make an additional allowance. To make a 2-inch heading allow 4 inches (a total of 12 inches per panel).

Cut curtains on the straight grain of the fabric. Straighten ends and remove selvages. Press the fabric. Working on a large, flat sur-

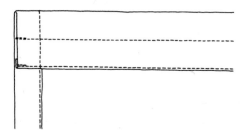

face, carefully measure lengths for your curtain. Pull a thread on the crosswise grain to mark cutting line for each length. Cut carefully, with long, even strokes. Do not tear the fabric, as this may distort the grain.

Join the panels with a very narrow French seam, encasing the raw edges. Long seams sewn on sheer fabrics may pucker. To avoid this, use a very fine needle, fine or synthetic thread, and light pressure on the presser foot. Experiment first by testing stitches on a lengthwise scrap of fabric. If the seam does pucker, loosen the tension and lengthen the stitch.

Finish the side hems first; turn the edge under 1 inch, press, and turn again, forming a double 1-inch hem. Press and pin. Stitch close to the edge. To make the top hem, turn under ½ inch and press. For a 1½-inch heading, turn under 3 inches for casing and heading. For a 2-inch heading, turn under 3½ inches for casing and heading. Press and pin. Stitch close to edge as shown. Backstitch at both ends.

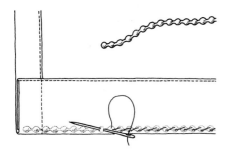

A 1½-inch casing is usually adequate, but check because rod widths vary. Insert the rod and hold against the stitching. With extension rods, use wide part of the rod. Place pins above rod to mark width of the casing. Allow enough space to adjust curtains on the rod. Remove the rod, and adjust the pins into a straight line. Stitch along pins, and backstitch at ends.

Turn a double 3-inch hem at bottom of the curtain and baste with long, running stitches. Do not press. Try the curtain on the rod, adjust the fullness, and hang for a few hours. Check the length. Full-length glass curtains should barely clear the floor. Glass curtains and draperies should be exactly the same length. If you have altered the width of the casing or heading, adjust the length. Remove the curtain rods, and adjust the hems. Then press and stitch the hems.

Because of the lightweight fabrics used, glass curtains tend to float and may need to be weighted for even hanging. Chain weights (small lead beads encased in a woven tube) are the best because they place even weight along the entire hemline. Purchase lengths of chain weights for the entire width of each of the finished curtains.

Insert round chain weights through the hem. Anchor the chain with short, loose stitches through the back of the hem. Close the ends of the chain with small stitches. This should prevent the beads from working out at the ends.

Casement Curtains

Made from sheer fabrics, these have a casing and heading at the top and the bottom. Select small round rods with short brackets and mount them on the window frame just above and below the glass. Measure from the top of the upper rod to the bottom of the lower rod. Add 2¾ inches to the top and bottom for casings and headings (5½ inches for each panel). Measure the width between brackets and double (or triple) for fullness. Allow ½-inch double hem on each side (2 inches for each curtain). Cut the panels and hem the sides. Turn under ½ inch at each end and press. Turn a 1½-inch hem and stitch. Insert rods and pin-mark the casing width. Mount the rods and adjust the casings at the top and bottom so curtains are taut. Remove the rods and stitch along the pinned lines.

Casement curtains are ideal for doors or casement-style windows that swing in to open.

How to Make Draperies

Don't let the word "draperies" frighten you—draperies are only flat pieces of fabric with straight seams. The fabric does all the draping. Drapery styles are as varied as the windows they cover. Usually floor length, they can also be apron or sill length. They can hang straight down from the rod or be held back with decorative holders or fabric tiebacks. Draperies can be used alone or in combination with glass curtains, cafe curtains, swags, cornices, shades, or blinds.

Use draperies as camouflage: small windows appear larger when draperies are extended beyond the window frame; two different-size windows appear the same when concealed with draperies. Long draperies, ceiling to floor, add importance to windows, as well as make ceiling appear higher.

Draperies can be formal or casual. Full-length silk draperies combined with swags and jabots will enhance the elegance of a formal room, while printed cotton draperies will add to the casual air of a family room.

Select draperies according to use and the style of the room. For privacy at night and light by day, choose lined draperies. Linings protect draperies from soiling and sun fading, add body to the fabric, and give all windows a more uniform appearance from the outside. However, unlined draperies are popular and are easier to construct.

Draperies—lined or unlined—must have adequate fullness to look attractive. Let the weight of your fabric determine the amount of fullness required. All draperies need to be at least double fullness—the width of the unpleated finished drapery is twice the width of the space to be covered. For lighter-weight fabrics, the fullness is 2½ to 3 times the width.

On the pages that follow, you will find directions for making lined and unlined panel and sheer draperies.

Lined Draperies

The first step in making lined draperies is selecting the correct rod and mounting it securely. Long draperies can be quite heavy, so a sturdy rod is a 'must.' When mounting rods, don't forget to allow for "stack-back"—the space needed for draperies when they are completely opened. If you are making draperies for sliding glass doors or windows where you will want the entire window exposed when the draperies are opened, extend the rod beyond the window frame by one-fourth the width of the window to allow "stack-back" space.

Measure the mounted rod and figure the yardage you'll need; see the basic directions on pages 36 and 37. Add the following allowances: to the length, add ½ inch for the top seam and 6 inches for a double 3-inch hem. For extremely long draperies you may wish to make a deeper hem, up to 5 inches. If draperies are to extend above the rod, allow ½ inch. If your fabric has a definite design, measure the repeat and add this amount to the length of each panel. To determine the length of the repeat, place a pin at a definite point in the design—the center of a flower, or the point of a color change, for example. Then let your eye travel straight down the fabric until that exact point is reached in the next design and mark it with a pin. Measure the distance between the two pins. This is the length of a repeat—and this amount must be added to each panel length to ensure accurate matching.

To the width, add the fullness—two to two-and-one-half times the width. Also add 1 inch for each seam and 2¼ inches for each side hem—a total of 10 inches for side hems on each pair of draperies. If you plan to use pleater tape, figure the width of draperies, following the directions on page 37.

You will need less lining fabric than drapery fabric because linings have no side hems, are slightly shorter than the drapery, and have no pattern. For example, the lining will be 5 inches shorter than the drapery lengths and 8 inches narrower than the total width of each panel.

*Make the most of a single tall window. Here, →
boldly patterned floor-length draperies dramatize a plain window. Fabric tiebacks hold the draperies in place and reveal a roller shade trimmed to match the draperies.*

If your hem allowance is wider than 6 inches, adjust the lining. Completed drapery will have 2-inch side hems, and lining will be 1½ inches shorter than drapery. Next, straighten ends of fabric. Carefully measure and mark the length of each panel with all panels having the design or nap facing in the same direction, and matching design placement on each panel.

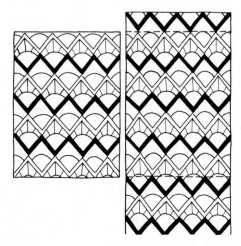

Cut the fabric on the true crosswise grain, then cut off the selvages. Cut the lining panels in the same manner. Press all panels. Join the panels with a ½-inch seam and press open. Seam the lining panels in the same manner. Compare the widths of drapery and lining; the lining must be exactly 8 inches narrower than the drapery for side hems.

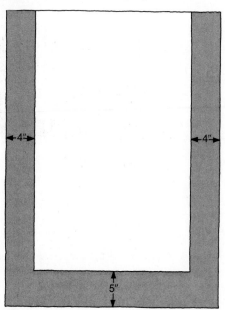

Hem the lining first; turn under ½ inch along the bottom and press. Turn again, forming a 2-inch hem. Pin and stitch by hand or machine. Place the lining over the drapery—right sides together—with top and right-hand edges even. Pin along right side, and stitch ½-inch seam—stopping at top of lining hem. Attach this portion of lining after the draperies are hemmed.

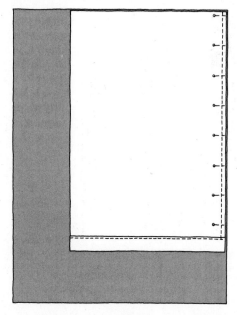

Pin and stitch the left-hand edges together in the same manner. The drapery fabric will bell out because it is wider than the lining.

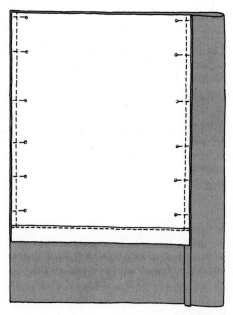

Press the seam allowances toward the lining. Smooth drapery out on a flat surface. Center the lining over the drapery so that the drapery extends 2 inches beyond either side of lining. Pin lining and drapery fabric together along the top edge, with edges even.

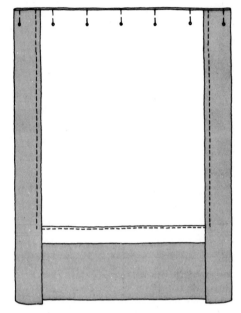

If you plan to pleat your draperies without pleater tape, add stiffening for a heading. Cut a 4-inch piece of buckram or stiffening the same width as the drapery. Pin it across the top on the drapery side. Stitch a ½-inch seam across the top; backstitch at the ends.

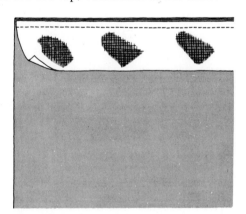

Turn the drapery right side out. The stiffening should now be concealed. Press along the top seam, making sure the lining does not show at the top of the seam. Press the side hems, being careful to keep them the same width from top to bottom. See page 52.

To pleat with pleater tape, stitch a ½-inch seam across the top of the drapery and turn it right side out. Press the top seam and side hems. Pin the premeasured tape to the lining side of drapery ½ inch from the top edge. Turn under ½ inch at the ends of the tape. Machine-stitch along edges of the tape.

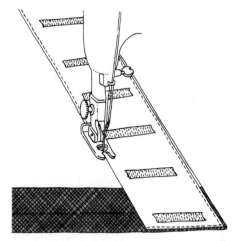

Insert pleater hooks as planned, being careful to keep the pleat pockets straight. Compare the lengths of all panels at the center and outside hems to be sure that they are identical. Adjust the hem allowance.

Leaded weights help draperies hang evenly and smoothly. They are available in various sizes and shapes, covered and uncovered. When selecting weights, keep in mind the weight of fabric and the length of draperies. Insert weighted tape in hems to ensure taut, non-floating draperies.

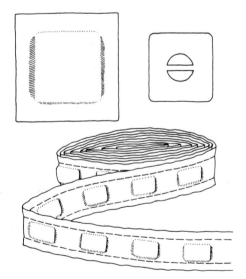

Weights should be attached inside the hem, and slightly above the bottom of the drapery. Unfold the side hem and—working on the wrong side of the drapery fabric—attach a weight along the seam allowance—just above the second fold of the bottom hem.

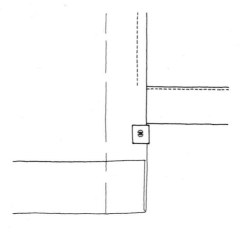

Attach weights to all seams where panels are joined to prevent the draperies from drawing. Attach uncovered weights like sew-through buttons. With covered weights, stitch through covering along top edge.

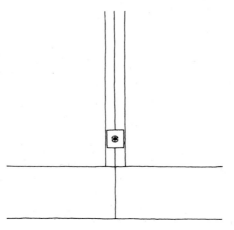

Fold a double 3-inch hem and miter the corners. Baste with long, running stitches. Do not press the hem at this point—adjustments may be needed later. Hang the draperies and arrange the pleats. Check the length—draperies should clear the floor by about ½ inch. Allow the draperies to hang for three or four days before stitching the hems, because some fabrics will stretch or shrink as they hang. Adjust the hem if necessary. Press hems, and if the fabric is bulky, trim excess at the corners. Hem draperies by hand

with a slip stitch or catch stitch; be careful to pick up only one or two threads of drapery. Slipstitch mitered corners to side hems.

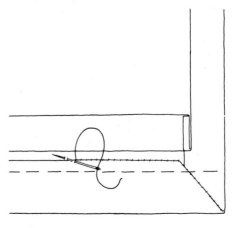

Remove the bastings and slipstitch the lining to seam allowance of the side hems.

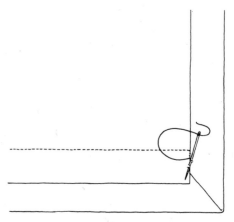

To ensure even hanging, anchor lining to drapery every 12 inches with a French tack.

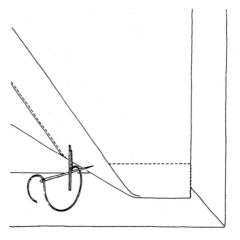

To make a French tack, take a small stitch in the hem of the drapery, and then take a small stitch in the hem of the lining—while holding the two fabrics about 1 inch apart. Take three or four stitches in the same manner and anchor the thread with a small stitch. Cover threads with a blanket stitch.

The outer edge of the draperies should hang in a perfectly straight line against the wall. Use cup hooks and small rings to stabilize this outer edge at the top and bottom. With traverse rods, you'll need a hook and ring at the bottom only, because the last drapery hook is fastened into a hole in the bracket, holding the drapery snugly against the wall. Sew small plastic rings near the bottom outer corners of each drapery. Mount cup hooks on the window frame, wall, or baseboard in line with the rings. Hook the draperies in place.

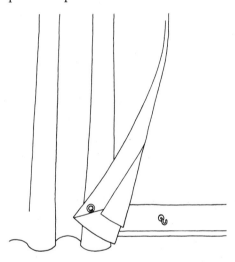

To hang on a plain rod, use hooks and rings at top and bottom. Sew rings at outer top corner of each drapery. Mount cup hooks in line with rings on window frame or wall.

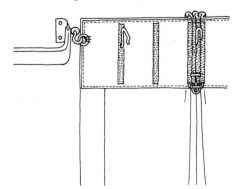

Perfect folds are the mark of excellence on draperies. After the draperies are hung, finger-pleat down the folds for a foot or two. Then tie them loosely with a tape. Don't use thread or twine because it might leave a mark on the draperies. Continue pleating downward and tie at intervals. Leave the tape tied for two or three days, and then untie. By then, your draperies will have conformed perfectly to your finger-pressed folds.

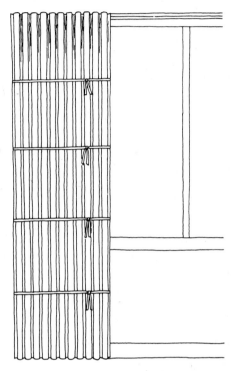

Extremely wide draperies often are cumbersome and difficult to handle. Make these draperies in separate lengths and hold together at the top with a double-prong slip-on hook. Insert one prong in the edge of the drapery and the other prong in the next-to-the-last pleat in the second panel. On the right side, sew a hook in the edge of the overlapping panel and a thread loop in the adjoining panel. Repeat at intervals along hem.

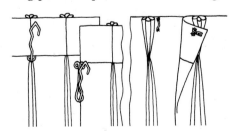

Here's how to pleat draperies without using pleater tape: start by selecting the type of pleat you wish to use. The most common types are the pinch pleat, French pleat, box pleat, and the cartridge pleat. The pinch pleat —consisting of three small pleats pinched together—has a crisp, creased appearance. The French pleat is like the pinched pleat, except that it is not creased and has a softer look. Box pleats are pressed flat against the draperies and have a very tailored look. Cartridge pleats are filled with a stiffening to give them a rounded or cartridge appearance—they are most attractive when the cartridge is small. They are often arranged in groups of three. Pinch and cartridge pleats are sewn by machine. French and box pleats require hand stitching.

Since windows and draperies vary in size, there's no set rule for pleat spacing. But there are a few guidelines to make your pleating project more professional looking. Pinch pleats and French pleats are usually 5 to 6 inches in width and are spaced 4 inches apart. Box pleats are approximately 4 inches wide and 4 inches apart. For cartridge pleat, allow 2½ inches for each pleat and 2 inches between pleats. Use these measurements only as a guide, and adjust them to fit your draperies.

To figure pleat depth and spacing, measure the space to be covered by a single drapery. Be sure to include any return or overlap. Subtract this from the width of your drapery to determine the total amount to be taken up in pleats. For example, if your drapery space is 46 inches, one drapery panel would be approximately 112 inches, and 66 inches (112 inches minus 46 inches) would need to be taken up with pleats. Figuring a depth of 6 inches per pleat, 11 pleats would be required. Distance between pleats is 4 inches.

Stationary panel draperies can be pleated with equally-spaced pleats, but draw draperies must be pleated to accommodate the center overlap. All styles of draperies should have pleats spaced so that a pleat comes at the corner of the return. For stationary draperies, measure 2 inches from the edge of the panel that will be the center edge of the finished draperies. Place a pin there, measure for the width of your pleat, and place a second pin. This locates the first pleat. On the opposite end of the drapery panel, measure the depth of the return. Place a pin there, and measure for that pleat. Place the third pleat in the center, between the two end pleats. All other pleats should be spaced between the first and third, and the second and third pleats.

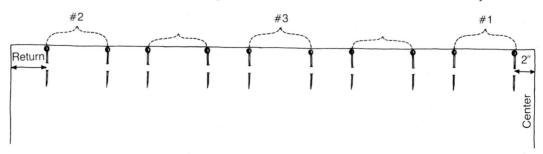

For draw draperies, follow the same procedure as explained above, except for the placement of the first pleat at the center of the window. Measure 3¼ inches from the center edge of the draperies and place a pin at that point. Measure for width of pleat and mark with a second pin. This locates the first pleat. Continue as directed above.

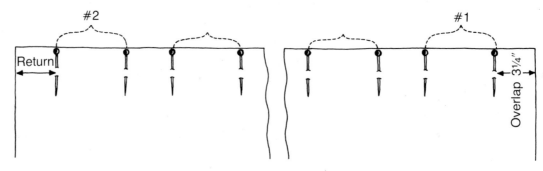

After all pleats are spaced, chalk-mark the stitching line for each pleat, stopping at the bottom of the stiffening. For straight pleats, all vertical lines must be parallel and perpendicular to the top edge of the drapery. To form a pleat, fold through the center of the space marked for the pleat and pin it down. Be sure to keep drapery, stiffening, and lining together while pleating and pinning. On the right side of the drapery, stitch from top edge to bottom edge of the stiffening. Backstitch to reinforce the pleat.

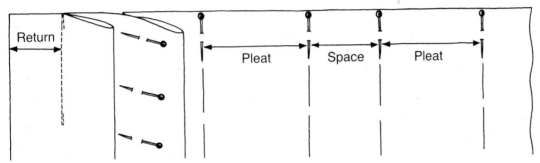

Pinch pleats are formed by dividing the large pleat into three smaller ones. With thumb and forefinger, pinch the edge of the fold and push back to the stitched line. This sets the "pinched" pleat in the middle— forming three pleats of equal depth.

French pleats are formed by dividing a large pleat into three smaller pleats, and then hand-sewing through the pleats at the bottom. Using heavy-duty thread, sew through the pleats several times with a back-and-forth or in-and-out needle motion. Then draw the thread up tightly. This pleat is not pressed, and gives a soft, triple-pleated look.

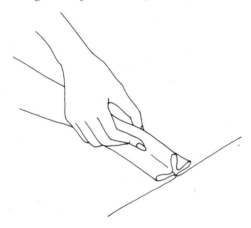

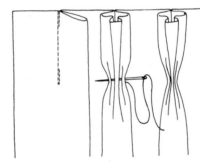

Press the pleats together from the base of the pleat to the top of the drapery, forming sharp creases. At the lower edge, stitch across the pleats or tack them together.

Box pleats are formed by pressing down the large pleats, so that the folds are equidistant from the center line of the pleat. Press each pleat flat. Tack at the top and bottom edges with small stitches through the edge of the pleat, and anchor them to the drapery.

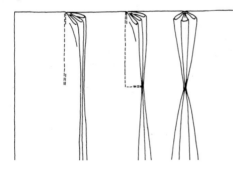

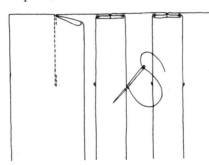

Cartridge pleats are similar to box pleats, but they're not pressed flat. To hold the smoothly rounded shape, the untacked pleat must be filled with a stiffening. Use rolls of stiff paper, buckram, or nonwoven interfacing as a filler. Cut a strip of stiffening 4 inches wide. Then cut the strip into 3- or 4-inch sections, one for each cartridge. Roll a section into a tight cylinder and insert it into the pleat. The cylinder will expand, fitting snugly inside the cartridge pleat.

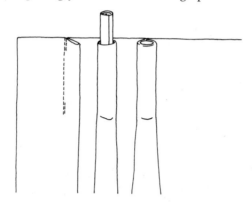

Variations of the four basic pleats can provide special effects. The draperies on the adjoining page are an adaptation of the box pleat. The draperies hang from a rod drawn through strap loops.

To create this window fashion, first mount the rod above the window frame. Measure the drapery length from about 1½ inches below the rod. When figuring the yardage, allow extra fabric for the loops. Construct the draperies and make the basic pleats, following the directions on page 52 — but do not tack them down. The strap loops should be the same width as the finished pleat. Cut strips of drapery fabric lengthwise—twice the width of the finished pleat, plus a seam allowance. For loops 2½ inches wide, allow 5 inches plus 1 inch for the seam—a total of 6 inches. You'll need lengths of about 9 inches for each pleat. Fold the fabric lengthwise with the right side out and press, while centering the seam at the back. Cut the strip into lengths, one for each pleat. Center the loops behind each pleat, and adjust the length to fit your rod. Pin. Fold the pleat to one side and stitch close to the center pleat stitching. Fold the pleat to opposite side and stitch. Press the box pleat flat—covering the stitching lines—and anchor it with hand stitches at the top and base of each pleat.

Hanging your draperies requires special care. First, choose the right drapery hook. For permanently pleated draperies, you can choose from a variety of hooks. Select the hooks that fit your rod; use over-rod hooks for plain curtain rods, and traverse hooks for traverse rods. Choose between the pin-in, sew-on, or slip-in types. The slip-in type fits, into the fold of each pleat. The pin-in type can be pinned into the drapery heading, at each pleat or in between pleats. Use the sew-on hook if you don't want to pin into the fabric. The slip-in and pin-on types have one important advantage: they remove easily for cleaning. If your draperies are long or heavy, purchase heavy-duty hooks.

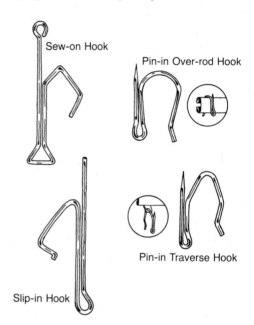

Sew-on Hook

Pin-in Over-rod Hook

Pin-in Traverse Hook

Slip-in Hook

Attach the hooks carefully, and be sure all hooks are the same distance from the top of the drapery. After you have attached three or four hooks, hang the drapery panel and check the length. Adjust hook placement. Attach all hooks, and check to make sure no hooks or stitches come through to front. Continue with steps for lined draperies.

Strong vertical lines are created by these drapery panels, giving this window wall the illusion of height while reducing the glare. The strap loops exposing the rod add interest at the top, increasing the feeling of height. →

56

Unlined Draperies

The first step in making unlined draperies—as with all other types of curtains or draperies—is selecting the correct rods and mounting them securely. Measure the mounted rod—following the basic directions on page 36—and add the following allowances: for draperies pleated with pleater tape, add 1 inch for the top seam; for draperies with handmade pleats, add 5½ inches. If draperies are to extend above the top of the rod, add this amount to the length. Also, add 6 inches for a double 3-inch hem or more for a wider hem. In the width measurement: include returns and overlap, and add the fullness—two to two-and-one-half times the width. If you plan to use pleater tape, figure the width for your draperies, following the directions on page 36. Also add 1 inch for each seam and 1½ inches for each side hem. Estimate the yardage you will need by using the chart on page 38. Don't forget to add the allowances for matching designs.

Straighten the fabric and mark the lengths for each panel, being careful to match the designs. Pull a crosswise thread to mark the cutting line for each panel, and cut carefully—do not tear the fabric. Cut off selvages. Stitch panels together, using a French seam.

For draperies with handmade pleats, cut a 4-inch strip of stiffening the width of the drapery minus the width of the side hems. Center the stiffening on the wrong side, 1 inch down from the top. Fold the top edge over stiffening and press. Stitch along edges.

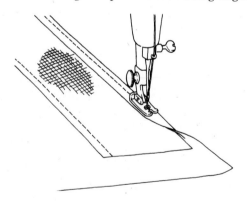

The stiffening will support the pleats, ensuring a neat, crisp heading on your finished draperies. To reduce bulk at the corners of the draperies, trim away the excess fabric and miter the corners.

Trim fabric at end of stiffening, starting ½ inch above the lower edge of the stiffening, and then cut along edge of stiffening.

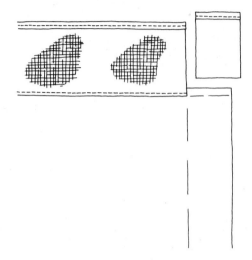

To form the miter at the corner, fold the top edge of the side hem down, at a right angle to the top hem, and press. Trim the fabric ½ inch from the fold, as illustrated.

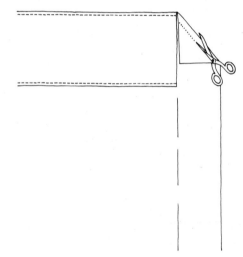

Fold the side hem under. The most convenient place to work on long side hems is on the ironing board. Place your ironing board next to a table or counter, to hold the excess fabric. If your ironing board is adjustable, you may wish to lower it so you can work while sitting. Use a hem gauge or a seam guide to measure the width of the hem. As you fold the hem, place a pin straight through the fabric and into the ironing board. Press the hems, placing the iron tip between pins. Then place pins along the hem for stitching.

Unlined draperies—made from an open weave fabric—enhance a special view. The light filtering through the weave of the fabric adds a complementary texture to the room, and the curve of the tied-back draperies softens the straight lines of the wide window walls.

Slip-stitch the mitered corner to the top hem. Stitch the side hems by hand, using a slip stitch, catch stitch, or hemming stitch. Machine hemming can be done with a straight stitch or zigzag blind stitch. Adjust machine tension to prevent puckering.

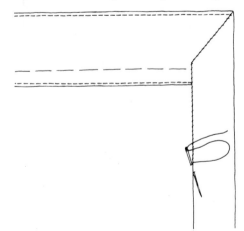

After finishing the heading and side seams, make the pleats. Pleats in unlined draperies are formed in the same manner as those in lined draperies. Refer to page 52 for illustrations of the most common pleats and instructions for constructing them. After the pleats are made, select the appropriate hooks and attach. The various types of hooks are illustrated on page 54.

Forming the hem and attaching the weights are the next steps. Mark a double 3-inch hem at the bottom of the draperies. Do not press the hemline, as it may be necessary to adjust the length. You'll probably need to add weights to the hemline of the draperies to make them hang smoothly. Use sew-on weights, or weighted tape. Attach them inside the hem at each seam and side hem; or you can use weighted tape. The weighted tape is pulled through the finished hem and tacked in place through the back of the hem. Tape should extend full width of each panel.

To reduce the bulk at the corners of the hem and allow the hem to lie flat and smooth, trim out the excess fabric and miter the corner. Cut away the side hem in the lower 3 inches of the bottom hem. Then fold a double 3-inch hem. To make a neatly mitered corner, fold under the outer edge of the hem at an angle that will meet the edge of the side hem. Pin corner at point where two hems meet.

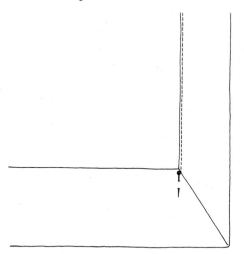

Baste the hem and the mitered corners. Hang the draperies and arrange the fullness. Allow the draperies to hang for a day or two. Then check the lengths and adjust the hems if needed. Stitch the hems. If you wish to use the weighted tape, insert it in the hem and tack it in place. Slip-stitch the mitered corners to the side hems. Hang the draperies and arrange the folds as illustrated on page 54.

Panel Draperies

Panel draperies are stationary panels that hang at both ends of a window and do not cover the full window. They are often used with glass curtains, cafe curtains, or shades. When panel draperies are used with glass curtains, both curtains are hung from the same rod. To hang panel draperies separately, use a decorative rod or select a custom-made rod that extends to end of draperies.

Panel draperies are constructed in the same manner as regular draperies, except for the pleat spacing. There is no overlap on panel draperies, so all pleats can be equally spaced. To make panel draperies, follow the directions for lined or unlined draperies, and make pleats by hand or with pleater tape.

Sheer Draperies

Sheer draperies are similar to unlined draperies, except all hems are made double. Allow 4 inches for each side hem, 8 inches for the heading, and 6 inches for a double 3-inch hem. On long draperies, you may wish to make hems deeper, up to a 5-inch double hem. Allow triple fullness for sheer fabrics. Figure yardage, cut, and join the panels, following the directions for unlined draperies.

Fold, press, and pin double 2-inch side hems. Stitch by hand or machine. For handmade pleats, cut a 4-inch piece of stiffening the exact width of the hemmed drapery. Pin stiffening to underside of the drapery, along top edge. Stitch stiffening to the drapery stitching close to lower edge of stiffening.

Fold the stiffening and the drapery fabric to the underside. Then fold it again. This forms a double hem, with the stiffening and raw edges completely enclosed.

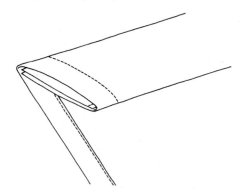

To pleat sheer draperies with pleater tape, fold a double 4-inch hem at the top and press. Then pin pleater tape over the hem and stitch it in place. Complete the draperies, following directions for unlined draperies.

Versatile draperies meet the needs of many windows. Sheer draperies (upper left) color-matched to the wall diffuse the light and help make this small room appear larger. Panel draperies combined with sheers (upper right) emphasize the color scheme. Tieback side draperies (lower left) combine with a valance and cafes to frame a lovely view. Overdraperies (lower right) can be closed at night for privacy; sheer underdraperies mask the view during the day.

How to Make Shades

Austrian shades provide an elegant window treatment. These glamorous shades are made from sheer or semisheer fabrics. They hang in graceful folds.

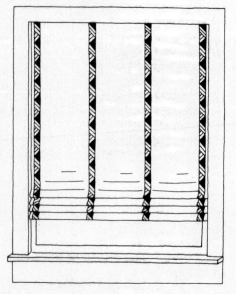

The **Roman shade**—made from flat fabric—can be drawn up to form a tailored, horizontally pleated window treatment.

Roller shades can be used in every room in the house and can be decorated to complement any mood or color scheme. Today's roller shades, available in many colors and styles, are as decorative as they are practical.

Austrian Shades

These decorative shades may look very complicated; but with careful attention to each detail, you can fit them to any window in your home. There are two ways to hang the Austrian shade: with a spring-tension rod, or for wide windows, hang the shade from a board mounted on the window frame. The shade is attached to the board with Velcro or snap tape.

First, determine the length and width of the finished shade. Measure the inside of the window frame from the top of the frame to sill; then measure the inside width of the frame. The length of the shade fabric should be two or three times the finished length plus 1 inch for the bottom hem. Add an additional 1½ inches to the top for the casing; if you plan to hang the shade from a tension rod, there is no heading. Use more fabric, and make the draping of the shade fuller.

To the finished width measurement, add 1½ inches for each side hem, plus two to four inches for each shirred section. Allow more space for each scallop to create deeper scallops. You can place the scallops in an Austrian shade from 10 to 15 inches apart—12 inches is the most common. Ready-made shirring tape for Austrian shades is sold by the yard. This tape has cords woven into it for shirring the shade, and rings for the pull cord. The tape is stitched to the underside of the fabric, along each side hem and at equally spaced points, separating the scallops.

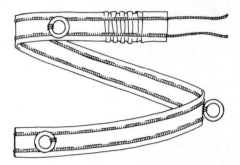

You'll need one strip of tape between each pair of scallops, and one strip for each outer edge. If you plan 3 scallops, you'll need 4 strips; for 5 scallops you'll need 6 strips. Cut each strip of the Austrian shade tape the same length as the fabric before hemming.

If it is necessary to join widths of fabric, plan seams to fall between the scallops. Join the sections with a plain seam and press open. You don't need to finish the raw edges —they'll be covered by shirring tape.

Hem sides of shades first, turn under ½ inch and press; then turn a 1-inch hem, press, and stitch. Pin strips of tape over the side hems ½ inch in from the finished outside edge. For a rod-mounted shade, start tape 3 inches from top to allow for casing.

The Austrian shade with its gracefully scalloped shirring adds a touch of elegance to this kitchen. These shades are made from sheer or semisheer fabrics such as pongee, silk, ninon, batiste, or sheer synthetics. They are usually white, but pastels and neutrals also work well.

For a board-mounted shade, start the tape 1½ inches from the top. Sew the tape in place, stitching down both sides of the tape—stop 1 inch from the bottom of the fabric. Allow the excess tape to hang below the shade. This tape will be stitched into loops for the bottom rod. Decide how many scallops you'll want in the shade, and divide the width of the shade by this number to determine where the rest of the shirring tapes should go. Pin and stitch tape to wrong side of the fabric (keep tapes parallel).

After all tapes are stitched, pull out the shirring cords about 2 inches and knot the cords loosely at the top and bottom.

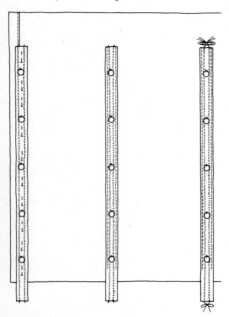

Hold the tape ends out of the way, and turn and stitch a double ½-inch hem at the bottom of the shade. Fold the tape ends and form loops to hold a small brass rod at the bottom. The bottom of the loop should be slightly above the hemline. Cut off the excess tape and stitch.

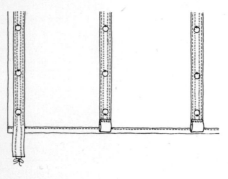

Next, finish the shade's top edge. To make the shade fit the window, fold small pleats at either side of the shirring tape strips to the exact width of the finished shade. Pin. Anchor pleats in place by stitching along the fold from the top of the tape to the top of the fabric. Backstitch at both ends.

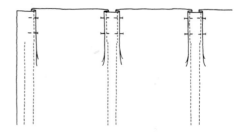

To finish the top of a shade with a rod-casing, turn under ½ inch; press. Then, turn under 1¼ inches, forming the casing; stitch.

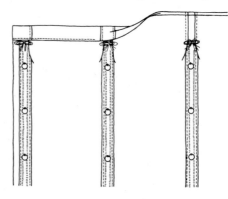

To finish the top for board mounting, turn under ½ inch along the top and press. Pin and stitch Velcro or snap tape over the hem.

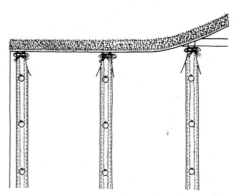

To weight the shade at the bottom, use a brass rod cut to the exact width of the finished shade. Cover the rod with a casing made from the shade fabric.

Slide the covered rod through the loops at the bottom of the shade. Space the tapes evenly along the rod, and tack the rod securely to the tapes.

The shirred look of an Austrian shade is created by pulling up the two cords in each strip of tape until the shade reaches the desired length. Make sure each tape is shirred to the same length and that the rings on the tapes are horizontally level. When the shirring is done, roll the cords into a small bundle and knot the cords together at the top of the shade, but don't cut them. Release them and unshirr the shade for cleaning.

To install your Austrian shade, cut a length of traverse cord for each strip of shirring tape on the shade. The cord should be long enough to attach to the brass rod, go up the shade, across the top, and down the side. Tie each cord to the covered rod at the bottom, and then thread the cord up through the rings.

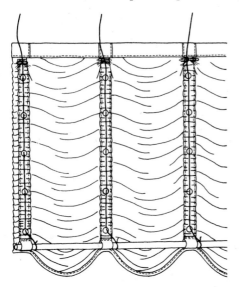

Before hanging your Austrian shade, attach screw eyes to the inside of the top of the window frame as guides for the pull cords.

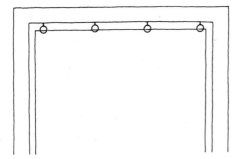

Attach screw eyes to top of window frame 1 inch from each of outside edges. Mount additional eyes in line with shade tapes.

To mount the shade, insert the tension rod through the casing and adjust to the proper width. Mount the shade in front of the screw eyes, against the top of the window frame. Thread the cords through the screw eyes.

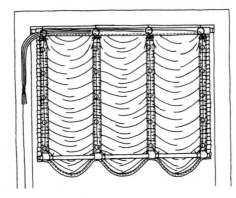

Lower the shade all the way and then knot all of the cords together, just below the last screw eye. Cut off all but one of the cords just below the knot. This long cord will be used for raising and lowering the shade. Mount a small awning cleat on the side of the window frame. Raise shade and fasten cord around cleat to hold shade in place.

To mount the shade on a board, cut a 1x1½-inch board the same width as the inside of the window frame and sand the edges smooth. Staple or glue Velcro or snap tape to one 1½-inch side. On the underside, attach screw eyes 1 inch from each end; fasten additional eyes, equally spaced, in line with tapes on shade. Mount board inside window frame with angle brackets, positioning board 1 inch below top of window.

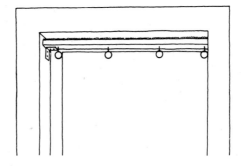

Attach the shade to the board with the Velcro or snap tape. Thread cords through screw eyes, adjust shade, and tie cords.

Roman Shades

Roman shades are similar to Austrian shades, but they are less formal. They are also easier to make, and require less than half the fabric. The Roman shade, like the Austrian shade, can be mounted on a spring-tension rod inside the window frame or on a board attached to the window frame. If you want the shade to cover the window frame, hang the shade from a board mounted on the front of the window frame and at the top of the frame.

Determine the size of the finished shade by measuring the area you wish the shade to cover. Add 2 inches to width measurement for side hems. Add 3 inches to length for hems. If you use a spring-tension rod, add 1½ inches for the casing at the top.

Ready-made Roman shade tape stitched to the back of the fabric makes it easy to raise and lower the shade to any height you wish.

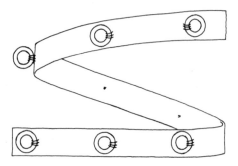

To determine the number of strips of shade tape you'll need, divide the finished width of the shade into equal portions. The tapes are

In this cheerful room, red and white plaid Roman shades are combined with a matching valance and cafe curtains. The white cafe curtains are trimmed to match. The straight lines of the Roman shades combine well with the clean, streamlined look of the contemporary furnishings.

usually spaced 10 to 14 inches apart. Each strip of shade tape will be the same length as the fabric before hemming.

Cut the fabric and tapes. When cutting the tape, be sure that the rings will be parallel on the strips. To sew Roman shades, finish the bottom hem first. Turn under ½ inch along the bottom edge. Then fold, press, and pin a 1-inch hem. Stitch.

To hem the sides, turn under 1 inch along the side and press. Pin tapes over side hems, starting 3 inches below the top edge for a rod-mounted shade or 1½ inches from the top for a board-mounted shade. Stitch down both sides of the tape, stopping 1 inch above the bottom hem. Sew additional strips of tape at evenly spaced intervals. When positioning the tapes, be sure the rings are parallel so the shade will pull up evenly. Let the excess tape hang below the bottom hem. After all strips are stitched in place, turn up the ends of the tape to form loops. Pin. The bottoms of the loops should be just above the bottom hem. Adjust the lengths and stitch in place.

If desired, add decorative braid trim to the front of the shade to conceal the pull tapes' stitching. Select a color-coordinated braid or ribbon and cut each braid the full length of the hemmed shade plus 1 inch to turn under — or 6 inches if you plan to form loops at the bottom to hold a decorative rod. Starting at the top, pin the braid to the right side of the shade over the stitching lines for the tapes. Allow excess braid to extend below the bottom of the shade. For plain hems, fold the ends of braid under, and stitch.

To weight the shade and make it hang smoothly, insert a brass rod the exact width of the shade through the tape loops at the back of the shade and anchor to the tape.

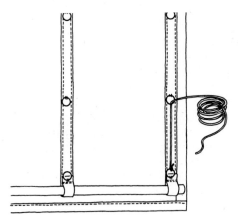

Cut lengths of traverse cord for each tape on the shade. The cords should be long enough to go up the shade, across the top and down the sides. Tie each cord to a bottom ring, then thread it through all the rings.

To finish the top edge, turn under ½ inch and press. For a rod-mounted shade, turn down 1¼ inches for a casing and stitch. If the shade will be hung from a board, stitch Velcro or snap tape along top edge.

To form braid loops at the bottom, pin the ends of the braid to the underside of the hem. Make sure all loops are the same length. Stitch in place by hand or machine.

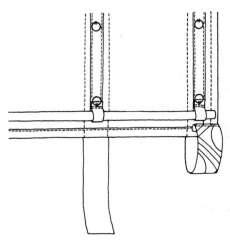

Then, insert the rod through braid loops.

To mount a Roman shade inside the window frame, follow the instructions for mounting Austrian shades. For those that extend over window frames, cut a board the width of finished shade and attach Velcro or snap tape and screw eyes. Mount on face of frame, even with top of window opening.

Roller Shades

Attractive roller shades will add decorative impact to your windows at little expense, and will perk up a drab room. Gone are the days when shades came only in white or dark green. They are now available in a wide range of colors and textures. Also available are kits that provide all the necessary materials and instructions to show you how to laminate your own fabric to the shade backing. Or, you can make your own shade with the aid of fabric fusing webs.

Whether you make your own shade or buy one ready-made, first take accurate measurements. Measure distance between the points where the brackets will be placed. Shades are usually mounted inside the window casing, next to the glass (inside mount). They can be mounted on the front of the window frame (outside mount). For the outside mounting, place the brackets so there is a 1½- to 2-inch overlap on each side of the casement. When purchasing shades, be sure to specify either inside- or outside-mounting brackets.

The shade length is the full length of the window opening plus 12 inches. This permits the shade to be drawn the full length without tearing it from the roller. Even though they appear identical, some windows may vary slightly in size, so measure each window carefully. To replace an old shade, measure your old roller from tip-to-tip, including the little metal pins on each end.

Ready-made shades are easy to personalize; simply use rows of fringe, braid, or ribbon. Attach the trimmings with fabric glue, which remains flexible even after it dries. Appliqued designs can give shades a very personal touch. Cut designs from firmly woven, light- to medium-weight fabrics such as chintz, polished cotton, or percale. To prevent the raw edges from raveling, paint the cutting line on the back with colorless nail polish before cutting; or, you can iron lightweight nonwoven iron-on interfacing to the back of the design. If you are using nail polish, try the polish on a scrap of the fabric to make sure that it won't damage the fibers. Arrange fabric cutouts in an attractive pattern on the lower portion of the shade, then glue the cutouts in place. Work on a flat surface so that the shade does not become wrinkled. Do not move the shade until motifs dry.

If you wish to make a shade, purchase an iron-on or press-on shade kit which contains the shade backing and complete instructions. Select a firmly woven, light- to medium-weight fabric. Follow the directions carefully.

Shades can also be made by fusing two fabrics together with an iron-on bonding web that fuses fabrics permanently and adds body to the fabric. Whether you make your own shade with the aid of a kit or use the fusing web, remember—you must work on a large, flat work area, and you must cut perfectly straight lines. The work area needs to be large enough to support the full length and width of the shade. Unless you have a very long dining room or kitchen table, the floor is the best work surface.

To make a shade using the bonding web, choose a fabric that is firmly woven and is light to medium weight. You can use a print, a solid, a plaid, or a stripe. Border prints and panel prints can also be used effectively. For the backing, use a medium-weight muslin or percale fabric. The finished shade should be the exact width of the shade roller. Measure the width of the roller. Cut the shade fabric 1 inch wider than the width of the roller and 20 inches longer than the length of the window. Cut the backing the same width but only 5 inches longer than the window. Cut the fusing web the same size as the backing, and piece together.

The lower edge of the shade can be shaped with points, squares, scallops, or curves. Select the design of your choice, and make a pattern from stiff paper. Fold 8 inches along the bottom of the shade to form a facing, with the right sides together. Pin close to the fold. Mark the stitching line for the shaped edge on the facing. To make the squared-edge design shown below, cut a rectangle from stiff paper and mark around it as illustrated.

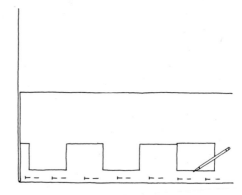

Machine-stitch on the marked line. Trim the seam allowance to ½ inch and clip into each corner, carefully clipping to—but not through—the stitching line. Turn the fabric right side out and gently pull the fabric out at the corners. Press along the edge, forming a sharp line. To form a casing for the shade slat (which acts as a weight for the shade), place two rows of stitching 1½ inches apart near the top edge of the facing.

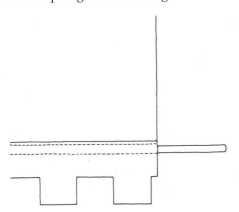

Press the shade and backing to be sure both fabrics are wrinkle-free. For best results in fusing the shade and backing fabrics, use a work surface equal to the total shade surface. A kitchen table or the floor are perfect. Protect the work surface with several layers of an old sheet or a blanket. Place the shade and the backing on the work surface, with wrong sides together and the fusing web between the two fabrics. The backing and the fusing web should just cover the upper edge of the facing. Follow the package directions for the proper heat setting and timing for the fusing web. First, partially fuse the two fabrics together, smoothing out any bubbles or wrinkles that form. Working from the center out, permanently fuse the two layers together. Do not remove the shade from the work surface; allow it to cool and dry completely before handling. Check the width of the shade, and mark the trimming lines along each side of the backing. The lines must be perfectly straight and parallel. Trim with sharp shears, and tack or staple the shade to the roller.

Two classic patterns, stripes and houndstooth checks, team up to dramatize this conversation area. The roller shades were made by laminating fabric to a special heat-sensitive shade backing. The twice-tied draperies conceal the window molding and separations between roller shades.

Special Treatments

In addition to curtains, draperies, and shades, there are special treatments that can enhance your window fashions. Cornices, valances, swags, and jabots are used to top draperies, curtains, and shades. Use tiebacks to hold curtains or draperies to side of a window, and sliding panels to create special effects and solve problems with sliding glass doors.

Cornices

Cornices are rigid structures made of wood, hardboard, or buckram. They can be painted or padded and covered with fabric.

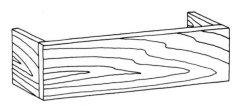

The box-type cornice board is the most common. To pad and cover the board, cut cotton flannel 1½ inches wider on all edges to allow for turn-under. For a more rounded look, use several layers of flannel. Place the flannel over front of board and staple to underside. Cover padded box in same manner.

Valances

Valances are made from fabric and can be hung from a rod or a valance board. Valance headings need not always match the headings of the companion curtains or draperies.

One of the easiest and most popular valances is a straight piece of fabric gathered on a regular rod. To pleat a valance, use pleater tape or follow the same method used for the draperies. When hanging the valance from a plain rod, anchor the top corner as shown.

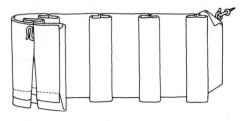

Plain, tailored valances are quick and easy to make if you hang them with a double rod. Determine the depth of the valance, allowing for a casing at both top and bottom. Slip the constructed valance onto the rods. The top rod holds the valance. The bottom rod, not anchored to window, acts as a weight.

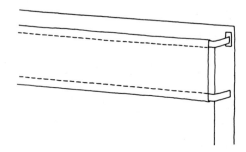

The same technique can be used to mount a simple valance on cafe rods. Just measure the width of rod and add side hem allowances. Leave valances plain or trimmed with braid or appliques after casings are stitched.

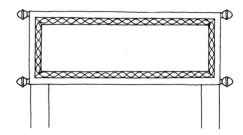

The shelf-type valance board provides a sturdy base for mounting swags, jabots, or shaped valances. The shelf board is mounted at the top of the window frame and snap tape or Velcro is attached onto the top of the shelf and along the top edge of the valance.

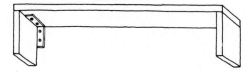

To make a shaped valance, measure the width of valance shelf and returns. Then make a paper pattern as illustrated below.

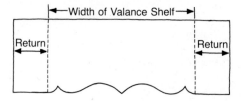

Width of Valance Shelf

Return   Return

A wall of windows is the center of attention in this bedroom. Striped fabric was used for draperies and roller shades on the three windows.

The box-style cornice board, covered in the same fabric, united the windows and shelves into an important feature of the room.

The simplest of valances—a straight piece of fabric with casing and heading at the top—is gathered on a rod to top plain curtains and frame the view in front of the small breakfast counter. The curtain fabric and the wallpaper are companion prints.

Mark the exact width and desired length of the valance. Mark the length and depth of the returns. Shape the lower edge of the valance between the returns; make sure the design is centered. Fit the pattern to the shelf. Cut stiffening to the exact size of the finished valance, using the pattern. Next, cut an interlining of cotton flannel 1 inch larger than the pattern on all sides. Cut the drapery fabric in the same manner as the interlining. Cut the lining ¼ inch larger than the stiffening. Baste drapery fabric and interlining together with long running stitches along all edges. For a professional look, stitch bias-covered cording along the shaped edge.

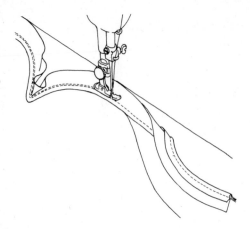

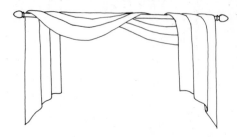

Trim the seam and clip the curves. Turn seam allowances to the underside and press. Place stiffening on the underside and pin in place, folding the drapery fabric over ends of stiffening. Turn under ¼ inch along the shaped edge and lining ends. Pin the lining to the back of the valance and slip-stitch it to the lower edge and ends. At the top, turn the drapery fabric over the lining and stitch. Attach snap tape or Velcro to the top of the valance shelf. Attach the other half of the tape or Velcro to the top of the valance.

Swags and Jabots

Very elegant and formal, swags can be used alone or to top off a regular drapery window treatment. There are two common methods of creating swags: they can be hung from a cafe curtain rod or they can be mounted on the shelf-type valance board (see page 68). The swag can be rounded, triangular, or any decorative shape that complements your decor.

Jabots—the hangings on either side of the swag—can go either in back or front of the swag. Jabots can be short or floor length.

When using a cafe rod for a simple swag, drape the curtain over the rod, with jabots

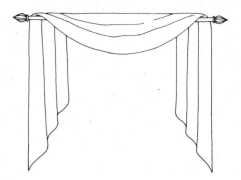

in back and the swag in front. To create a double swag for a large window, drape the swag as shown in the illustration below.

A double swag is made in four pieces: two swags and two jabots are sewn or fastened to each other with Velcro or snap tape. To make a swag, measure the width of the area to be covered to find the top measurement. However, to drape nicely, a swag must be larger at the bottom than the top. This bottom measurement is figured according to how deep you want the swag at the center or lowest part.

Using a diagonal line pattern is a sure way to make a perfect swag. Lay the paper, muslin, or the swag fabric if you're an expert, on the floor right side up. Start with material one-half to one yard wider than the top measurement of the swag. In the center of the material, mark the width of the swag top. From each outside mark, drop a line straight down the fabric to the bottom edge. Measure 15 inches down this line and mark. From this mark, measure 4 inches toward the outside edges of the material. Then draw a diagonal line from the mark to the top edge marking. For a swag 16 inches deep, mark 5 inches out from the base line; for a 17-inch swag the mark should be 6 inches out. Increase an inch in width on both sides of the swag for each added inch of depth that you desire.

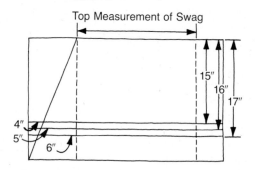

Next, decide how many folds the swag will have. For example: for four folds, you would divide the diagonal line into five parts.

Gracefully draped swags and jabots mounted on a shelf valance set a mood of elegance in this formal dining room. These and the draperies and tiebacks are trimmed with the same warm, rich tones found in the furniture. Tiebacks hold the draperies in place.

Cut out the paper or muslin pattern, using notched markings for the folds, and pin it to the swag fabric (which is right side up). Transfer markings from the pattern to the fabric.

When the swag is outlined on the fabric, pin the top of the swag to the edge of a bed or the back of a sofa, so it hangs straight down. Then pin the markings for the first fold by taking the fabric at the point of the first mark and bringing it to the top of the swag. Do this on both sides and smooth the first fold from the center of the swag outward toward the sides. Next, bring up and pin the second fold. Continue these steps until all folds are pinned securely in place.

Cut off any excess fabric (along the diagonal line) and trim the bottom of the swag to leave three inches below the last fold.

Make a ¼-inch hem at the top, and tack the sides to keep the folds in place. Next, add the decorative trim by hand or machine.

Jabots are usually made 25 inches wide and 27 inches long. The inside edge is usually the depth of the swag, and the bottom horizontal edge is four inches wide.

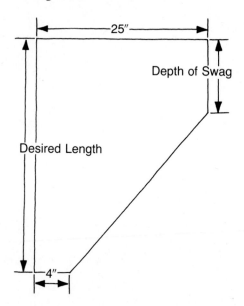

Finish the jabot by turning a ¼-inch hem or by lining the entire section. If you plan to line the jabot, cut the lining fabric the same size and shape as the jabot, and stitch the two right sides together. Sew on all sides but the top. Then turn it right side out and blindstitch the ends. If you're trimming a lined jabot, sew the trim on now. Trimmings can be attached by hand or machine. Pleat

the jabot with three pleats. Fold the first pleat 4 inches from the outside edge (to allow for the side return). Fold over the remaining two pleats, one on top of the other, to achieve the desired width. Stitch the pleats in place. Reverse the pleating for the jabot on the other side of the swag.

If you hang the swag on a cafe curtain rod, attach snap tape or Velcro to the top of the jabots and to each end of the swag.

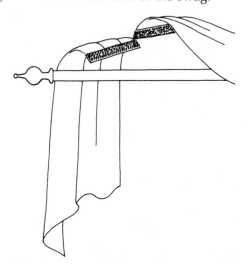

If you're attaching swag to a valance shelf, glue or staple snap tape or Velcro to the top of the valance shelf. Sew the other half of the tape or Velcro to the top of the jabot and swag after they have been attached to each other. Mount the valance shelf on the window frame and attach swags and jabots.

Tiebacks

Although curtain and drapery tiebacks are a very minor part of window fashion, they deserve careful consideration. Tiebacks hold curtains and draperies out of the way so that light and air can enter the room. They also serve as a means of draping curtains in graceful curves. Tiebacks can be constructed from matching or contrasting fabric and are often trimmed with braid or fringe. The tieback must be appropriate to the style of your curtain. Priscillas require ruffled tiebacks; plain, straight-edged tiebacks are best for pleated draperies. Sew small plastic rings to both ends of the tieback, and mount a cup hook on the window frame. Slip the rings over the hooks to hold the curtains in place. Decorative rope can also be used for tiebacks.

Sliding Fabric Panels

Fabric panels that slide—one in front of the other—offer an inexpensive and practical treatment for sliding glass doors. A special track containing sliding strips attaches to the ceiling. Panels of fabric are attached to the sliding strips with Velcro.

First, mount the track on the ceiling. Then, measure from the top of the track to the floor (or to your desired length). Measure the width of the sliding strip. To the length measurement, add 6 inches for a double 3-inch hem at the bottom, and add 1 inch for the top hem. To the width, add 2 inches for the side hems. Cut one panel of fabric for each sliding strip. Fold under the side hem allowances, turning under the raw edge. Press and stitch. Fold and press a double 3-inch hem at the bottom. Stitch the hem in place by hand or machine. Hems can also be secured with fabric fusing strips. Fold and press the hems, and then place fusing web strips between the hem and the outer fabric. Fuse the hems in place, carefully following the fusing instructions.

Insert drapery weights in the bottom hem to keep the panels hanging straight. Weighted drapery tapes or small brass rods work best because they distribute the weight evenly across the entire width of the panel.

Sew strips of Velcro to the top of each panel on the wrong side (the other half of the tape will be on the sliders). Press the panels to the sliders at the top. For an opaque window treatment, the panels can be lined with a firmly woven lining fabric.

Sliding fabric panels are a thrifty and unique way to treat a sliding glass door. The fabric panels attach to sliding tracks attached to the ceiling and create the impression of a total fabric wall when closed. To open the panels, simply slide one behind the other.

Chapter 4

Bedspreads, Canopies, and Bed Linens

Make your own bedspread? Why not! Most of the seams are straight, and you don't need to worry about zippers or intricate closings. The selection of fabrics is nearly unlimited, and any combination of color, texture, and bedspread style makes it possible for you to create a one-of-a-kind bedroom.

Because the bed is often the bedroom's center of attention, you must give careful consideration to its covering. The fabric you select should match or complement the decor of the room, and the style should reflect the personality of the room's occupants. For example, a fitted spread with a ruffled flounce may be just right for your pre-teen daughter. Choose a more masculine (and durable) style for your son, such as a tailored box spread. Or, for the teen-age daughter who 'redecorates' frequently, try a plain dust ruffle. This design allows her to change the coverlet or the throw to match her many moods. And, don't forget the master bedroom—it's your special place to get away from it all. Decorate it with soothing tones and a style to match your personality.

Top off your bedroom decor with a full canopy— you'll be surprised at how effectively it can change the mood of the entire room. Or, give your tired room a new look with a partial canopy/headboard combination.

Green and white polka dots set the theme for this cool, restful bedroom. The polka dot coverlet doubles as a light quilt on cool evenings. The polka dot theme is carried to the dust ruffle, the pillow shams, the sofa pillow, and the draperies.

Basic Bedspread Styles and Variations

There are two basic styles of bedspreads—fitted spreads and throw spreads. Each has many variations. On a fitted bedspread, the center section is the same size as the top of the mattress. Additional fabric is sewn around this rectangle and can be plain, gathered, or pleated. The throwstyle spread is a flat rectangle that drapes down the sides and at the foot of the bed. A coverlet is a throw that does not reach the floor. The coverlet and dust ruffle team up in a combination of different styles. Select the style that best suits your needs, and adapt it to your situation.

Start with a good-quality mattress and springs. Buy the best quality you can afford. It will last you many years. If you must economize, invest in a top-quality mattress and economize on the covering rather than purchasing a poor-quality mattress and covering it with an expensive spread. Remember, a good mattress will make any spread look better.

All of the following fabrics are suitable for bedspreads: chintz, velveteen, corduroy, polished cotton, antique satin, sailcloth, denim, organdy, screen-printed linen, or gingham.

Bedspreads can be lined or unlined. Lining will conceal the raw edges of the seams and give a nice finish to the inside of the spread. However, many of the sturdy fabrics will work well without being lined.

You may wish to combine two or more fabrics for your spread. Often a gaily colored quilted fabric is used for the top and the sides are made from a plain fabric. The effect is colorful as well as dramatic. To color-coordinate your bed with the bedroom's

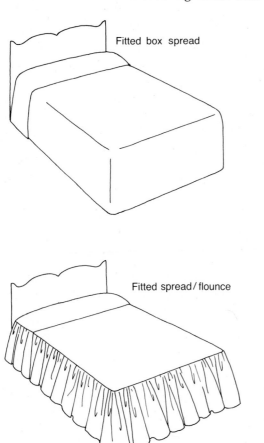
Fitted box spread

Throw spread

Fitted spread/flounce

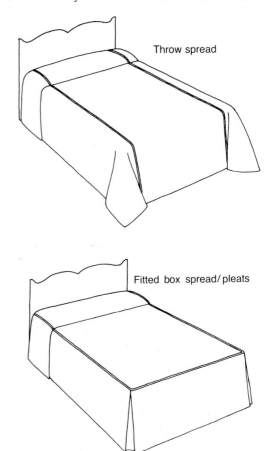
Fitted box spread/pleats

color scheme, match the bedspread fabric with the draperies or slipcovers, or use a different but complementary color.

When selecting the fabric, consider the care requirements of your bedspread. For children's spreads, which will take a lot of hard use, use easy-care, washable fabrics. In guest rooms and the master bedroom, where bedspreads will not get hard use, care is not as important a factor.

How to measure for bedspreads: After you've decided on the style of your spread, you'll need to measure your bed. Make the bed with sheets and blankets, and take these measurements: **Length (A)**—measure from the head of the bed to the foot, across the top of the mattress. **Width (B)**—measure from side to side across the top of the mattress. **Height (C)**—measure from the top of the mattress to the floor. (This is also called drop.) **Depth of the mattress (D)**—measure from the top of the mattress to the top of the springs. **Depth for dust ruffle (E)**—measure from the top of springs to floor.

To find out which measurements are needed, check the instructions carefully for the style of bedspread you wish to make.

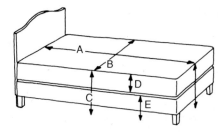

Use an accurate, nonstretchable tape for measuring. If the tape will not extend the full length of the bed, pin-mark the point where the tape ends. Then, move the tape and continue measuring from the pin. Write down each measurement as you take it. To these measurements, add allowances for seams, hems, and fullness before estimating the total yardage. Remember—you'll need additional fabric for cording seams, and for matching designs if fabric is patterned.

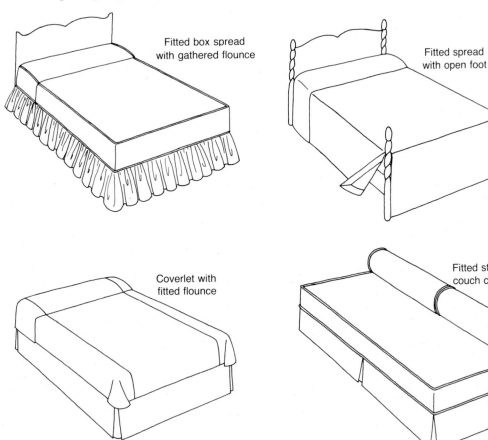

Fitted box spread with gathered flounce

Fitted spread with open foot

Coverlet with fitted flounce

Fitted studio couch cover

Fitted Bedspreads

The tailored box spread and the feminine, ruffled spread are both variations of the basic fitted bedspread. The top of the spread is the same size as the top of the bed, and can be plain, quilted, appliqued, or monogrammed. The side sections or drops can be plain, pleated, or gathered. You can either fit this spread to the length of the bed (with bolsters or shams to cover the pillows), or you can extend the spread to provide adequate coverage and tuck-in for the pillows.

The exact yardage needed depends on the type of spread, the height and width of the bed, and the width of the fabric you select. If you are making a spread for a twin bed and your fabric is 44 inches or wider, one width will be sufficient for the top. For a double,

queen-, or king-size bed you will need to piece the top section. To do this, center one width of the fabric on the top of the bed. Then cut identical strips for either side; be sure to allow for seams.

The seams on the top of your spread can be plain, corded, or covered with trim. Bands of trimming stitched over the seam lines will add a custom-made touch to the spread. If you use trim, repeat the same trim around the hem or on bolsters or pillow shams.

The type of fabric you select will determine whether the spread should be lined. Sheets make an ideal lining; their generous size reduces seams to a minimum. You also can line spreads with muslin or firmly woven broadcloth. If you decide not to line your bedspread, construct it with self-finished seams, or bind or overcast the seams to pre-

Fitted box bedspreads with their clean-cut lines are the perfect style for this smartly tailored bedroom. Bolsters and decorative pillows soften *the straight lines and add color accents. See the following pages for directions on how to make this and other styles.*

vent raveling. Flat-fell or self-bound seams are good for medium- to heavyweight fabrics. For lightweight fabrics, use French seams. When using plain or corded seams, overcast the raw edges by hand or machine for most fabrics. However, if the fabric ravels badly, a bias binding will provide the best finish.

On the following pages are instructions for making the tailored box spread, the fitted spread with a gathered or pleated flounce, and a fitted spread for a studio couch. All three of these styles may be lined.

Tailored box spreads are usually made with welting (often called cording) in the seams along the top edge, creating a neat, crisp seam around the top of the bed. To determine the amount of yardage you'll need, measure the length, width, and height of your bed, following the basic measurement directions on page 77. Then, add these necessary allowances for seams and hems:

To the length measurement **(A),** add 2 inches for the hem at the head and ½ inch for the seam at the foot of the bed. If you plan to have your bedspread cover the pillows, add 30 inches. To the width measurement **(B),** add 1 inch for the side seams. These will be the measurements for the bedspread top.

Next, figure the size of the drop or side sections. To the height measurement **(C),** add 2 inches for the hem and ½ inch for the seam. The length of the side drop sections will be the same as the length of the top section of your spread. You will need two side drop sections; the foot section of the drop will be the same height as the side drop sections, and the width will be the same as the width of the top section.

If you are using a solid color or an overall design fabric without a nap, cut the side sections and the foot section on the lengthwise grain. However, if you are using a napped fabric or a fabric with a one-directional design, remember that you need to allow enough fabric so you can cut the side and foot sections on the crosswise grain.

If you plan to cover your own cord for the welting, allow adequate additional fabric yardage for cutting bias strips.

Cut one length of fabric for the center of the top section and cut off the selvages. Cut two strips (one for each side) the same length as the center section and the width needed to cover the top of the bed. Add 1½ inches to each side section for seams. Cut the drop sec-

tions. From the remaining fabric, cut bias strips for covering the cord. The weight of the fabric will determine the size of the cord. For lightweight fabrics, use a fine cord; for heavier fabrics use a thicker cord. The width of the bias strips needed to cover the cord must be one inch plus three times the width of the cord. Cut the bias strips and cover the cord, following the directions that are given on pages 24 and 25.

Seam the top sections together. If these seams are to have welting, stitch the welting to either side of the center section. Then attach the side sections. (See corded seams, page 25.) If these seams will be plain, a French, self-bound, or flat-fell seam will work best—so there will be no raw edges on the underside. If you plan on using trim over the seams, stitch it in place now. To prevent welted seams from fraying, overcast them by hand or machine, or bind them with bias tape.

Lay the bedspread top on the bed to check the size. Seam allowances should extend ½ inch beyond the sides and foot of the bed. To get a good fit, you must round the corners slightly. Carefully pin-mark the curve at the corner of the bed. On the right side, chalk-mark the line of the pins to mark the stitching line for the corner. Compare the two corners; both curves must be exactly the same. If necessary, correct the chalk lines.

If the top seam will have welting, pin the welting to the seam line of the top section, with right sides together. Place the stitching line of the welting on the chalk line marking the corner curve. Ease the welting around the corner, being careful not to stretch the cording. Clip where necessary (see page 26). Stitch in place, using a cording foot.

Next, join side and foot drop sections in one long strip. Hem the lower edge by hand or machine. Carefully pin the boxing strip to the top, along the foot and sides of the top section. Be sure the corner seams are at the center of the curve on the top of the spread. Ease the drop section to the top around the corners. Stitch the seam, notch seam allowances around the corners, overcast raw edges, or bind seam allowances with ready-made bias tape. If the fabric is bulky, trim out seam allowances of the cording before binding seams. To finish, turn under ½ inch across the head of the bedspread, and press. Then, turn a 1½-inch hem across center section and both drop sections. Hem by hand or machine.

Fitted box spreads are often made with inverted pleats or mock pleats at the corners. The pleats will allow the bedspread to adjust to a change in the weight of the bedding used under the spread. On light- and medium-weight fabrics, use the inverted pleat. The mock pleat works better for heavier or quilted fabrics, because it is not as bulky.

To make inverted pleats, add 12 inches to the length of the side drop sections, and 8 inches to length of foot section of the bed.

First, construct the top of the spread. Next, join the three drop sections together with a ½-inch seam, and hem the lower edge. Lay the inverted pleats at the corners, making each pleat 4 inches deep. Seams joining the flounce sections should fall at the back of the pleats. Pin the pleats in place.

Check the fit by placing the bedspread top on the bed. Be sure that the seam allowances extend beyond the edges of the bed. To ensure a proper fit, round the corners of the spread top to match the curve of the bed. Mark the curve line on the top of the spread with chalk. Pin the welting along the seam line—following the curve at the corners—and stitch it in place. Pin the flounce to the top of the spread along the sides and the foot to check the fit. Adjust the depth of the pleats, if necessary. The pleats should open exactly at the corners. Remove flounce and press the pleats, clipping seam allowance at the top of the hem, as shown below. Then stitch along seam line to secure pleats.

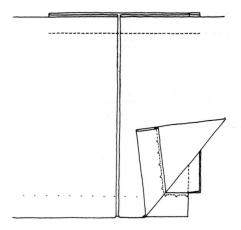

Pin flounce to spread top with right sides together. Ease the drop around the corners, and stitch. To reduce bulk, trim out seam allowances of welting. Bind or overcast seams. Turn under a hem along top, and stitch.

Make a mock pleat by leaving the corner seam open and inserting a separate piece of fabric under the opening.

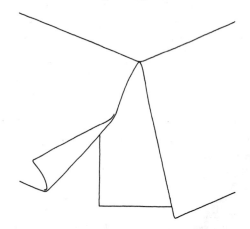

To make mock pleats, cut drop sections—following the directions for the basic fitted spread—but add an additional 2 inches to each side section and 4 inches to the foot section. Then, cut two separate sections for the underlays—12 inches wide and the depth of the drop sections. Do not stitch the drop sections together. Hem the bottom of the underlay and finish the two sides with a narrow hem, or overcast the edges. Hem the lower edge of each drop section separately.

Hem the vertical edges that will fall at the corners in the same way. Construct the spread top the same as a plain fitted spread. Pin the drop sections to the spread, with vertical hems meeting at the corners. Stitch. Mark the center of the raw edge of the underlay. With the right sides of the underlay to the wrong side of the drop section, pin the unfinished edge of the underlay along the seam line. Match center mark to corner opening. Stitch on seam line. Complete the spread the same way as the fitted box spread.

A gathered flounce on the fitted spread gives a soft look. The top of the spread is made exactly the same as the fitted box spread. The fullness of the flounce will be determined by the weight of your fabric. For medium or heavyweight fabrics, 1½ to 2 times fullness is usually used, but for light-weight fabric, use 2½ to 3 times the length for fullness. If you are using a lightweight fabric such as a gingham or organdy, you will want to line and perhaps underline the top of the spread. This will add strength and prevent show-through from sheets or blankets.

Lining the top also covers the raw edges of the seam allowances, leaving the underside of the spread neatly finished. The flounce need not be lined because the gathers will prevent the bedding from showing through. Underlining the top will add body, increase durability, and help prevent wrinkles.

To underline, cut firmly woven fabric the same size as the top pieces. Baste the underlining to the wrong side of each outer fabric piece, and then handle as a single piece.

Cut the fabric for the flounce into lengthwise sections, seam into a long strip, then gather. To find the correct yardage, measure around the three sides of the bed. Divide this measurement by the width of the fabric to find the number of panels. For triple fullness, multiply the number of panels by 3. Then, multiply this figure by length of skirt, and divide by 36 inches to obtain the number of yards needed for a shirred skirt.

For example, a full-size bed will measure about 204 inches around the three sides — or approximately 4 lengths of 50-inch fabric. Multiply this by 3. The resulting figure shows that 12 lengths are needed for shirring. Skirts are usually 22 inches long, including hem and seam allowance. Multiply the 12 lengths needed by 22 inches (the length needed for each piece) to find the total amount of fabric needed for the flounce. In this case, the total would be 264 inches or 7 yards and 12 inches of fabric. Remember, this is the yardage for the flounce only. Measure the top of the bed, and add the amount needed for the top of the spread. This spread will cover just the bed.

If you want to make a spread that will also cover the bed pillows, add another 60 inches to the bed measurement before figuring the yardage for the flounce. To save yardage and make the shirring hang more gracefully, cut a shirred skirt on the crosswise grain.

A colorful print bedspread brightens the bed in this child's room. The fitted spread is made extra long in order to cover the pillow. With this spread, making the bed is a snap, even for a child. Always select washable, easy-care fabrics for children's rooms.

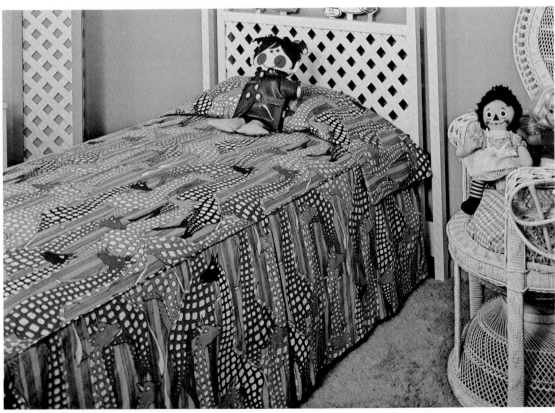

To assemble the spread, make the top section, and mark the corners as for the fitted box spread. Stitch the flounce sections together, using a French seam. Hem the lower edge. Gather the top edge using the gathering foot, or follow the directions on page 27. With the right sides together, pin the flounce to the top section at the corners, at the center of the foot, and at the center of each side. Pull up the gathering threads, or ease the gathered fabric to fit the top section. Stitch with the gathered side up.

To line the top section, use a firmly woven fabric such as broadcloth, muslin, or a bed sheet. Cut the lining the same size as the top. If you need to seam the lining, make sure the seams match those of the top. Press the seams open. Fold the flounce sections over the top of the spread. Place the lining over the top section, with the right sides together, and with the flounce in between. Pin along the side and foot seam lines. Stitch. Trim off the excess lining at the corners, and turn right side out. Hem the top of the spread, stitching straight across the ends of the flounce and the top of the spread.

Pleated flounces also make for attractive bedspreads, and present a slightly more tailored appearance than gathered flounces. The pleats can run continuously around the spread, or they can be evenly spaced, with one at each corner and one halfway between the head and foot on either side. If you are using a print with a definite repeat, center the design on each pleat. Measure the length of the skirt piece needed, including the hem and seam allowances. Decide on the best placement of the design for economical fabric cuts. Pleat a strip of fabric to determine the amount needed for the size of the pleat you are going to use.

Then, measure and space the pleats to fit the sides of the bed. For a better fit, plan inverted pleats at the corners. To determine the yardage needed, figure the number of pleats needed for the perimeter of the bed and the number of lengths required for pleating.

Construct the spread top. Then stitch the lengths together for the pleated flounce. Hem the lower edge of the flounce by hand or machine. Pin the pleats in place. Lay the top of the spread on the bed and mark the curve at the corners of the bed. Pin the pleated flounce around the top section to check the fit. If necessary, adjust the pleats.

Remove the flounce and press the pleats in place. Machine-baste along the seam line to hold the pleats.

With the right sides together, pin the pleated flounce to the top of the spread, easing the flounce around the corners. Machine-stitch. Bind or overcast seam allowances; or line the top, enclosing the seams. Turn under ½ inch across the head of the spread, including the two flounce sections. Turn under a 1½-inch hem, and press. Stitch the hem in place by hand or by machine.

Linings add body and increase the durability of bedspreads. Although many fabrics —such as corduroy, sailcloth, ribcord, and denim—do not require a lining for durability, a lining will ensure a neat finish to the inside. Another reason is to prevent snagging the long floats of intricately woven fabrics. You also should line all lightweight and sheer fabric bedspreads.

Select a lining fabric that is compatible with your bedspread fabric in both weight and color. Select from muslin, polished cotton, chintz, taffeta, batiste, and bed sheet.

Cut the lining for the top of the spread the same size as the top section. If it is necessary to piece the lining, be sure the seams match the seams on the spread. Cut the drop sections the same size as the drop sections of the spread, minus the hem allowance. To assemble, stitch the top sections of the spread together and press the seams open. Stitch seams in the top lining sections, and press open. Place the spread top on the bed, and mark the corner curves. Mark the same curves on the lining. Stitch the three drop sections together at the corner seams, but do not hem. Press seams open. Repeat with lining.

With wrong sides together, baste the spread drop and lining drop sections together, matching the upper edges and the corner seams. Pin the drop around the top of the spread, right side of drop to right side of the spread top. Ease drop sections at the corners, and stitch in place. Place the right side of the top lining section over the spread top with the drop and drop lining in between. Pin along sides and foot. Stitch. Trim the excess out of the corners, and turn right side out. Press. To hem, fold under ½ inch around the lower edge of spread, and press. Turn a 1½-inch hem over the lining; press and pin. Hem to the lining by hand. Turn and hem the spread across the top.

Separate pillow covers are needed when bedspreads are fitted to the bed length and do not have a pillow covering allowance. You can make *shams, bolsters* (see Chapter 6), or *special covers* to match or complement this type of bedspread.

One easy way to make a pillow *cover* is to sew a separate piece of fabric at the head of the bedspread to fold over the pillows.

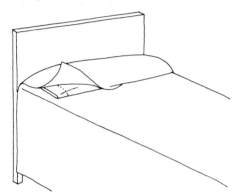

To do this, cut a piece of fabric 32 inches long and the width of the bed plus 4 inches for hems. To cover standard-size pillows, 32 inches will be adequate; however, if you have oversize pillows, cut the strip longer. If the spread top is pieced, seam the pillow cover to match. Hem the pillow cover along the sides and the bottom. Fold under ½ inch along the top and press. Pin the folded edge along the top hem of the bedspread and top-stitch in place.

Pillow shams are separate covers for pillows that usually match the bedspread and often have a flange hem or a ruffled edge.

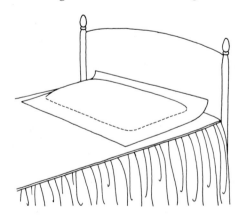

To make a pillow sham with a flange hem, measure the length and the width of the pillow over the center of the pillow. Add 1 inch to each measurement for ease allowance. To determine the width of the flange, place the pillow on the bed and measure the distance from the pillow to the edge of the bed. Add this amount to the width and length measurements all around. Then, add 1 inch more to both the length and width for the seam allowances. The finished pillow sham should cover the entire width of a single bed or half the width of a double bed.

Cut the top section following the instructions above. Cut two back sections half the width of the top and add 2 inches for overlap. Hem one edge of each back section with a narrow hem. With right sides together, pin the back sections over the top, overlapping hemmed edges at the center. Stitch a ½-inch seam around the outside edge. Trim the seam and clip the corners. Turn right side out and press. Measure and chalk-mark the width of the flange, allowing for pillow measurements plus ease. Topstitch on the marked line. Insert pillow through the lapped opening.

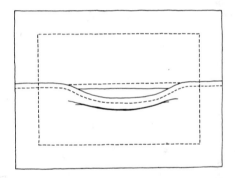

For a ruffle-edged sham, measure pillow length and width over fullest part. Add 1 inch for ease and 1 inch for seam allowances to both the length and width measurements. Cut one piece for the top. Cut two back-pieces half the width of the front plus 2 inches for the hem and overlap. Cut bias strips for ruffles. Piece the ruffle strips, if necessary. Hem one edge. Gather the strips, using the ruffler or by pulling up gathering threads (see page 27). Pin the ruffled strip to the top of the sham, with right sides together. Stitch with the ruffled side up. Pin the backing pieces over the ruffles and the top section. The right side of the back sections will be against the right side of the top section, with ruffles in between. The backpieces will overlap along hemmed edges. Stitch. Trim seams, turn right side out, and insert pillow.

A fitted spread for a studio couch is constructed similarly to the fitted box spread, except that the studio couch cover encloses all four sides.

Select a fabric that coordinates with other furnishings in the room. Chintz, linen, corduroy, velveteen, sailcloth, denim, and duck are all good choices. The more firmly woven the fabric is, the better it will hold its shape. Also, be sure to consider carefully the weight, texture, color, and design of the fabric that you choose.

Solid colors are the easiest to work with because there is no design to match. Floral prints or prints with a one-directional design require a little more planning because you must match and center the designs. Handle allover prints the same as solid-colored fabrics. You'll need to match striped fabric on the lengthwise grain. If you work with plaid fabrics, you must match them on both lengthwise and crosswise grains.

You can style studio couch covers to fit any decor. Make a fitted box cover, as illustrated on page 77, using these instructions.

Measure your studio couch, following the general directions on page 77. Measure the length (A), the width (B), the depth of the mattress (D), and the distance from the bottom of the mattress to the floor (E). If you want to make covers for the bolsters or cushions, refer to the chapter on pillows.

To the above measurements, add the following allowances for the seams and hems: add 1 inch to the length (A) and 1 inch to the width (B) for seam allowances around the top. For the boxing strips, add 1 inch to the mattress depth measurement (D) for seam allowances. You'll also need two boxing strips the length of the mattress plus 1 inch for the seams, and two strips the width of the mattress plus 1 inch for the seams. To the flounce measurement (E), add ½ inch for the seam and 2 inches for the hem. The length of the flounce pieces must include the allowances for the pleats. Remember that each pleat requires 16 inches.

If you have seams joining the flounce pieces, they should be at the back fold of the pleats so they will not be conspicuous. For front and back flounce pieces, add 24 inches to the length measurement (A) for the pleats and 1 inch for the seams. For the end flounce pieces, add 24 inches to the width measurement (B) and 1 inch for the seams. Also, keep in mind that you'll need additional fabric for cutting the bias strips to cover the cord for the welting.

Cut the pieces for the studio couch cover, matching the designs where necessary. Cut the bias strips for the cord covering. Cut the bias strips three times the width of the cording, plus 1 inch for the seam allowances. Join the bias strips and cover the cord, following the directions given on pages 24 and 25.

Lay the top piece over the mattress, and pin mark the curve at the corners. Compare the pin markings and perfect the curve. Then, chalk-mark the same curve on each corner. Pin the welting around the top piece, easing it around the corners. Do not pull the cording; pulling will cause the seams to pucker. Stitch the welting in place. Join boxing strips with ½-inch seams at the corners.

Press the seams open. Machine-stitch along the upper seam line (½ inch from the edge) for approximately 4 inches on either side of the corner seam. With the right sides together, pin the boxing strip to the top piece, matching corner seams with the corners of the top. Ease the boxing strip around the corners. Clip the seam allowance of boxing strip so the seam will lay flat. Stitch with boxing strip on top. Turn right side out and press the seam toward the boxing strip.

If your fabric tends to ravel, overcast the seams by hand or machine, or bind the raw edges with bias tape. Pin welting to lower edge of the boxing strip and stitch it in place. Place a pin at the seam line, marking the exact center of each of the four sides.

Join the flounce strips end to end with ½-inch seams. Turn under the 2-inch hem allowance along the lower edge and press. Turn under the raw edge of the hem and stitch by hand or machine around the entire flounce. Place a pin along the top seam line, marking the center of each of the flounce sections: front, back and the two ends.

Pin flounce to boxing strip, matching center markings. Then, fold the pleats in place — each pleat should be 4 inches deep. Pin the center front and center back pleats in place, then pin pleats at each corner. See the illustration on page 80 for forming pleats.

Clip seam allowances at top of hem so that seams will lay flat. Adjust pleats until the flounce fits smoothly. Remove the pleated flounce and press the pleats, keeping vertical folds straight. Machine-baste each pleat

85

along the seam line. With right sides together, pin the pleated flounce to the boxing
strip and stitch in place with a ½-inch seam.
Press the seam up, toward the boxing strip.
Bind or overcast the edges, if necessary. Press
the cover and place it over the studio couch.

Use these basic instructions as a starting
point and create the design best suited to
your decor. Your studio couch probably
leads a double life. It may be a seating space
in a sewing room or den by day, and then a
bed at night when guests arrive. This dual-
purpose existence calls for special attention
when selecting a style and fabric.

For a softer, less tailored look, follow the
same basic directions, but substitute a gathered flounce for the pleated one described on
the previous page. You can also cover the
welting with fabric of a contrasting color.
This treatment will provide a custom-made
look. Select cushions or bolsters from the
wide variety of shapes available—box- or
wedge-shaped pillows, round or square
bolsters, or rectangular cushions. For a uni-

fied look, cover them to match the couch. Or,
add color accents with decorative pillows in
different sizes and shapes.

To create a professionally upholstered
look, make separate covers for the mattress
and the box spring. Cover the mattress on
both sides with cording around the boxing
strip, like a cushion. Use a long zipper to run
the full length of the back of the cover. Make
a separate fitted box cover for the spring
section. The boxing strip should be the depth
of the box spring, and the flounce should be
equal to the distance from the spring to the
floor. This will give the flounce the short-
skirted look that is often found on upholstered furniture.

This method does require additional fabric, but it is more durable and practical. You
can cover both sides of the mattress and turn
it frequently so that the fabric wears evenly.
Measure carefully for each piece. Remember
that you'll need three pieces the size of the
top of the mattress, one for each side of the
mattress, and one to cover the top of the box

*Decorative tabs with buckles and buttons trim
this studio couch cover. The red and blue colors
are picked up from the plaid fabric that covers*
*the alcove in the wall. An assortment of deco-
rative pillows makes this couch a great place
to curl up with a good book.*

spring. Make the mattress cover, following the cushion directions in chapter 7. Then, make the spring cover, using these basic directions as a guide.

Throw or Draped Bedspreads

The throw-style bedspread or draped spread is a flat piece of fabric that is thrown or draped over the bed. It's easy to make and is an ideal project for a beginner. There are two seams and a hem. The full length of the spread, from floor to the head including the pillow cover, is cut in one piece. Another length is split and sewn to each side of the center section.

The straight lines of this bedspread allow countless possibilities for one-of-a-kind decorating. The plain center section is ideal for appliqueing or monogramming. For a bold contemporary look, make the center section one color and the outer strips a contrasting color. You can have a plain hem or trim it with fringe, braid, or tassels. Or, consider using binding to finish the outer edges. If you simply attach decorative fold-over braid, there's no hemming needed. Or give this versatile throw a soft, feminine look by sewing ruffles around the hemline.

Fabrics suitable for the throw-style spread range from elegant silk to plush deep-pile to sturdy denim. Strong, firmly woven fabrics are the best choice for beds that will get a lot of use. Reserve delicate fabrics for use in rooms where bedspreads will not be used a great deal. Throws can be lined or unlined. Line lightweight or sheer fabrics to prevent patterned sheets and blankets from showing through. The lining will also help to prevent wrinkles and prolong the life of the spread.

How to measure: To estimate the amount of fabric required, measure the length, width, and height of your bed. The length of the throw is equal to the length of the bed plus the height. To this measurement add 4 inches for hems and 30 inches to cover the pillows. This is the total length needed for each section. If you plan to bind the edges, omit the hem allowances. To determine the total width you'll need, double the height measurement and add it to the width measurement. Then, add 4 inches for seams and another 4 inches for hems, unless you plan to bind the edges. From these two measurements, estimate the yardage you'll need.

For example, a standard bed with bedding measures approximately 76 inches long, 55 inches wide, and 21 inches high. Therefore, 76+21+30+4=131 inches, or almost four yards. The width will require 55+42 (the doubled height) +4=101 inches. Always figure one full width for the center of the spread, then add pieces on either side to meet the width requirement. If you select a bolt 54 inches wide, you'll need 8 yards.

How to make a throw: First cut one length for the center of the spread and cut off the selvages. Then cut the sections for each side, matching the design if necessary.

If you plan to decorate the center of the spread, apply the applique or monogram before joining the side seams. Be sure your design is in proper proportion.

Seam the sections together with ½-inch seams. On unlined spreads use a French seam, a self-bound seam, or a flat-fell seam to enclose the raw edges.

Leave the corners at the foot of the bed either square or rounded. Square corners will stand out, tent-style. Rounded corners will hang in graceful folds and will just clear the floor. To round the corners, place the spread on the bed and mark the outline of the edge of the mattress along the foot and sides. Remove the spread from the bed and lay it out on a flat surface. Measure the distance between the marked line and the edge of the spread. At the corner of the mattress marking, measure out the same distance and mark a rounded corner.

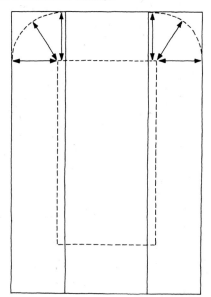

The throw-style bedspread adapts well to many decorating themes. Its simple lines do not interfere with the pattern-on-pattern theme featured *in the room above. Different prints that feature the same blue-and-white scheme create a crisp, uncluttered look in the room.*

Then, fold one corner in half by bringing the side edges to meet the end, and check the curve to make sure it is even and smooth. Fold the bedspread lengthwise—bringing the corners together—and mark both corners the same. Fit the bedspread on the bed before cutting off the excess. If there are posts, these rounded corners may be slit diagonally up to the edge of the mattress so that they will flare and overlap; or, the corners may be cut out, allowing 1 inch for hems.

If you plan to trim the seams with braid or ribbons, pin the trimmings in place over the top of the seams and topstitch them in place, stitching close to either side.

To hem the spread, turn under a 1-inch double hem on all sides and press. Ease fullness at the curves and miter the hem at the corners. Hem by hand or machine.

If you plan to bind the edges, purchase ready-made binding or cut bias strips twice the finished width of the binding plus 1 inch for seam allowances. With right sides to-

gether, pin the binding ½ inch from the edge, and stitch 1 inch from the outer edge. Turn the binding to the underside and press. Then, turn under the raw edge and blind-stitch to the seam on the underside.

How to line your bedspread: Cut the lining sections the same size as the spread sections. Stitch the seams of the lining and press open. In order to keep the spread and the lining smooth, you will need to attach the lining to the spread along the seam lines. Loosely catch-stitch the seam allowances together.

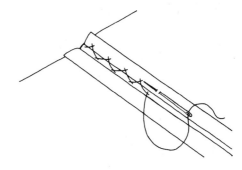

Pin the lining to the spread, with wrong sides together. Starting at the center, pin from the top to the bottom. Smooth the lining out to the seams and pin along the seam lines. Fold back the outer sections of the lining and catch-stitch the lining to the spread along the seams. Smooth the lining over the spread again, and pin the outer edges of the spread and the lining together, making sure that both layers are smooth.

For a plain edge, turn under the hem of the spread, press, and stitch. Trim the lining to within ½ inch of the finished edge. Turn under the raw edge and slip-stitch the lining to the hem of the spread.

If the edges are to be bound, baste the outer edges of the spread and the lining together. Then, when attaching the binding, handle it as a single fabric.

Handling special fabrics such as fake fur, designer prints, or your own tie-dyed originals is easy when you're dealing with throw-style bedspreads. This is true because of the simple lines of the throw, and because there are no complex seams to interfere with the beauty of the fabric.

Fake-fur fabrics make handsome bedspreads. These 'furs' are not difficult to work with, but a few special techniques will make the job easier, and make your spread more professional-looking.

Fake furs have a nap or direction unless the fur pile is brushed in a swirled pattern. Brush your hand lightly over the surface of the fabric. The smoother feel is the nap or direction of the pile. Make sure that the nap runs in the same direction on all pieces.

If your fabric has a very thick pile—or if it is quite expensive—you might want to make your throw to cover just the bed and use separate covers for the pillows. To make 'fur' shams for your pillows, follow the directions on page 83. Make the back section from the lining fabric or another coordinated fabric.

Use sharp shears to cut fake-fur fabrics. If the pile is thick, cut through the backing fabric with a single-edged razor blade. Carefully brush the hairs away from the seam line, and hand-baste the seams securely.

To sew fake fur, test the machine stitching on scraps of the fabric, using a medium to long stitch (8 to 10 stitches per inch). If the hair is long, loosen the pressure on the presser foot, and adjust the tension. Use the point of a needle to carefully pull out any

hairs that are caught in the stitching. Finger-press the seams open. If the 'fur' is bulky, shear the hair from the seam allowances. Catch-stitch the open seam allowances to the backing to keep the seams flat.

Never press the nap on fake-fur fabrics. If the fabric requires pressing, use a dry iron only on the backing.

To line your 'fur' throw, cut the lining fabric the same size as the 'fur' sections. Seam the sections together and press the seams open. Attach the lining to the seams with a catch-stitch.

'Fur' throws can be hemmed or finished with a binding around the edges. To hem the 'fur,' turn the cut edge to the underside and catch-stitch it to the backing. Trim the lining to within ½ inch of the hem. Turn the raw edge under ½ inch shorter than the 'fur,' and blindstitch it to the hem.

If the pile is thick, bind the outer edges rather than turning under a hem. Baste the lining and the 'fur' fabric together, close to the edge. Bind the edges with ready-made fold-over braid, or cut bias strips and bind by hand or machine.

To finish your 'fur' throw without a lining, trim the seam allowances to ¼ inch, and cover them with twill tape or bias tape. Pin the tape to the backing on either side of the seam, encasing the seam allowances. Blind-stitch the edges of the tape to the backing. Bind the outer edges of the throw.

Vinyl fabrics also make excellent special-effect coverings. They are suited particularly well to dual-purpose rooms, such as a den-guest room, because the vinyl throw provides a neat, tailored look. Select vinyls that are fused to a knitted or woven fabric backing because these are generally more durable and easier to work with. Although vinyl fabrics cannot be dry-cleaned, they are easy to clean with a damp, soapy sponge, so line a vinyl throw with a drip-dry fabric.

Following the general directions for making a throw, cut the sections for your vinyl spread. Unless you have an extremely soft vinyl fabric, make your spread without a pillow covering allowance. Then make separate covers for the pillows. To make matching vinyl bolster covers, follow the directions in chapter 6.

Many different techniques will simplify stitching vinyl. Do not pin through the vinyl because this leaves marks. Use paper clips instead. Handling large pieces of vinyl can be difficult, so use a special roller foot attachment which will help move the fabric; or, cut pieces of tissue paper and place them on either side of the vinyl to help feed the material smoothly through the machine. Also, use a fine machine needle, mercerized thread, and a long stitch.

Never press vinyl with an iron. Finger-press the seams open. If they will not lay flat, hold the seam allowances in place by topstitching on either side of the seam or by gluing the seam allowances to the backing. Be sure to use a special fabric glue that will not become stiff when it dries. Finish the edges with a single narrow hem or bind the edges with ready-made fold-over braid.

A tie-dyed bedspread can be the center of interest in a bedroom. And what better way is there to display your favorite hobby than draping it over your bed? Use a fabric (white or a pale neutral color) that is sturdy and closely woven. Make sure that the fiber you're using is one that will dye easily. Most washable fabrics—except some polyesters and acrylics—will accept dye.

To make a tie-dyed spread, cut the section for the throw, allowing 2 extra inches for shrinkage and frayed edges. Stitch the seams. Then, tie-dye in your favorite designs and colors. Press the throw after it has dried. Trim it to the correct size, and follow the instructions for the basic throw.

Designer prints, batik fabrics, and silk-screened print or block-printed fabrics all make charming throw-style bedspreads. Follow the instructions for the basic throw.

For a custom-made look, trim the outer edges with several rows of braid or fringe. The trimmings will also act as weights and help the throw hang smoothly.

Make the spread long enough to cover the pillows. Or, if you wish, select coordinated fabrics for bolsters or pillow shams.

Fabulous 'fur' to throw across your bed—what luxury! Create your own 'fur' bedspread with the use of fake-fur fabric. It's easy to seam it together in a simple throw-style bedspread. For added textural interest, make the pillow shams from contrasting fabrics.

90

Coverlets

Coverlets, or bedspreads that have a short drop, can be fitted or throw-style and combined with either a dust ruffle or a fitted flounce. Because coverlets use less fabric than a full bedspread, you can change them more often. They can double as a blanket, too.

The length of the drop of a coverlet will depend on the height of your bed, and whether or not it is combined with a flounce. The standard drop is approximately 10 inches from the top of the bed—usually about 4 inches below the bottom of the mattress along the sides and the foot. However, determine the exact depth of the drop by the proportions of your bed. If you have an antique bed, which may be quite high, you may want a coverlet drop deeper than 4 inches below the bottom of the mattress.

Extend the coverlet to cover the pillows, or use it with separate pillow covers. To make a fitted coverlet, follow the instructions for fitted bedspread and adjust depth of drop.

It often is possible to make a throw-style coverlet for a twin or single bed from one width of fabric.

Determine the depth of the drop needed, then follow the directions for the throw-style bedspread.

How to make a coverlet: The eye-catching coverlet below is an example of one of the many ways you can make a coverlet. This coverlet is made with 12 alternating strips of tangerine velveteen and purple ribless corduroy with a tailored flounce.

To make this beautiful coverlet, measure your bed and determine the width of the completed coverlet. Divide this measurement by the finished width of the strips (8 or 9 inches) to determine the number of strips you'll need. An even number of strips will give you a spread with alternating colors on the outside edges. An uneven number will result in matching colors along outside edges.

Allow ¾ inch for seam allowances on either side of each strip (if the finished width is 8 inches, cut the strips 9½ inches wide; for 9-inch finished strips, cut each strip 10½ inches wide). To determine the length of each strip, measure the length of your bed. Then, add the depth of the drop and 1½ inches for seam allowance and hem. If the spread is to cover the pillows, add another

Velveteen and ribless corduroy combine to give the coverlet shown below a soft, inviting texture. Cording stitched along the strips adds a

professional, custom-made look. To perk up a dull room, select fabric in the colors of your choice, and sew a special coverlet for your bed.

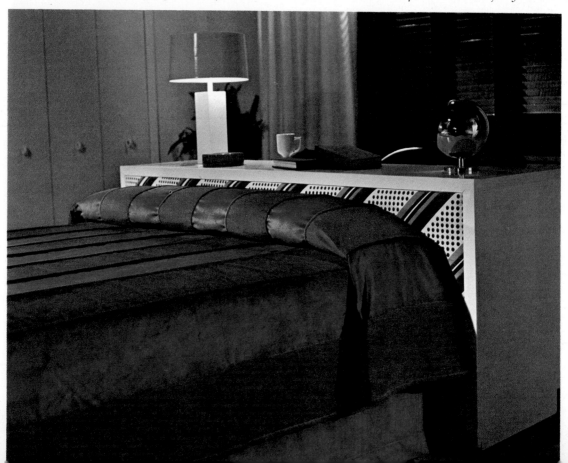

30 inches. Edge each strip with cording, and finish the outer edge of the coverlet with bias-covered cording. Don't forget to allow additional velveteen for covering the cording around the outer edge of the spread.

You'll also need ¼-inch cord between each strip and ½-inch cord to be sewn to the sides and foot of the spread. The amounts of cord that are needed will vary, naturally, according to the size of your bed and the depth of the drop. A queen-size bed with allowances for covering the pillows requires approximately 5 yards of ½-inch cord and 36 yards of ¼-inch cord.

Cut the necessary number of strips. Then, cut the bias strips 4¾ inches wide to cover the cording that will finish outer edges.

Before stitching, check to make sure the nap on all strips runs in the same direction. With right sides together, baste one purple and one tangerine strip together, just inside the seam allowance. With the tangerine side up, lay the ¼-inch cord over the basting. Fold the velveteen over the cording and pin in place. Machine-stitch close to the cord, using a cording foot.

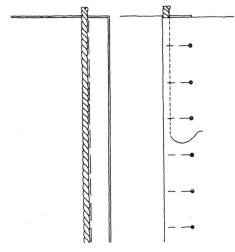

Continue to add strips, alternating the colors until the width of the spread is completed. Always use the tangerine velveteen to cover the cording. Place the coverlet on the bed to check the fit. Round the corners at the foot of the bed, marking the curve with pins. Fold one corner in half and bring the side edges to meet the end. Then, check the curve to make sure it is even and smooth. Fold bedspread lengthwise, bringing corners together, and make both curves the same.

Sew 4¾-inch bias strips together and press seams open. Cover ½-inch cording with bias strips, leaving ½ inch fabric on one side of cording and 2¾ inches on the other. Gently stretch bias as you stitch. Pin cording around outer edge of spread with narrow seam to inside. Stitch, using a cording foot, easing cording around corners. Turn one inch of the 2¾-inch allowance under and slip-stitch in place. Fold over seam allowance at top twice and stitch ½ inch from edge.

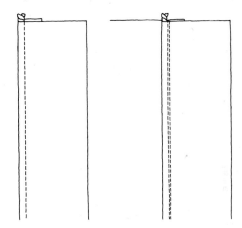

Clip the seam allowances around the curves, and turn the folded side of the strip to the underside. Ease the excess around the corners. Turn 1 inch of the 2¾-inch allowance under, and press. Pin to the underside of the throw, and slip-stitch in place.

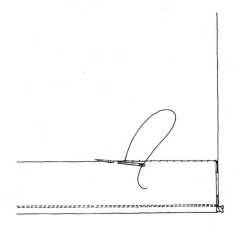

Overcast seams by hand or machine, or bind them with bias tape. To reduce the bulk at the top hem, gently pull approximately ½ inch of the cording out of each seam, and trim off. Turn under a narrow hem and machine-stitch ½ inch from the folded edge.

Dust Ruffles and Tailored Flounces

A dust ruffle or a tailored flounce is used with a coverlet to conceal the springs and the legs of a bed. The dust ruffle is gathered around three sides of the bed; the tailored flounce is plain and is fitted around the bed with pleats at the corners. You also can place pleats at the center of each side and in the center of the foot section on a king-size bed.

The ruffle or flounce extends from the top of the spring to ½ inch above the floor or carpet. Sew the ruffle or flounce to the piece of sheeting or muslin that covers the spring. To prevent the muslin from showing when the coverlet is removed, join the skirt to the center section with a 4-inch-wide strip of matching fabric. Or, attach the dust ruffle or flounce directly to the box spring with snap tape or Velcro.

You can use a variety of fabrics and colors. Select a fabric that will coordinate with the other fabrics and furnishings in the bedroom. Match the coverlet, curtains, or slipcovers or use a neutral color. Sheets are ideal for making dust ruffles because you can coordinate them with the bed linens.

How to make a gathered dust ruffle: Attach the dust ruffle to a piece of muslin or a section of sheeting cut to the size of the spring. When the mattress is placed on top, the muslin is anchored between the spring and the mattress, allowing the dust ruffle to fall evenly on all sides. Standard dust ruffles require double fullness. For extra fullness, triple the length of the area to be covered. The depth of the dust ruffle—depending on the height of the spring—will be anywhere from 10 to 18 inches.

Measure the width and the length of your box spring. Then measure the height, from the top of the spring to ½ inch above the floor.

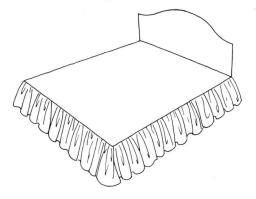

To the height measurement, add 4½ inches for seam and hem. The length of the ruffle is twice the bed length plus the width. Multiply the length measurement by two for double fullness; multiply by three if the fabric is lightweight or sheer. Add 1 inch for each joining seam and 4 inches for hems at the ends.

Seam the strips together with French seams, forming one long strip. Make a 1-inch double hem along both ends. Make a double 2-inch hem along one long side and run two rows of gathering stitches along the edge of the opposite side, or gather, using the ruffler attachment on your sewing machine.

If you wish to conceal the muslin, cut three strips of the ruffle fabric 4 inches wide, two strips the length of the bed plus 1 inch for seams, and one the width of the bed plus 1 inch. Press under ½ inch along one long side of each strip. Cut the muslin or sheeting to the length and width of the spring plus a ½-inch seam allowance on all four sides.

Remove the mattress and place the muslin piece over the spring to check the fit. Pin the raw edges of the strip along the outer edge of the muslin piece, wrong side of strip to right side of muslin. Miter the corners at the foot of the bed. Pin. Remove the muslin cover and stitch the strips in place. Baste along the outer edges and topstitch close to the folded edges; topstitch the mitered corners in place.

Turn under a ½-inch hem along the top, folding ends of strips into the hem. Stitch.

With right sides together, pin the skirt to the muslin section, pulling up gathers or adjusting the ruffled fullness to fit around the three sides. Stitch the ruffle to the center section. Place the completed dust ruffle over the box spring, slipcover-fashion, and replace the mattress.

How to make a tailored flounce: Measure the bed, as directed for gathered skirt. Then, determine the number of pleats you want in the skirt. To the length of the flounce strips, add 10 inches for each pleat plus 4 inches to hem the ends and 1 inch for each joining seam.

Plan the joining seams so that they will fall at the back fold of the pleats. Join the strips with ½-inch plain seams. Hem the lower edge. Fold the pleats in place, making each pleat 2½ inches deep, and pin along the seam line. Pin the pleated flounce around the bed to check the fit. Adjust pleats, if necessary. Remove the flounce from bed and press pleats.

Clip the seams at the top of the hem so they will lay flat. Machine-baste along the top seam line to hold the pleats in place. Cut the top section and attach the pleated flounce, following the directions for the gathered dust ruffle on page 92.

To attach a dust ruffle or a flounce directly to the mattress, cut and construct either the gathered or the pleated skirt. Hem the lower edge and both ends, and arrange the pleats or gathers.

Cut a strip of fabric 2½ inches wide and equal to the distance around the three sides of the bed, plus 1 inch for hems at the ends. With right sides together, pin the top of the skirt to one side of the strip and stitch. Press the seam allowances to the strip side.

Turn under ½ inch on the opposite side of the strip and press. Remove the mattress and place the skirt around the bed to check the fit. Pin the strip to the top of the spring, and miter the corners so they will lay flat. With a piece of chalk, mark a line on the mattress along the edge of the strip. Remove the skirt

and stitch the corners to hold the miter in place. Pin Velcro or the receiving side of snap tape along the underside of the strip. Clip the Velcro or snap tape to form square corners.

Pin the other half of the snap tape or Velcro to the top of the box spring, placing the inside edge of the tape along the marked line. Stitch it in place, using a curved upholstery needle, or glue it to the box spring cover with fabric glue.

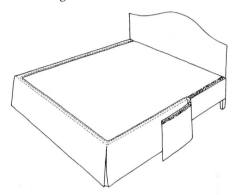

In the bedroom below, a fitted coverlet and a gathered dust ruffle combine to make a charming bed cover. The clever use of a print, a stripe, and plush pillows gives this bedroom a sitting room atmosphere. The room is ideal for studying, reading, or just plain relaxing.

Canopies For All Bed Styles

The four-poster canopy is truly king of the beds. The decorative and dramatic canopy beds of today have little in common with their ancestors. Functional canopies with the side curtains to draw as a protection against the cold night air are no longer needed. Today, canopies are strictly decorative; they do however add drama, elegance, and excitement to a bedroom.

There is a canopy for every type of decorating theme, from the quaint antique to the most contemporary setting. Modern furniture with its sleek lines can be enhanced with a tailored canopy. A gracefully curved or gathered canopy adds charm and warmth to traditional furniture. For the budget-minded homemaker whose bedroom is furnished with attic and basement furniture, an easy-to-make partial canopy can add excitement to an otherwise dull, unimaginative room.

If the idea of a canopy delights you but you don't have a canopy bed, don't despair. You can easily construct a canopy with standard lumber and a little skill. Partial canopies are easy to make from curtain rods mounted to the wall and ceiling.

There are two major types of canopy beds, the curved style and the flat style. The canopy hangs from a framework attached to the four posts of the bed. Construct the posts and canopy frame in such a way that the posts extend above the canopy. Slats or crosspieces join the sides of the canopy and act as a support for the fabric. Canopy beds are some-

times made with a solid wooden top, usually decorated with molding. These canopies can be fitted with rods on the inside to hold curtains or a valance. When curtains are used, they are tied to the posts at the bed top.

The traditional curved or arched canopy usually is topped by a ruffled canopy that matches either the bedspread or the dust ruffle. Chintz prints, checked gingham, and calico prints are all appropriate for use on this canopy bed. For a feminine look, trim the canopy with embroidered eyelet or organdy.

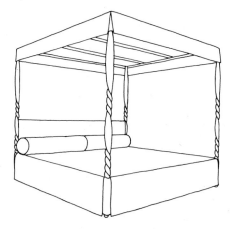

The flat-style canopy lends itself to more tailored treatments. Documentary prints, stripes, plaids, or bold floral prints, as well as solid-color fabrics, are all good choices. The sides of this canopy are usually plain with inverted pleats or vents at the corners.

The decorative impact of a canopy bed is felt strongly in any bedroom. So, if you have a canopy bed, carefully plan your bedroom decor with the bed as the center of interest. Place it along the center of a plain wall where it can be easily seen. Consider the style and the basic design of the furnishings in the room, too.

A hand-stenciled bedspread is the key to the color scheme in this traditional bedroom. The bold blue canopy with matching pillow shams and dust ruffle repeats the blue in the spread and draws attention to the graceful canopy. →

Following are directions for constructing various types of canopies. Use these instructions as a guide to create the canopy that will best suit your bed because canopy beds vary a great deal in their basic construction.

Arched Canopies

The arched canopy is a straight piece of fabric with a ruffle attached. The framework of the bed gives the canopy its shape. To make an arched canopy, first use a flexible tape to measure the distance along the top of the arch. Then, measure the width of the canopy frame, and determine the depth of the ruffle. This will run from 6 inches to 12 inches, depending on the size of your bed and the type of fabric you select. Make the ruffle with either double or triple fullness. The lighter the fabric, the more fullness you'll need.

Cut a section of fabric to cover the top of the canopy (length times width), plus 1 inch around all sides. If necessary, seam the fabric to achieve the proper width. Cut the lining fabric to the same size. Make the lining of the same fabric or a coordinated color because it will be seen from the underside of the canopy.

Place the lining over the frame to check the fit. Use masking tape to hold the fabric in place while you mark the corners around the posts. Remove the lining and trim the corners ½ inch from the marked line. Mark and trim the corners of the outer fabric to match the lining. Pin the lining and canopy fabrics right sides together and stitch a ½-inch seam all around, leaving an opening along one side for turning. Clip the seam allowances at the corners. Turn right side out and press. Turn in raw edges of the opening, and slip-stitch the edges together.

Cut the strips for the ruffle, allowing a 1-inch heading and 1 inch for narrow hems. Cut the strips on the crosswise grain because this saves fabric and the ruffles will hang better. Join the ruffle sections with French seams or a narrow flat-fell seam. Seam the ends together, forming a circle. Hem both sides of the ruffle with a narrow hem. For efficiency in hemming, use the narrow hemmer foot. Gather the ruffle by using the ruffler attachment, or two rows of gathering threads. Stitch one row 1 inch from the top edge and the second row 1½ inches from the top edge.

With the wrong side of the ruffle to the right side of the canopy top, pin the ruffle around the canopy. Place the top row of gathering threads ½ inch from the edge of the top section, with the heading toward the center and the ruffle extending beyond the edge. Do not attach the ruffle to the corners.

Allow enough space between the corner area and the ruffle for the post to slip through. Adjust the ruffle or pull up the gathers to fit the canopy. Topstitch the ruffle to the top section, continuing to stitch on the ruffle section around the corner. This will anchor the gathers in place. Slip the canopy over the posts and adjust it on the framework. Thumbtack the canopy to the top of the frame to secure it.

Flat-Style Canopies

The flat-style canopy can be made with a gathered flounce or a plain flounce. To make the gathered style, follow the directions above. The plain, tailored-style canopy is fully lined, and features small pleats at the corners and a welted seam around the top.

To make the tailored canopy, first measure the length and the width of the canopy frame. Cut the fabric for the top section, allowing a ½-inch seam allowance around all sides. Seam strips of the fabric together, if necessary, to achieve the correct width. Cut the lining the same as the top section.

Determine the depth of the flounce and add 1 inch for seams at the top and the bottom. To the end length measurement, add 13 inches for the pleats and seams. To the side length measurement, add 5 inches for pleats and seams. This will make 4-inch inverted pleats at each corner, with the joining seams at the back inside fold of each pleat. Cut the four flounce sections—two sides and two ends. Cut the lining sections the same. Stitch the flounce sections end to end with ½-inch seams, forming a circle. Be sure to alternate the pieces, one side, then one end, then the second side and the second end. Join the

Warm brown and gold tones intensify the beauty → *of this handsomely tailored canopy bed. The matching bolsters and canopy repeat the mellow golden tone from the bedspread and set the mood for quiet relaxation in this room.*

lining sections in the same manner. Press the seams open. With right sides facing, pin lining and the outer fabric together along the lower edge. Stitch a ½-inch seam. Trim the seam, turn right side out, and press. Fold the pleats at each corner, making each fold 2 inches deep. Pin and press.

Cut bias strips to cover the cord. Strips must be three times the width of the cord plus 1 inch for seam allowances. Seam the strips together and press the seams open. Cover the cord, using the cording foot. Stretch the bias slightly as you stitch. Pin the welting to the right side of the top section, with raw edges even. Place over the canopy frame to check the fit. Set the welting right along the outer edge of the frame.

If the posts extend above the frame, fold back the top corners, leaving an opening between the cording and the top section. Slip the posts through the opening, and mark the top snugly around the post. Remove from the frame and trim out the corners ½ inch from the marked line. Fold under on the marked line and press. Trim, fold, and press the lining corners to match. Stitch the welting in place, using the cording foot.

With the right sides together, pin the pleated flounce to the top section and the welting, keeping the raw edges even. Adjust the pleats, if necessary. Stitch. If corners are open, stitch the flounce to the welting only around the corner areas.

Place the canopy right side up on a flat surface, with the flounce folded to the center as when stitching. Lay lining right side down over the canopy, smooth out from the center, and pin to the seam line. Stitch along the seam line, leaving an opening at one end for turning. If the corners are cut out, stitch across the corners on creased line, joining the lining and the top sections only. Trim and clip seam allowances and turn right side out. Press, folding in raw edges at the opening. Slip-stitch the open edges together.

To finish the welted edge at the open corners, clip the seam allowances at the edge of the top section and press down. Trim out the excess seam allowances and whipstitch the raw edge to flounce lining. For a special, personalized effect, attach decorative ribbon or braid to the flounce. Press the entire canopy, creasing the corner pleats firmly. Place the canopy over canopy frame, and thumbtack it to the frame.

Partial Canopies

Partial canopies can deliver the same decorative punch as the true canopy bed. There are several ways to create a partial canopy. Pictured on the next page is a simple, yet exciting canopy created with dramatic fabric and curtain rods. For this canopy/headboard effect, use a fabric that is coordinated with your bedspread. The wider fabrics work best because with them there is no need for seams in the center section of the canopy.

Measure the width of the bed to determine the finished width of the canopy. Purchase three brass or wooden rods the width of the bed. Mount one rod on the ceiling directly over the bed, 1 inch from the sidewall. Mount the second rod on the ceiling approximately 30 inches (more or less, depending on the effect you wish to achieve) from the wall. Make sure the two rods are parallel.

Measure the height of the wall and the distance between the rods. Then, determine the amount of drop you want at the front of the canopy and the amount of drape desired between the two rods. Add these four figures to find the total length of the fabric needed. Add an additional 4 inches for the casing for the rod weight, which hangs behind the bed.

Make the canopy double, so that it will hang and drape well. Cut two lengths of fabric the total length needed. To trim the edges or add width to the fabric, cut a 9-inch-wide strip according to the width of your fabric. (In the canopy pictured, the trimming strip matches the bedspread.)

Pin the two canopy sections together, right sides out, and baste close to the edges on all sides. Be sure the fabrics are perfectly smooth. Pin a trimming strip along one long side of the canopy, keeping the outer edges even. Let the trimming strip extend beyond the end that will be the top when you finish the canopy. Stitch a ½-inch seam along one long side to within ½ inch of the corner. Backstitch. Attach the strip to the opposite side in the same manner.

Pin and stitch the trimming strip to the top of the canopy, letting the strip extend equally at both ends. Start and stop stitching ½ inch from each edge. Press the seams toward the trimming. Turn under ½ inch along the free edge of the strips and press. Fold the strips to the underside, pinning the pressed edge along the seam line.

Miter the corners and slip-stitch in place. Blindstitch by hand, or machine-topstitch the binding to the back. Turn under ¼ inch along the bottom of the canopy. Then, turn again, forming a 1¾-inch casing. Press the canopy. Slip the third rod through the casing at the bottom. Drape the canopy over the two mounted rods. If the fabric slips out of place, use double-faced masking tape to anchor the fabric to the curtain rods.

You can make this same canopy with felt. Felt requires no lining and is available in width wide enough to equal the width of a king-size bed. Simply cut the felt to the proper length and make a casing at the bottom. Leave the felt plain or trim it with bands of braid. Or, if you wish, you can applique felt cutouts to the headboard area.

Valances mounted to the ceiling form another type of partial canopy. Choose the kind of heading you prefer and make the valance in the desired length. To hang this canopy, attach a 1-inch strip to the ceiling to form the size of the canopy. Staple or glue one side of snap tape or Velcro to the sides of the wood strip. Sew the other side of the tape to the top of the valance. You can easily remove the canopy when it is time for cleaning.

To hold side draperies, attach small curtain rods to the frame or to the ceiling inside the frame. Remember that draperies will be seen from both sides, so either make them double thickness or line them with a color-coordinated fabric.

Plain canopy frames can be built by anyone with a little woodworking skill. Make the posts from 4x4 posts or dowels at least 2 inches in diameter. Build a box frame from plywood and attach it to the top of the posts. Brace the frame with crosspieces attached to either side, flush with the top of the frame. Attach the posts to the frame of the bed or box spring, or let them stand free. Paint the frame or finish it to match the decorating style or color of other furnishings in the room. Cover it with a fitted canopy.

Boldly printed fabric makes a unique and inexpensive headboard/canopy that makes a plain bed the center of attention in this room. The canopy is draped over two curtain rods, which have been mounted on the ceiling. A third rod, behind the bed, holds the fabric taut.

Making Pillow Cases and Bed Linens

Bed linens require special attention in a truly coordinated bedroom. The wide array of color-coordinated sheets and pillow cases available today is a far cry from the total white of a few years ago. By combining printed and solid-color bed linens as well as by adding your own touches, you can give each bedroom a linen wardrobe all its own.

For your linens, pick up colors from the room's color scheme, and repeat with rows of rickrack or braid, or decorative machine-stitching along the hem lines.

Applique also can dress up linens. If you have used prints for curtains, dust ruffle, or bedspread, cut some of the motifs from the fabric and applique them along the border of a sheet. Do the applique by hand or machine, or with the use of an iron-on bonding web. And trim the borders of pillow cases to match.

How to make pillow cases: The yardages given here are for two pillows. If you use 36-inch fabric, you will need 4 yards for regular-size, 4½ yards for queen-size, and 5½ yards for king-size. If you use 45-inch fabric, you'll need 2 yards for regular-size pillows, 2¼ yards for queen-size pillows, and 2⅔ yards for king-size pillows.

When cutting the fabric, make sure the lengthwise grain runs from top to bottom of the cases, not from side to side. If you use 36-inch fabric, you'll fold and sew the cases differently than if you use 45-inch fabric.

The following chart gives the measurements for cutting the various sizes:

Pillow Size	Fabric Width	Size to Cut
Regular	36 inches	21x72 inches
Queen	36 inches	21x80 inches
King	36 inches	21x92 inches
Regular	45 inches	42x36 inches
Queen	45 inches	42x40 inches
King	45 inches	42x46 inches

To sew regular-size pillow cases, fold fabric in half, right sides together. If working with 36-inch fabric, fold the 21x72-inch piece of fabric to measure 21x36 inches, with the fold on the end. For 45-inch fabric, fold the 42x36-inch fabric to measure 21x36 inches, with the fold on one side.

With 45-inch fabric, stitch one end and open side to form the case. With 36-inch fabric, stitch the two open sides. Use a ⅜-inch seam and overcast the edges, or stitch seams with the narrow hemmer foot. For the hem, fold up 2½ inches, then fold over again for a double hem. Press and stitch.

Sheet trimming to match the pillowcase will vary in width according to the depth of your design. If you use a patterned fabric, allow for one pattern repeat. The yardage also will vary according to the width of the sheet. Cut the fabric strip 1 inch longer than the width of the sheet and 1 inch deeper than the desired depth of the trim. Allow an extra inch for piecing fabric. When strip is pieced, press under ½ inch on all sides. Trim off excess at corners where turned edges overlap. Place trimming strip on top of sheet.

If fabric pattern is a one-directional design, the top edge of the sheet will be the bottom edge at the foot of the bed when bed is made and the sheet is turned back. Pin strip in place and topstitch around edges.

How to make linens: Custom-made beds, odd-size antique beds, and special cots often create a problem when it comes to buying sheets to fit. For these unusual sizes, make your own fitted sheets rather than struggling with sizes that are too long or too wide. Ready-made flat sheets are best for making your own fitted sheets.

First, measure mattress length, width, and depth. For a fitted bottom sheet, add twice the depth of the mattress plus 4 inches for hems and tuck-ins to both length and width measurements. This gives the total size needed before finishing edges. Top sheets should have an overhang of 12 to 18 inches. Add the amount of overhang to either side for the total width. To the length, add the amount needed for tuckins at the foot of the bed and the amount of fold-back at the head. Add 4 inches for the top hem and 1¼ inches for the bottom hem. Compare these measurements to the sizes of standard sheets to determine which size is the most economical to use.

Cut the pieces, being sure to cut on the straight grain. If you use ready-made sheets, remove the hems and press flat.

Center the bottom sheet over the mattress. Make sure the overhang is the same on all sides. To fit the corners, hold the tip of one corner straight out from the mattress and pin the overhang side and end sections together exactly at the corner (edges must be even at the bottom). Allow a ½-inch seam allowance and trim off the excess fabric. Remove the pins, then fold the sheet into quarters with the cut corner on top. Following the cut edges, cut the remaining corners to match.

Pin the cut edges together at each corner, wrong sides of fabric out. Stitch a ½-inch corner seam. Overcast or bind the raw edges. Mark the exact center of each end.

Pin narrow elastic (¼ to ⅜ inch) to the boxing area on one side of the mattress approximately 6 inches from the corner. Stretch the elastic around the corner, across the end, and 6 inches down the other side and cut. Be sure elastic is stretched and taut. Cut a second piece of elastic the same size. Mark the center of each strip. Pin the center of the elastic to the center mark on the sheet, placing the elastic along the edge on the underside. Pin ends of the elastic 6 inches down the side from each corner. Then, stretch the elastic to fit the sheet and stitch to the edge. Hold the elastic and sheeting firmly both in front and in back of the needle as you stitch along the center of the elastic. Stitch with a regular or small zigzag stitch. Stitch elastic to the other end in the same manner. Turn the elastic and the fabric over, then turn again forming a hem around the elastic. Hem, stretching elastic as you stitch. Repeat at the other end. Turn under narrow hems along both sides and stitch.

To make the top sheet, fold and stitch a narrow hem along both sides. Fold a 4-inch hem across the top and a 1¼-inch hem across the bottom. Press and stitch.

Bright pillow cases and matching sheet trim wake up the bedroom below. These custom-made linens look costly, but are inexpensive and simple to make. The same fabric is used for the dust ruffle and the wall covering to create a totally coordinated decorating scheme.

Chapter 5

Quilts and Quilting Techniques

It's no wonder the quilting craft is enjoying a great revival as women of all ages try their hands at Grandma's favorite needlework. Color and variety of design have always been trademarks of quilts. Each one is unique and expresses the personal taste of its maker.

With today's choice of methods, there is a way for anyone to make a quilt. Whatever construction method you prefer, each quilt calls for careful planning and precise cutting and stitching. These basics are covered step-by-step on the following pages, along with complete directions for making many special quilt types.

If you wish to make a quilt by the time-honored piece method, with many small pieces of different colors and patterns joined to make a pattern, sewn, and quilted by hand, you'll find instructions here.
Or make an appliqued quilt with attractive patterns in plain colors and prints repeated over the quilt top.

For fine results more quickly, use the sewing machine. No special attachments or stitches are required, and a quilt can be made on the machine from start to finish.

In addition, there are easy patchwork techniques using new iron-on products to tempt a beginner or the needleworker who has more enthusiasm than time. These techniques also can be used to make other decorative items, such as pillows and wall hangings.

Many patchwork patterns are used to make this bedroom out of the ordinary: a Blazing Star quilt in contemporary colors on the bed, a Log Cabin quilt used as a wall hanging, and pillows that illustrate many of the traditional quilt designs.

Traditional Quilts

Quilts are as American as apple pie and are deeply rooted in American history. They were made in earlier times by thrifty housewives who cut patches from unworn portions of used clothing and linens and pieced them together to form quilt tops. These quilts were inexpensive, but warm, durable, and washable.

After the top was pieced together, the quilting was often done at a quilting bee, where friends and neighbors could meet and exchange pieces of work and the latest news. A supply of quilts was an important part of every girl's hope chest.

Today, you can re-create a piece of history for your own home and family. A handmade quilt is a treasure in any age.

Pieced Quilts

A pieced quilt top is made of many small pieces of fabric joined to make a definite pattern. Most patterns are based on 12-inch squares, but blocks can be made in almost any size you choose.

There are hundreds of traditional quilt patterns. Shown here are four of the simpler ones. Each drawing represents one block. To use one of these patterns, trace it and then enlarge it to the size you need.

The Eight-Pointed Star consists of eight diamond-shaped pieces, four squares, and four half-squares. Use two different prints or a variety of prints. These blocks usually are set together with plain blocks or with strips separating the pieced blocks.

Square in Square is made from one square and two different triangular shapes. Use a variety of prints or a combination of prints and solids. This pattern is set with solid squares separating the pieced blocks. The separating blocks often repeat a print used in an inner square.

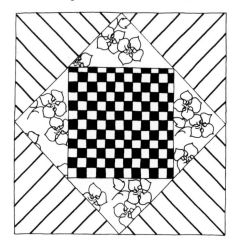

Baby's Block is a continuous geometric pattern. The entire quilt is made from one pattern piece. It is most effective when it is made in three different values—light, medium, and dark—arranged as shown in the drawing below. All of the patches need not be of the same color or print just so long as the values remain the same. You can finish Baby's Block with a border, or you may want to leave it in points with the edge bound along the points.

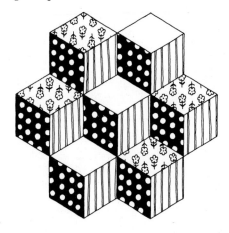

Log Cabin is one of the most popular of the traditional quilt patterns and has long been a favorite for using scraps. The narrow pieces of various lengths make good use of snips of ribbon and old silk neckties.

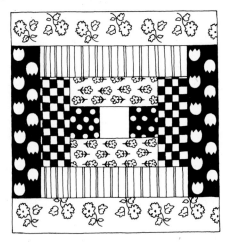

Try taffeta, velvet, and lightweight woolens as well. Variety of texture and subtle shading of colors have made nineteenth-century Log Cabin quilts sought-after antiques. It looks tricky to piece, but begin in center and add pieces two at a time.

Many quilt patterns are effective when pieced blocks are alternated with solid-color blocks or bands of plain fabric. You can also use a solid-color border with pieced blocks in most patterns. This reduces the number of pieced blocks necessary to make the quilt — something to consider if your supply of scraps is limited or if you wish to speed the construction of a quilt top. However, it is important to make sure that the width of these bands and borders is in proportion to the size of the quilt.

You can use most patterns to make a quilt for any size bed by adjusting the number of blocks. The exception is a pattern with a large design in the center, such as the Blazing Star quilt on page 102, which is not suitable for a twin bed-size quilt because much of the design would hang over the edge and detract from the total effect.

Quilts may be made bedspread size — to fit from floor to floor on either side and the foot of the bed and over the pillow — or they can be coverlet size. If you plan to use the quilt with a dust ruffle, subtract about 18 inches from the width and approximately 9 inches from the length of the measurements given on the following chart.

This bedspread is a typical traditional quilt. Light and dark calico patches are arranged in large blocks of 36 patches each. The light patches are arranged in the center with the darker patches along the outer edges. Bright red squares spark each corner.

Bed	Mattress Measures	Bedspread		Coverlet	
		22" skirt	18" skirt	22" skirt	18" skirt
Twin	39"x75"	83"x114"	75"x114"	83"x97"	75"x97"
Double	54"x75"	98"x114"	90"x114"	98"x97"	90"x97"
Queen	60"x80"	104"x119"	96"x119"	104"x102"	96"x102"
King	76"x80"	120"x119"	112"x119"	120"x102"	112"x102"
Throw size is 48" by 72"					

Quilt Sizes

Fabrics for quilt pieces should be firmly woven and have a soft texture. Avoid using fabrics that tend to ravel. Prints should be fairly small. Cottons and cotton-synthetic blends are the best choices, as they wear and wash well. All fabrics used in the quilt top should be about the same weight.

Cut quilt pieces from unworn portions of used fabrics, as Grandmother did, or from scraps of new fabric left from sewing. If your supply of scraps is limited or you plan a special color scheme, you will need to buy remnants or other new fabrics. Make sure all fabrics are colorfast, and preshrink new fabrics before cutting pieces.

Patterns for quilt pieces must be accurate. Trace the different size pieces and cut out the paper patterns. Then, trace around the patterns on heavy cardboard or on the smooth side of medium sandpaper, which makes an excellent pattern because it does not slip while you are marking the fabric. As you mark, the edges will become worn, so cut several patterns for each piece. Discard a pattern as soon as the edges show wear because accuracy is important.

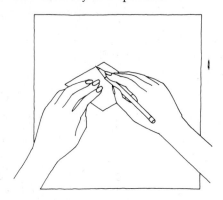

Find the straight grain of the fabric by observing the selvage or, on pieces with no selvage, by pulling a thread. Place the pattern on the straight grain of the fabric. For square or rectangular pieces, all edges should be on the lengthwise and crosswise grain; any diamond-shaped pieces should be cut with two edges on the straight grain; and right-angle triangles should have two sides on the straight grain. All other shapes should have the straight grain running through the center of the piece.

Mark around the pattern pieces on the back of the fabric, being careful not to stretch the fabric. Use light-colored pencils on dark fabrics and dark-colored pencils on light fabric. *These marked lines will be the stitching lines, not the cutting lines.*

Allow a ¼-inch seam allowance on all sides. For the most economical use of the fabric, mark the patterns ½ inch apart and cut in the center of the allowance.

Cut out the pieces with sharp sewing shears, cutting accurately and being sure not to stretch bias or curved edges.

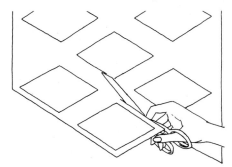

After you have cut a number of blocks, it's a good idea to sort and string them. Place all of the blocks of the same size, shape, and color together on a single thread. Tie a knot in the end of the single thread and pull the needle through the center of each block. After stringing all the identical blocks onto the thread, remove the needle. Do this for each different group of size, shape, and color. As you need the blocks, simply slip them off the thread one at a time. This not only keeps your work area organized, it also makes it easy to find just the piece you want as the blocks are sewn together.

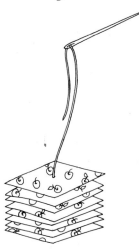

Piecing the quilt—sewing the pieces together to form blocks—requires little sewing skill but must be done accurately. Hold the pieces firmly in place with the right sides together. Longer seams may be pinned if you wish. Make a knot at the beginning of each seam and sew with tiny running stitches along the marked lines. Fasten the thread at the end of the seam with several backstitches. When two bias edges are sewn together, be careful not to stretch the seams. Pull the thread taut to prevent stretching. Finger press the seams open as you go, making sure each seam is open before crossing with another seam. Trim out excess fabric where seams cross to reduce bulk.

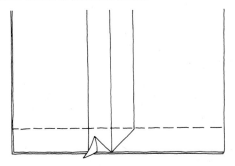

Piece one entire block at a time. Then, press the block, making sure all the seams are open and laying flat and smooth.

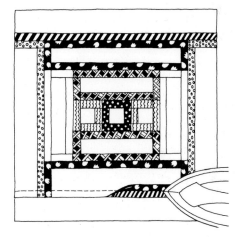

Compare all of the finished blocks to make sure that they are all the same size. If the block sizes vary, adjust the seams wherever necessary to make them uniform.

Setting together means sewing the blocks together to form the quilt top. Lay the completed blocks out on the floor and arrange them into the design of your choice. Add alternate solid-color blocks or strips at this time, if you are using them. Sew the blocks together, a row at a time; then join the rows. This may be done on the sewing machine, if you wish. If desired, add borders around all edges, mitering the corners. Carefully press the entire quilt top.

Appliqued Quilts

Appliqueing is decorating by sewing small pieces of fabric to a background fabric. The applique can be any shape or design. It can be sewn to blocks, or the top of the quilt may be made up of a single sheet of fabric with the designs applied to the entire surface area, with no piecing necessary. The applique is applied by hand with a blind stitch or a decorative stitch, or by machine with a zig-zag stitch.

Hand applique designs vary from traditional flowers and fruits to contemporary art. First, choose or create the design you wish to use and determine the size needed for your finished quilt. Draw the design to scale. Next, select soft but firmly woven fabrics that will not fray easily or stretch out of shape. Cotton and cotton blends, calico, percale, broadcloth, and muslin work well. If the quilt will be dry-cleaned, you may use wools, velvets, and silks to create special effects. Trace the design to be appliqued and cut out the patterns. Mark around the pattern on the right side of the fabric.

If you are marking several pieces on the same fabric, be sure to leave at least ½ inch between the marked lines. Machine-stitch around the design following the marked line, using matching thread and small stitches. This machine stitching makes it easier to turn under the raw edges, especially along curved areas. Cut out the design ¼ inch beyond the stitched line. Clip the seam allowance almost to the stitching line along curves, and trim the corners. Fold under the raw edges, rolling the stitching line to the underside. Pin the applique pieces in place on the background fabric, and baste them to hold in position while hand appliqueing.

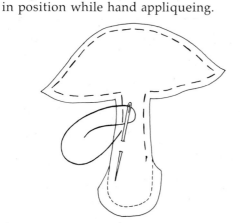

Using thread that matches the applique, blindstitch the applique to the base fabric; take very tiny stitches, close together. Be careful not to pull the thread too tightly.

Appliques can also be applied using the blanket stitch. Use embroidery floss to match or contrast the applique piece. To do the blanket stitch, work from left to right. Bring the needle up at the edge of the applique. Hold the thread down with the left thumb. Insert the needle a little to the right of the starting point, about ⅛ to ¼ inch from the folded edge. Bring the needle out directly below the edge of applique, being sure to go through base fabric. Draw the needle through the overloop of the thread.

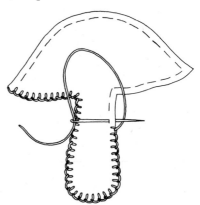

Machine applique, like hand applique, can be done in blocks or directly on the entire quilt top. Select the design for your quilt and make the patterns. Again, choose soft but firmly woven fabrics.

Mark around the patterns on the right side of the applique fabric. Cut out, allowing at least ½ inch on all sides. Position the applique on the base fabric and hand-baste just inside the marked line. Using a short straight stitch and matching thread, machine-stitch on the marked line. Then, set your machine for satin stitching. Test the width on fabric scraps. Zigzag over stitched line.

Pull the ends of the threads to the underside and tie. Using embroidery scissors with sharp points, cut away the excess fabric very close to the stitching line.

If the fabrics you have chosen are light-weight and tend to draw during the machine stitching, place a piece of organdy under the base fabric. Trim away the excess after stitching the applique.

After the top of the applique quilt is completed, assemble and prepare for quilting as for a pieced quilt. To give added depth to the appliqued designs, quilting is usually done only on the outside of the appliqued shapes, unless they are large.

Quilting

When the quilt top is completed and ready for quilting, choose a quilting pattern that enhances the pattern of the quilt top. Most quilting patterns must be marked on the quilt top before putting the quilt top together with the batting and backing.

The simplest quilt pattern, often used on pieced quilts, involves quilting ⅛ to ¼ inch on either side of each seam line. These lines need not be marked on the quilt top.

Another easy pattern uses two sets of diagonal lines that cross to form diamonds. Mark the lines on the quilt top, using a yardstick and tailor's chalk or a chalk pencil.

The shell or scallop makes a lovely quilting design, and the pattern is easy to make. Trace a row of half-circles of the desired size on a strip of cardboard. Then, cut them out carefully on the traced line.

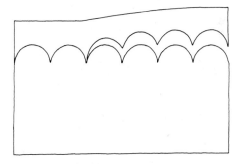

Lay the pattern flat on the quilt top and trace along the scalloped edge. When one row is completed, lay the pattern close to the first row—half a scallop to one side so that the dip of the first row meets the center of the scallop in the second row—and mark again. Repeat until the area to be quilted is filled with scallops.

For more complex patterns, such as scrolls, flowers, or plumes, buy a commercial pattern or draw one of your own. Draw the pattern to scale and transfer to the quilt top with a tracing wheel and dressmaker's carbon. Use a carbon color that can be seen easily, but not a color of such strong contrast that it will be difficult to remove.

Another transfer method uses a perforated pattern. Trace the pattern onto wrapping paper; then with the machine unthreaded, stitch along the lines. Lay this pattern on the quilt top and mark by rubbing stamping powder or paste through the holes.

Several different quilting patterns are often combined in one quilt. Pieced blocks may be quilted along the seam lines, the plain blocks separating them may be quilted in a wreath pattern, and the border may be done in diamonds or scallops.

Assemble the quilt for quilting, beginning with the backing. The backing fabric should be the same type and weight as the quilt top. It may be plain white or neutral, but prints or colors may be used if they coordinate with the quilt top. Make the backing larger than the quilt top by about 1 inch on all sides. Stitch strips of fabric together to make the proper width. Press seams open. Lay backing, wrong side up, on a flat surface and smooth it out. Over this, place one layer of cotton or polyester batting cut to the same size as the backing. (Two or more layers of batting can be used for additional warmth; however, thicker batting will make quilting more difficult.) Smooth out wrinkles. Center the quilt top over the batting.

Pin the layers together, being sure to go through all three layers. Then, baste the layers together. First, baste on the lengthwise and crosswise grain through the center of the quilt. Then, baste diagonally from corner to corner and around the outside edges of the quilt.

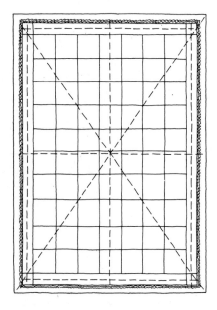

If you plan to quilt on a quilting hoop, or in your lap without a hoop, additional basting will be necessary.

Hand quilting can be done on a floor frame, on a quilting hoop, or on your lap without a hoop. *The floor frame* allows several persons to work on the quilt at one time, as at a traditional quilting bee. It consists of two long poles onto which the quilt is attached and stretched between the two side braces. The frame is held on a stand at table height. Attach the quilt to the poles and roll it to one side, until the exposed area is tightly stretched. Begin quilting about 12 inches from edge and quilt toward yourself. When the quilting in one area is finished, roll it under and expose a new unquilted area, making sure that the area is tightly stretched.

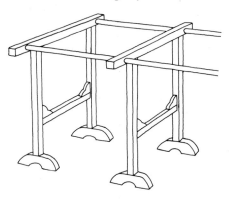

The quilting hoop is similar to an embroidery hoop but is much larger. The inner hoop is placed under the area to be quilted and the outer hoop is placed over it, stretching the quilt tightly.

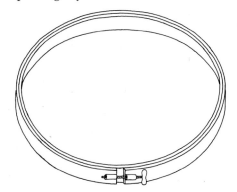

The thumbscrew adjusts the outer hoop to hold any thickness of quilt. When using the hoop, begin quilting in the center of the quilt and work outward in all directions.

You may also work on your lap without a hoop. If you choose to work in this way, begin in the center and work toward all sides.

Quilting stitches should be short and even. The secret of expert quilting is to make sure each stitch goes through all three layers of the quilt. Select needles with which you feel most comfortable, preferably a number 8 or 9, and discard any that are dull or rough on the top. A thimble is very helpful in quilting. Use a strong white thread or a color to match the fabric. Thread the needle with a single thread approximately 18 inches long, because longer threads tend to tangle. To begin, knot the thread at the end and bring the needle up through all three layers of the quilt. Pull the knot through the backing until it is concealed in the batting.

There are two methods of making the quilting stitch. One method is done with the left hand above the quilt and the right hand below the quilt. Push the needle down through all thicknesses with the left hand, then push it up with the right hand—very close to the first stitch. The stitches should be the same length on both sides. If you are left-handed, work with the left hand below the quilt and the right hand above.

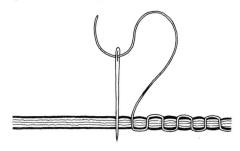

The other method is to take two or three running stitches at a time, before pulling the thread through.

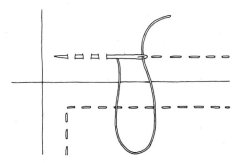

When all the quilting is completed, remove the quilt from the frame or hoop; remove the basting threads, being careful not to pull any of the quilting threads.

Trim the edges of the quilt even with the quilt top. To bind the edges, cut 2½-inch bias strips from the same fabric as the backing or a plain fabric that harmonizes with the quilt top. Piece the bias strip to make a strip long enough to go around the quilt. Press the seams open, and fold the strip in half lengthwise (seams on inside). Place the raw edges of the bias strip even with the edge of the quilt top, and stitch through all thicknesses in a ¼-inch seam. Turn the bias binding to the wrong side of the quilt, and blindstitch the folded edge by hand.

Machine quilting can be done in most quilting patterns; however, avoid intricate patterns. Machine quilting and hand quilting should not be combined in the same quilt.

Assemble the quilt as you would for hand quilting. Additional basting is necessary for machine quilting. Baste horizontal and vertical rows approximately 4 inches apart over the entire quilt. Use a fairly short basting stitch when you're doing this.

Although machine quilting can be done without special attachments, a quilting foot simplifies the stitching of straight patterns. The space bar may be placed to the right or to the left of the needle to guide the spacing of the lines of quilting.

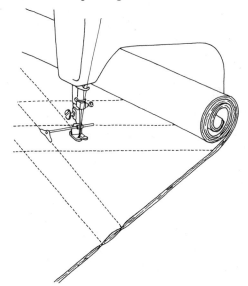

If you are using a portable machine, place it on a large table; extend cabinet models with card tables to make a large work surface to support the quilt. Use regular mercerized sewing thread. Set the machine at 6 to 8 stitches per inch, and loosen the pressure.

Roll the quilt crosswise to the center and place the roll under the arm of the sewing machine. Work—row by row—from the center to the edge. Do not pull the quilt; guide it gently and stitch at a slow, even pace. When half the quilt is finished, remove from the sewing machine, roll the completed area and unroll the unquilted portion. Again place the roll under the arm of the machine and quilt from the center toward the edge. When the quilt is finished, remove the basting, trim the edges, and bind with bias.

Comforters

A comforter has a pieced top like a quilt, usually in a simple pattern. It is smaller than a quilt and is thicker because it contains two or three layers of batting. When polyester batting is used, a comforter is very light despite its thickness. Comforters are tied or tufted, rather than quilted.

Tufting is done with pearl cotton, knitting worsted, or embroidery floss. Use the yarn doubled, but do not tie a knot. Working from the top, push the needle down through all layers and bring the needle back up ¼ inch away. Tie the yarns firmly in a double knot. Clip the ends, leaving at least ½-inch tufts. Make tufts at evenly spaced points about 6 inches apart.

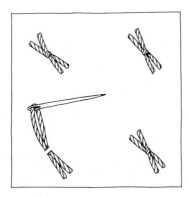

Crazy Quilts

Odd-shaped pieces sewn together in an apparently haphazard way form crazy quilts. The seams are usually trimmed with decorative embroidery stitches, and small designs such as flowers and butterflies may be embroidered on larger pieces. Antique crazy quilts were usually made of woolens or scraps of bright silk, satin, and velvet.

Although a crazy quilt appears to have been put together in a haphazard fashion, it requires time and planning to arrange the variety of shapes, colors, and textures into an eye-pleasing design. Crazy quilts made from cotton and similar fabrics usually are quilted along the seam lines. If the quilt is made from woolens or dressy fabrics, it usually is tufted.

To make an heirloom crazy quilt, select fabrics in rich colors and differing textures: velvets, satins, taffetas, and ribbons. Lay the fabrics out on a large, flat surface; cut the scraps into squares, rectangles, triangles, and other shapes that will fit together, allowing a ¼-inch seam allowance around each piece. Curved shapes may be used but are more difficult to work with. Carefully select adjoining colors for a pleasing effect. Stitch the pieces together, forming shapes that are approximately 15 inches square. Press the seams open. Then, decorate the seams with the featherstitch or another stitch.

Featherstitching adds a decorative touch to the seams. Use silk buttonhole twist, embroidery floss, or pearl cotton. The stitches can be done in one color or in a variety of colors to complement the blocks.

To make the featherstitch, bring the needle up a little to the left of the seam line. Hold the thread down with the left thumb; make a slanting stitch to the right of the seam and a little below the point where the thread came out, with the needle pointing to the left. Draw the needle through the fabric and over the working thread. Carry the thread to the left of the seam and make a similar stitch a little below this spot, with the needle pointing to the right. Draw the needle through, over the working thread. Do make sure that all of the stitches cross the seam lines and that they are centered.

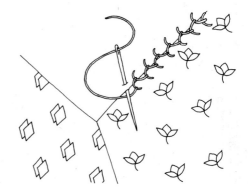

When several sections have been pieced and embroidered, set them together and decorate the joining seams. Continue in this manner until the quilt top is the needed size.

Crazy quilts of this type are sometimes trimmed with a ruffle around the outer edge and are used as throws or comforters.

Cut the fabric for the backing the same size as the top. Seam if necessary, and press the seams open. For the ruffle, cut bias strips of the backing fabric approximately 8 to 10 inches wide. Join the strips to make a length twice that of the distance around the quilt. Fold the ruffle in half lengthwise—wrong sides together—and gather along the raw edges. Place the ruffle over the quilt top, right sides together, and pin around the outer edges. Stitch. Press the seam toward the quilt top.

Place the quilt top, wrong side up, on a smooth, flat surface and cover it with a layer of batting the exact size of the finished quilt top, excluding the ruffle. Place the backing, right side up, over the batting and pin at the corners. Smooth out the three layers and baste together through the center crosswise, lengthwise, and from corner to corner. Baste about 1 inch from the outer edge. Trim away any batting that extends beyond the seam line of the quilt top. Turn under the edges

of the backing; blind-stitch to the seam line of the ruffle and the quilt top. Then tie the quilt with tufts, using embroidery thread.

If you do not wish to finish the edge with a ruffle, bind the edges with bias strips cut from the backing fabric or a plain fabric that harmonizes with the quilt top.

A crazy quilt may also be made from 12-inch blocks. You may find it easier to plan your quilt in this way. All blocks can be made from the same pattern, or you may use two or three basic patterns. To make your patterns, cut cardboard into 12-inch squares. Then, cut the squares into a number of triangles, squares, and rectangles. For easy handling, keep curved shapes to a minimum.

Place the patterns on the right side of the fabric and draw around them. Cut out, allowing ¼ inch for seams. Keep pieces for each block together until all blocks are cut to avoid confusion. Piece together in blocks. Press the seams open. Embroider over the seams on the right side with the featherstitch. Then, join the blocks to make a quilt top the needed size; work the featherstitch over these seams as well.

This quilt may be finished with a ruffle and tied like the heirloom crazy quilt, or the edges may be bound with bias and the quilt tied with tufts.

Scraps of many sizes, shapes, and textures are carefully put together to create this Crazy Quilt. Featherstitches add to the charm.

A large frame holds this quilt taut while several people finish it by tufting (tieing the layers of the quilt together with yarn).

Puff Pillow Quilts

This cloud-light quilt is made by stitching together tiny pillows, each sewn and stuffed separately. It is then tied like a comforter. This quilt is often made from scraps of luxury fabrics. Smooth surfaces of satin catch and reflect the light, giving a shimmering look. Made in soft, deep-toned velvet or velveteen, the quilt gives the effect of richness. For a feminine bedroom, choose soft pastels, dainty print cottons, or pale ginghams.

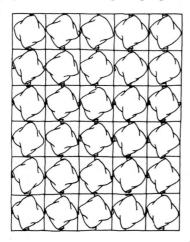

The quilt is made of 1¾-inch squares. For the double bed size—approximately 60x70 inches—you'll need 1,360 squares: 40 squares long and 34 squares wide. For the twin bed size—approximately 45x70 inches—you'll need 1,040 squares: 40 squares long and 26 squares wide. To alter the size of the quilt, simply add or subtract rows of squares. In addition to scraps for the pillows, you will need unbleached muslin for the lining of each square, backing for the underside and edge binding, polyester quilt batting (single or double size), and polyester fiber stuffing. You will also need some pearl cotton and sewing thread. As a guide to the amount of material that you will need, figure 144 3-inch squares per yard of 36-inch fabric and 256 2½-inch squares per yard of muslin.

To make the quilt, a 3-inch square of fabric is stitched to a 2¼-inch square of muslin and stuffed. The squares are sewn together to form the quilt top, which is backed with quilt batting and a backing. The outer edges are bound with the backing fabric.

Cut the 2¼-inch muslin squares, then the 3-inch from fabrics of your choice.

To make the pillows, pin corners of a 3-inch square to corners of a 2¼-inch muslin square as shown, with wrong sides together.

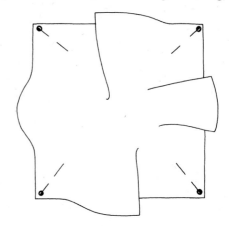

Fold small pleats in top fabric on three sides and pin to muslin, keeping edges even.

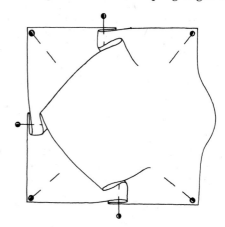

Insert fiber filling through the open side. The amount of filling you use will depend on how thick you want to make the pillows. Don't pack the filling because this will make the quilt feel hard. Baste around all four sides.

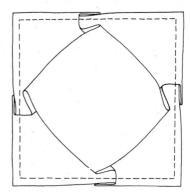

To create an updated Victorian mood, many patterns were combined in this bedroom. The spread is a contemporary version of the puff pillow quilt, made from large pillows of multistriped seersucker. Directions for making this beautiful quilt are given below.

Complete all the pillows, and arrange them in a pleasing color pattern. Place puffs into rows, 34 pillows to a row for the double bed size; 26 to a row for the twin bed size. With right sides together, sew pillows together with a ¼-inch seam. Press the seams open. Complete all 40 rows and then sew the rows together, making sure the seams match. Measure the completed quilt top. Cut the backing to the same size as the quilt top; seam two lengths together, if it is necessary to do so. Then, press the seams open.

Place backing wrong side up on a flat surface. Cut the batting to the same size and place it over the backing. Carefully smooth out any wrinkles. Place quilt top over the batting, right side up. Pin all three layers together. Baste the quilt lengthwise and crosswise through the center, being sure to go through all three layers.

Trim the edges of the quilt even with the quilt top. To bind the edges, cut 2½-inch bias strips. Piece the bias strip to make a strip long enough to go around the quilt. Press the seams open, and fold the strip in half lengthwise (seams on inside). Place the raw edges of the bias strip even with the edge of the quilt top, and stitch through all thicknesses in a ¼-inch seam. Turn bias binding to wrong side of quilt, and blind stitch by hand. Tie at 10- to 12-inch intervals.

Pillow Spread

The spread pictured above is a contemporary version of the puff pillow quilt. The construction is basically the same, but the pillows used here are much larger. The fabric is seersucker.

To duplicate this spread, cut 11-inch lining squares and 12-inch squares for the top. Place a top square over a lining square, and pin at the corners. Pin small tucks on either side of each corner. Stuff with fiber filling or 10-inch squares of batting. Baste top and lining together, ½ inch from the edge. Continue as for the puff pillow quilt, using ½-inch seams throughout.

Contemporary Quilts

Large patches, shortcut techniques, and machine sewing methods all work together in creating contemporary and easy-to-make quilts. The basic steps are the same as for the traditional quilt, but the additional steps are simplified. Included in this section are instructions for making a twin-size quilt and an appliqued coverlet for a double bed, plus several timesaving patchwork techniques.

Making a Twin-Size Quilt

To make this handsome quilt (see picture at left), start with 48 pieces of medium-weight fabric (cut into 12-inch squares) for the top of the quilt, 6½ yards of 36- or 45-inch fabric for the backing, and three 72x90x1-inch polyester batts or 18½ yards of ½-inch-thick, 48-inch bonded polyester batting. The finished quilt is 72x92 inches. The pillow sham requires six pieces of fabric cut into 12-inch squares, 2 yards of 36- or 45-inch fabric for the backing, 2½ yards of 48-inch polyester batting, and a 28-inch heavy-duty zipper.

To assemble the quilt, lay the 48 squares out and arrange them 8 squares long and 6 squares wide. Stitch six crosswise squares together in a row with ¼-inch seams. Press seams open. Stitch the other rows the same way. Stitch strips together; press seams open.

Cut the batting into 11-inch squares. Each fabric square requires 4 pieces of ½-inch batting or 2 pieces of 1-inch batting. Loosely tack the batting pieces to the fabric squares on the wrong side, keeping the batting ½ inch from the seams.

For the backing, cut two pieces of backing fabric 95 inches long. Seam together along one long edge. Press the seam open and trim to the same size as the quilt top. From the remaining fabrics, cut about 9¼ yards of 2-inch-wide bias strips for binding the edges.

For fast-paced contemporary style, create a quilt that is quick and easy to do—and has the clock-stopping quality of an heirloom. The quilt shown here was machine-stitched from large blocks of bright fabrics.

Place backing wrong side up on the floor and place one large continuous layer of batting over it. Trim batting to the same size as backing. Place the quilt top right side up over this. With an extra-long darning needle, baste through all thicknesses, starting with the center lengthwise seam. Straighten wrinkles as they form. Baste all vertical seams; then baste the horizontal ones. Also baste around outside edge of the quilt. Trim excess batting and backing from the edges and slightly round the corners of the quilt.

Use a large table or folding tables to increase the work area. On your machine, ease the top pressure and tension control slightly; set the stitch length at 6 to 8 stitches per inch. Start stitching the quilt top at the center, working lengthwise along the seam. Stitch all lengthwise seams first; then do the horizontal seams, working from the center out to the edges. Stitch around the outer edge of the quilt, ⅜ inch from the edge.

To bind the edges, sew the bias strips together to make one long strip. Stitch the strip to the top of the entire quilt edge—with the right sides together—⅜ inch from the edge. Turn the bias strip under ½ inch and fold over the raw edge. Slip-stitch it to the quilt back. Remove the basting threads.

Construct the pillow sham in the same manner as the quilt, with the addition of a zipper opening through which the pillow is inserted. Cut a 24x36-inch piece of backing fabric, 3½ yards of 2-inch-wide bias strips, and six 12-inch squares for the pillow top. Cut batting for each square and assemble like the quilt, but don't bind outer edges.

To make the zippered section, cut two 13x 36-inch pieces of the backing fabric. Stitch the long edges together in a 1-inch seam, 4 inches in from each end. Press seams open, continuing to press the seam allowances along the open section of the seam. Center the zipper face down over the open section, baste to the seam allowances, and stitch in place. Lay the zippered section on the quilted sham top, wrong sides together, and baste around edges. Trim excess fabric from edges and stitch ⅜ inch from edge. Join bias strips into one long strip and bind edges.

Appliqued Double Bed Coverlet

The coverlet below is a contemporary version of the appliqued quilt. Make it, using all of the quick tricks available and a very bold modernistic design.

The following directions and materials are for a double-bed-size coverlet. The finished size is approximately 76x100 inches.

Select firmly woven fabrics of light to medium weight. All-cotton or cotton and synthetic blends are the best choices.

If you are going to use 45-inch fabric, you'll need 6¾ yards of purple, 2 yards of turquoise, 2 yards of lime green, ½ yard of pink, ½ yard of deep pink, ¼ yard of orange, and ¼ yard of red. You will also need 2 large spools of green and turquoise thread, and one spool of each of the other colors. In addition, you'll need a 90x108-inch piece of polyester fiber batting and one double sheet or 6 yards of 45-inch fabric for the quilt back.

Cut two 45x100-inch pieces of the purple, and seam the pieces together along one side. Clip the selvages and press the seam open. Trim to 76x100 inches, making sure the seam is in the exact center.

Make the applique patterns according to the drawing (each square equals 4½ inches). Add 1 inch to the center ends of the green pieces, which will be tucked under the bright circles. Mark around the patterns on the right side of the fabric. If you will be using a zig-zag stitch, cut the pieces right on the marked line. If the applique is to be done by hand, allow ¼ inch around each piece to turn under. Cut out all but the turquoise pieces.

If seam allowances have been allowed, stitch around each shape with matching thread right on the marked line. This will make turning under the edges easier. Pin and baste the applique pieces to the turquoise piece; pin the green pieces in place first and overlap with the bright circles.

The stunning coverlet below features a large, bold applique. Large pieces of fabric are easier to handle than tiny appliques, and the results are usually more exciting. You can use the design shown here or create an original in your favorite colors and patterns.

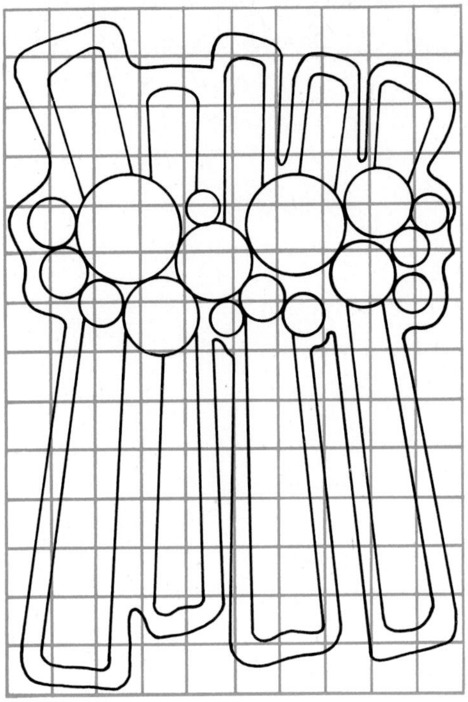

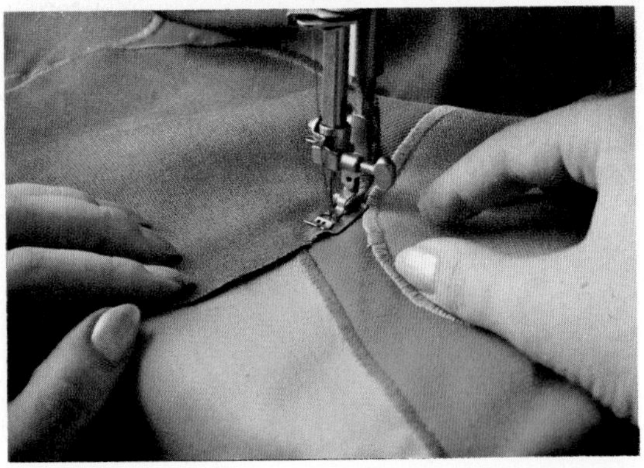

This design can be appliqued by machine. Place the pieces on the coverlet top and encase the edges with a wide satin stitch.

For machine zigzag applique, use a wide satin stitch and encase the edges of each piece. To applique by hand, turn under the edges of each piece before basting. Blindstitch the appliques, as shown on page 112. When all the pieces are in place on the turquoise fabric, cut out the turquoise piece and place it in the center of the purple. Pin the turquoise applique to the purple, allowing 12 inches at the bottom and sides.

Baste and zigzag over the outer edges or turn under the edges and blindstitch to the coverlet top. Cut the lining the same size as the coverlet top. If you are using a sheet, simply cut it to the same size as the top. To make the lining using 45-inch fabric, cut two lengths 45x100 inches and seam together along one long side. Clip the selvages and press the seam open. Place the backing on a large flat surface, wrong side up. Cut the batting the same size as the lining and place on top of the lining, smoothing out any wrinkles. Place quilt top right side up over the batting, and pin the layers together.

With a long needle, baste all layers together crosswise, lengthwise, diagonally from corner to corner, and around the outer edge. Baste around the applique, ¼ inch from the turquoise. Keep all layers smooth and catch all three layers with each stitch.

Machine quilting on large pieces requires additional work area. If your machine is portable, place it on a large table; if it is a cabinet style, place it next to a table or counter, or surround it with smaller tables to increase the work area. The additional area will help to support the quilt and make it easier to handle. Set the machine for a long stitch, and quilt around the design.

Start from the center and work out, stitching next to the edges of the applique. To make handling the quilt easier, roll the portion of the quilt that is under the arm of the machine like a sleeping bag. Stitch at a slow and even pace, and support the quilt at all times so you don't create too much stress on the needle.

Cut 4-inch-wide bias strips from the remaining purple fabric. You'll need enough to make a continuous 352-inch strip—the distance around the coverlet. Stitch the bias pieces together. To bind the edges, pin the strip to the top of the coverlet, right sides together, with the edges even. Stitch 1 inch from the edges, and miter the corners as shown on page 26. Press the bias over the seam and turn it to the underside. Fold under the raw edge and blindstitch to the stitching line on the underside.

If desired, quilt the area outside the applique in large flowing lines, following the shape of the outside edges of the applique. Chalk the lines and stitch. These rows of stitching will help prevent the batting from shifting. To finish the project, carefully remove the basting threads.

Patchwork pillows are fun to create and fun to use for decorating. Cover inexpensive pillows with fabric remnants and heap them on sofa, *bed, or in a hanging latticework chair. Patchwork pillows are quick and easy to make when you use the shortcuts described below.*

Quick and Easy Patchwork

If you love the look of patchwork, but lack the time and patience to do the real thing, try these timesaving ideas. The pillow covers are made quickly, without special skills, and require only small amounts of fabric. Watch the remnant counters for small pieces of fabric—they're ideal for pillow pieces. The fabrics shown on this and the following page are all-cotton or cotton and synthetic blends; however, you need not limit yourself to these. Select the fabrics that best suit your decor. Combinations of gingham checks, scraps of chintz, and pieces of polished cotton all work well for the iron-on patchwork. Try the stitched patchwork using alternating strips of imitation leather and fake fur to create texture variety.

Iron-on patchwork is the easiest of all the patchwork techniques. The heat-sensitive bonding web holds the patches together, and the only sewing involved is in the seams along the edges. For a 12-inch square pillow, cut two 13-inch squares of fabric. With right sides facing, seam the two pieces together along three sides using a ½-inch seam. Clip corners, turn right side out, and press.

Cut patches of contrasting fabrics. The one shown here has patches in different sizes. Repeat this design or develop your own, but keep the shapes simple. Turn under ¼ inch along all edges and press. Place the patch over the bonding web and cut the web to the exact size of the patch. Cut a layer of the bonding web to fit each of the patches.

Starting with the largest block, center it in the middle of the pillow cover, with the web between the patch and the pillow cover. Following the webbing instructions, very carefully iron the patch in place. Then place the second largest patch in the center and bond it in the same manner. Continue placing one patch over the other until all the patches are in place. Allow the pillow cover to cool completely before removing it from the ironing board.

Stuff the pillow or insert a pillow form. Fold in ½ inch along the open edges and pin. Blindstitch the edges together.

Make patchwork pillows quickly by sewing the patches together in strips. For an 18-inch pillow, cut three strips each of two contrasting fabrics. Each strip should be 48 inches long and 4 inches wide. With right sides together, join the strips lengthwise

Iron-on patchwork is the easiest way to make patchwork pillow covers. Squares of contrasting fabrics are bonded together with iron-on webbing.

2. *The stitched strips of fabric are carefully measured and are cut into horizontal strips; then the new strips are stitched together.*

with ½-inch seams, alternating the colors. You now have a "striped" piece of material 19 inches wide and 48 inches long. Press the seams open.

Lay out the fabric so that the stripes run crosswise in front of you. Using a yardstick and tailor's chalk or a chalk pencil, mark twelve 4-inch-wide strips. Cut on the marked lines. Pin the strips together again, right sides facing, reverse every other strip so that alternating blocks of the fabric meet to form a patchwork. Be sure the seams between the patches meet.

Restitch the 4-inch-wide strips together with ½-inch seams. You now have a piece of patchwork fabric 37 inches long and 19 inches wide. Press the seams open. Fold the fabric in half, right sides together; stitch a ½-inch seam on two sides. Clip the corners and turn the pillow cover right side out. Press. Stuff or insert a pillow form. Turn in ½ inch along both sides of the opening and pin. Blind-stitch the edges together.

1. *Quick and easy patchwork pillows start by stitching strips of the fabrics together in a long, vertical strip, as shown below.*

3. *Every other strip of fabric is reversed so that the alternating blocks of the fabric meet to simulate an authentic patchwork effect.*

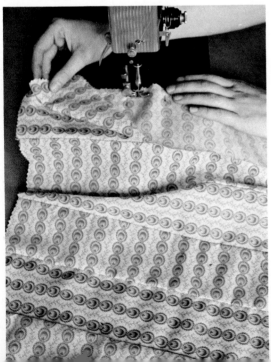

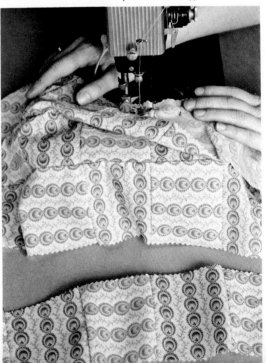

Chapter 6

How to Make Pillows and Cushions

Using decorative pillows is a quick and inexpensive way to add beauty and comfort to your home. They will add a spot of color, lend a feeling of luxury, or provide a contrast in texture. Create a plush mood with pillow covers of velvet, deep-pile fabrics, or velour bath towels. Use fake fur, vinyl, burlap, corduroy, and satin covers to add textural interest.

Pillows also provide a good outlet for showing off your handiwork. Design your very own pillow top if you do embroidery, crewel work, or needlepoint. Complete the needlework first, and then construct the pillow cover.

Pillows are easy to make. If you are a beginner, start with the knife-edge pillow—it's the most popular and the easiest to make. Making your own pillows allows you to select just the fabric and color you want.

Since most decorative pillows are small, you can afford to use expensive fabric. It's no problem at all to cover a pillow with less than a yard of fabric.

Follow the directions for making knife-edge pillows, box-type cushions, bolsters, and chair cushions that are given in this chapter. If you would like to sew a furniture-sized pillow, make a pillow sofa; or make an accordion-folded pillow that serves as a chair, a chaise lounge, or a floor mattress.

An array of plush pillows decorate the day bed in this game room. These pillow covers are a snap to make from bath and hand towels. To create your own velvet-textured pillows, use towels with a velour finish and follow directions for knife-edge pillows.

Pillow Basics

Ready-made pillow and cushion forms are available in a variety of shapes and sizes. Of these forms, there are two basic types: knife-edge and box-edge. Either type can be round, square, rectangular, or oblong. Forms are molded polyurethane foam or made of shredded foam, polyester fiber fill, or kapok with a muslin covering. Molded polyester forms, which are softer and less rigid than the foam forms, are also available in several sizes.

Bolster forms are usually molded and come in various sizes, lengths, and shapes (triangular, tubular, wedge, or five-sided).

You can construct almost any shape pillow if you make your own form. For filling, use shredded foam, polyester fiber fill, or kapok. Or use cotton or polyester batting that's sold in a roll about 16 inches wide and 1 inch thick. It can be cut and stacked, or rolled for round bolsters. Use styrofoam pellets for floor pillows and for pillow furniture.

To make your own form, first decide on the type, shape, and size. To make a knife-edge form, cut two pieces of muslin the size and shape desired. Add 1 inch for seams. Stitch together, leaving an opening. Clip the curved edges or trim the corner points; turn to the right side and stuff with filling. Turn edges of the opening to the inside and slipstitch.

The box-edge form consists of a top and bottom section joined together by a length of fabric called a boxing strip. The length of the strip is determined by the measurement of the perimeter of the shape, plus 1 inch seam allowance. The width of the strip depends upon the thickness of the cushion.

Make bolster forms by joining endpieces to a tube or center section. To make a round form, first determine the diameter of the circle for the endpieces. Add 1 inch for a ½-inch seam allowance and cut two circles from muslin. On the crosswise grain of the muslin, cut a rectangle (the short side corresponds to the bolster length measurement plus 1 inch). Cut the diameter measurement plus 1 inch on the lengthwise grain. Fold the rectangle in half with the crosswise grain edges together. Stitch a ½-inch seam, leaving a 6-inch to an 8-inch opening near one end for turning. Pin and stitch the endpieces to the tube. Turn right side out and pack in the filling smoothly and firmly to ensure a round form. Turn in raw edges and stitch the opening.

Construct forms that have square, triangular, or wedge-shaped ends in a similar manner. Make the pattern for the end piece by tracing around the end. The length of the bolster and the perimeter of the endpiece will give you the dimensions of the center section. Add 1 inch for seams. Cut out the endpieces and the center section. Fold the rectangle in half, with the crosswise grain edges together. Stitch a ½-inch seam, leaving a 6- to 8-inch opening. Run a line of machine basting ½ inch from the raw edge on each end of the center section. Pin this section to the ends, right sides together. Start stitching at one corner and clip the seam allowance to the machine basting. Pivot the needle, continue stitching to the next corner, and repeat procedure at each corner. Trim corner points, turn to the right side, and stuff the bolster with filling. Slip-stitch the open edges.

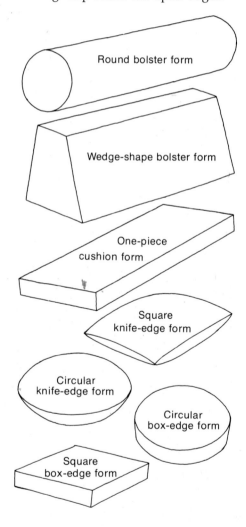

Round bolster form

Wedge-shape bolster form

One-piece cushion form

Square knife-edge form

Circular knife-edge form

Circular box-edge form

Square box-edge form

Knife-Edge Pillows

These pillows, because of their simple construction, are a good choice for those who are just beginning to sew.

To cover a basic knife-edge form, first measure across the width of the pillow from side seam to side seam, keeping the measur-

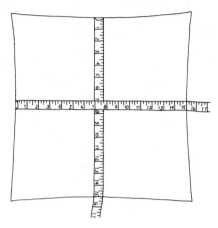

ing tape pulled taut, and add 1 inch for the seam allowances. Measure the height in the same manner and add 1 inch for seams.

On fabric's straight grain, cut two pieces to these dimensions. Down one side of each section, machine baste ½ inch from edge. Leave these edges open for turning.

With right sides together and edges even, pin the pieces together. Stitch ½ inch from the edges, starting and stopping on the machine basting as shown in the illustration on page 126. To ensure sharp corners, pivot the fabric on the needle and take a stitch diagonally across the point at the corners. Then continue stitching down that side. Clip across the corners and into the seam allowance at the basted opening. Blend seam allowance to the clip at basted opening. Turn cover right side out and press the seams.

Insert the pillow form. Along the basting, turn the edges of the opening to the inside and pin. Blindstitch edges together, catching material so basting is hidden in the seam.

The knife-edge pillow is the easiest kind of pillow to make. You can use lush fur fabrics or other novelty materials for a truly stunning effect.

Finish the top with embroidery or applique. Sew a fringe or an edging into the seam if you want a more decorative effect.

A cluster of Indian-print pillows creates a Far-Eastern mood in this sitting room. The pillow covers are made from printed cotton throws from India; additional throws are used to cover the bed and walls. The bright pillow on the right is made from men's silk neckties.

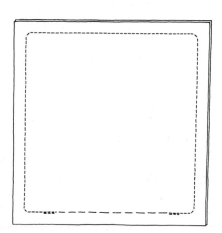

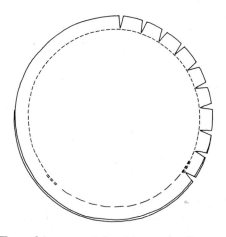

To make a cover for a round knife-edge form, measure the diameter of the form and cut two circles 1 inch larger than the measurement. On each piece, stitch an 8-inch length of machine basting ½ inch from the raw edge. With the right sides together, align the basted seam allowances of each piece and pin the pieces together. Stitch ½ inch from the edges, starting and stopping on the machine basting, as shown in the illustration at the right. Backstitch to reinforce edges of opening. Clip into seam allowance at basted area, blend, and notch the remaining seam allowance.

Turn the cover right side out and press the seams. Insert the pillow form. Turn in the seam allowance of the opening along basting stitches, pin, and blindstitch opening.

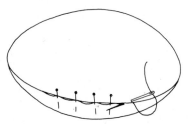

Knife-edge pillow covers with lap-back or zipper closures are easy to make, too. The seams can be plain or corded, fringed, ruffled, or trimmed.

The lap-back or envelope closure is not sewn or closed by a zipper. Instead, the cover back is made of two overlapping sections.

Prepare the front, following the directions for a knife-edge cover. For the back, measure the pillow height. Then measure the pillow width, divide in half, and add 3½ inches more to each half. Cut the two back pieces to fit these measurements. Turn the center edges of each half under ½ inch. Press and turn again, forming a 1½-inch hem. Press, pin, and stitch close to the hem edge. With right sides together, overlap and position the back pieces over the front. Be sure that all sides are even. Pin. Stitch the side seams, making a ½-inch seam allowance. Miter the corner points and blend the seam allowances on all sides. Turn right side out and press.

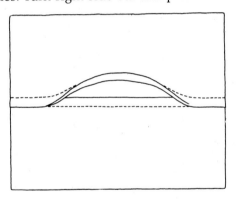

If you decide on a knife-edge cover with a corded edge, determine the amount of cording needed by measuring the circumference or the perimeter of the pillow form; add 3 inches. Purchase ready-made cording or follow the directions for making covered cording in Chapter 2.

Before joining the back and front pieces of the cover, machine-baste the cording to the right side of either piece. Start by pinning the cording to one edge and stitch to within ½ inch of the corner. Raise the presser foot and clip the cording seam allowance to the needle. Turn the fabric, pivoting on the needle, and take a diagonal stitch. Raise the presser foot and complete the turn. Continue stitching each side, clipping and pivoting at each corner. Overlap the cording ends as shown above right. Trim the ends.

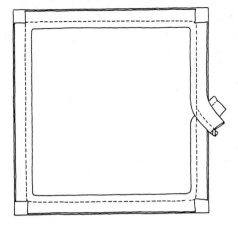

For a zipper closure, place open zipper face down on the right side of the cover front; the zipper teeth should be even with the cording. Pin and stitch close to the teeth.

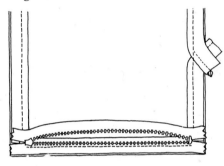

Fold tape and seam allowance to the wrong side of the cover. Close the zipper. Press under ½ inch along one edge of the cover back. Pin this fold over the zipper teeth. Stitch.

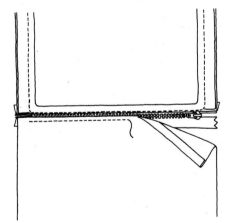

Open the zipper and fold the back section over the front with corners and edges even. Stitch the other three sides. Clip and blend the seams. Turn right side out, and press.

Box-Edge Cushions

To measure for this type of cover, follow the procedure described on page 124. Measure across the center for the width, around the sides for the length of the boxing strip, and down the side for the depth. To each measurement be sure that you add 1 inch for the seam allowances.

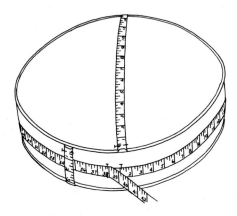

To make a boxing strip with a zipper insert, cut a length of fabric that is 1 inch longer than the zipper and 2 inches wider than the boxing strip. Cut the strip lengthwise through the center. With right sides together, machine baste the center edges, making a 1-inch seam. Press the seam open and insert the zipper, following the directions given on the zipper package.

To determine the remaining length to be cut for the boxing strip, subtract the zipper section length from the basic measurement around the cushion; add 1 inch for the seams. If desired, apply cording to the right sides of the top and bottom pieces.

Join the zipper section to the boxing strip, making ½-inch seams. Open the zipper. Stitch the boxing strip to the top and bottom pieces. Trim the seams. Turn the cover right side out, press, and insert the cushion form.

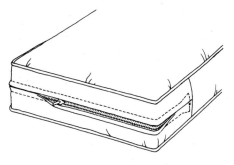

One-piece cushion covers are easy to make because they require less fabric and time than do other types. These are suitable for fur or plush fabrics. To determine the amount of fabric needed, measure each cushion as shown. Wrap the tape snugly around the width **(A)**, the height **(B)**, and the depth **(C)**. Mark off a rectangle on the wrong side of the fabric. Use the full amount of measurement **B** plus a 1½-inch seam allowance for the length of the rectangle, and one-half of measurement **A** plus a 1-inch seam allowance for the width of the rectangle. Cut out the piece. You will also need a zipper that is 2 inches shorter than the width of the cushion.

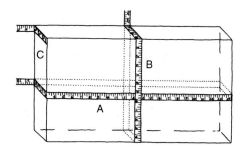

With right sides together, fold the rectangle in half crosswise. Center the zipper on the ¾-inch end seam and mark off the zipper opening. Making ¾-inch seams, stitch to these points from the edges and reinforce with backstitching. Machine-baste the opening and press open. Center the zipper over the basted seam and baste. Turn the cover to the right side and stitch the zipper in place. Remove the basting and open the zipper. Turn the cover to the wrong side again, and stitch the side seams with ½-inch seam allowances.

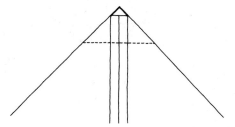

To shape the corners, fold one corner with the side seam centered, as shown. Across the point, draw a line to mark the depth measurement. Cut off the corner ½ inch above the line and stitch on the line; backstitch to reinforce. Repeat on remaining corners. Turn right side out and insert the cushion.

These folding cushion chairs are versatile. Ideal for porch, patio, or poolside, they can form a cube, a chair, a chaise lounge, or a floor mattress. Cover the foam squares with bright, durable fabrics such as duck, denim, or sailcloth. The covers remove easily for cleaning.

The folding chairs pictured above consist of three covered cushions that are hinged together. For each chair, you will need six molded foam forms, 24x24x2 inches; 5½ yards of muslin for the inner covers; 5½ yards of 42- to 48-inch-wide fabric (or 4½ yards of 54-inch-wide fabric) for the outer covers; three 24-inch heavy-duty zippers; and 18 yards of cording.

To prepare the cushions, stack two foam forms with the edges even and tape or glue them in position. Next, make three muslin inner covers. Cut six 25-inch squares along the lengthwise grain of the muslin. From the remaining muslin, cut enough strips from the lengthwise grain to join to make three boxing strips 97 inches long and 9 inches wide. Construct each cover, following the directions for box-edge covers that are given on page 128. Then, insert the foam form and sew up the opening.

Cut out the pieces for the outer cover, following the muslin cutting directions; make three corded box-edge-type covers with zippers (see page 128). To attach the hinges to the covers, leave one 24-inch side open on two of the covers, and two opposite sides open on the third cover.

To prepare the hinges, cut three 25x2-inch strips. Hem the 2-inch sides by turning ½ inch, another ½ inch, and stitching. Insert one raw edge of the hinge strip into the seam allowance of the cover opening. Pin in place. Topstitch all the seams together as close to the cording as possible. Insert the other raw edge of the hinge into the corresponding open seam in the next cover. Stitch. Repeat this procedure to join the remaining covers together—accordion fashion. (The illustration below shows the position of the hinges on the covers.)

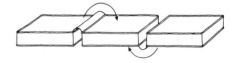

130

Bolster Covers

The size of your bolsters will depend on their intended use. Use round or wedge shapes as a backrest on a studio couch. Smaller bolsters add variety in pillow groupings.

Wedge-shaped and five-sided forms are measured following the same procedure described on page 124 for making muslin forms. When constructing covers for complicated forms, it is best to first make a paper pattern. Close the bottom seam with snap tape for easy removal. Use this closure method for any flat bottom form.

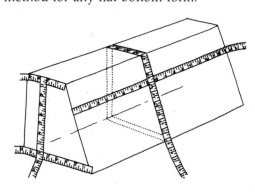

First, measure the length of the form and add 1 inch. Starting at the front bottom edge, take the measurement around the form (as shown) and add 1 inch. These two measurements will make up the center section, which is cut from one piece of fabric. Prepare a paper pattern for the endpieces, either by measuring the sides or standing the bolster on end on a piece of paper and tracing around it. Extend the pattern ½ inch on all sides.

Cut out the cover sections and stitch the cording to the endpieces. With right sides together, pin and stitch the back, top, and front edges of the endpieces to the center section. Turn the cover right side out and press the remaining seam allowances to the wrong side. Pin and stitch snap tape over the seam allowances, mitering the corners.

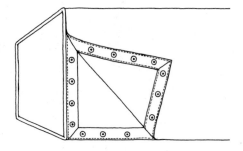

Round bolster covers can be attached permanently or made removable.

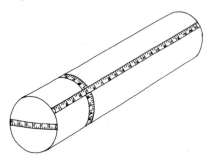

For nonremovable covers, make a circular pattern 1 inch larger than the diameter of the end section. To make the center section, measure the length of the form and add 1 inch; measure the circumference and add 1 inch. Cut a rectangle by these measurements.

To make a zippered removable cover, cut the endpieces as above. The zipper is inserted into a separate strip 7 inches wide and the length of the bolster plus 1 inch. Cut this strip in half lengthwise. Pin and machine-baste 1 inch from the cut edge. Press the seam open and insert the zipper. To determine the dimensions of the remaining cover section, subtract 4 inches from the circumference measurement and add 1 inch for the seams. Remove the basting and open the zipper. Join the zipper section to the center section with ½-inch seams, forming a tube. Machine-baste ½ inch from each end of the tube. Clip the seam allowances close to the basting. With right sides together, pin ends to bolster.

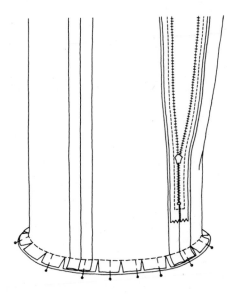

Hold the center section upright and turn it as you stitch. Turn the cover right side out, press, and insert the bolster form.

To make a gathered endpiece, cut two strips one-half the diameter of the end plus 1 inch, and as long as the circumference plus 1 inch. Stitch ends of each strip together. With right sides facing, join one edge of the strip to the tube with a ½-inch seam. Gather the remaining edge of the strip by hand. Draw the gathers tightly and tie the thread. Finish by attaching a covered button or a tassel.

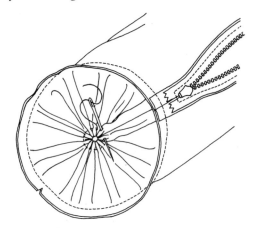

Pillow Furniture

Sew gigantic pillows that are large enough to be used as furniture in just a few short hours. The pillow sofa pictured below has only one seam. Simply stitch a muslin liner and stuff it with Styrofoam pellets. Cover your pillow with the fabric of your choice.

First, you'll need to decide on the length of your new piece of furniture. The one pictured is nearly 18 feet long, but yours can be any length you need. For the liner you'll need two pieces of sturdy fabric—heavy-weight muslin, sateen, or canvas—54 inches wide and the length you desire. Round the ends and stitch the two pieces together, leaving an opening on one side for stuffing. Double-stitch the seam with heavy-duty thread and turn right side out. Stuff the bag with Styrofoam pellets and carefully close the opening.

For the cover, select a durable, attractive upholstery fabric. Cut two pieces the same size as the liner. Insert a 54-inch zipper, or use two 36-inch zippers with the open ends together in the back seam near one end. Stitch the remainder of the seam in the cover, turn right side out, and insert the pillow.

A supersized pillow provides ample seating space or an ideal place to stretch out and relax. This easy-to-sew "pillow sofa" can be made any length and even can be curved around a corner. Select a fabric to complement your other furnishings, stitch one seam, and stuff.

Chair Cushions

Cushions that tie onto chair seats and backs give a custom-made look to ordinary chairs. If your chairs have square- or rectangular-shaped seats, simply measure the area to be covered by the cushion. For irregularly shaped chair seats, follow the procedure illustrated below and explained in the next column.

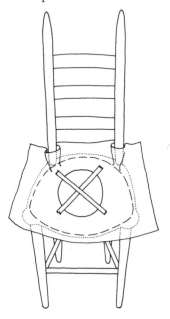

Determine the seat center from the front edge to the back, and mark it with chalk. Fold a large piece of paper in half and cut a hole on the folded edge. Open the paper and align the fold with the seat center mark, and tape it securely, as shown. Mark the outline for cushion on the paper, remove the paper, and refold it. Extend the marked line ½ inch to allow for seams, and cut out pattern along this line. From this pattern, cut two pieces of muslin and cover fabric for each cushion.

To make a corded knife-edge cushion, measure the perimeter of the pattern to determine the amount of cording needed, and add 3 inches. To make a box-edge corded cushion, also use the perimeter of the pattern to determine the length of the boxing strip. Double this amount for the cording, and allow 1 inch for each of the necessary seams. Construct a basic muslin form for each cushion, and stuff.

The ties that secure the cushion to the chair can be made from matching fabric, purchased cord, braid, or ribbon. To make matching ties, cut strips of fabric that are long enough to tie around the chair posts. Fold the strips in half lengthwise, turn in the seam allowances, and topstitch the ends and edges. Sew the ties into the seams at the back corners. Construct the knife- or box-edge cushion following the directions given earlier in this chapter.

Chair cushions are easy to make from terry towels. Here, floral towels are backed with blue towels and trimmed with green cording and ties.

Tie-on cushions made from red-and-white checked fabrics brighten this breakfast area. Cushions are tufted with self-covered buttons.

Trimming Pillows

The possibilities for decorating pillow covers are almost limitless. Let the color scheme and mood of your room be the guide in selecting a theme for your pillow decorations. Embroider your own designs by hand or machine. Patchwork and quilting are great ways to turn fabric scraps into bright accent pillows. Applique fabric or felt cutouts by hand or machine. For a quick applique technique, use the heat-activated bonding web or cut the shapes from iron-on mending fabrics. Arrange novelty trims, braids, or ribbons in attractive geometric patterns. Create dramatic stripes by alternating grosgrain and velvet or embroidered ribbons. Whichever method you choose to finish a pillow, make sure to complete the work before you join the pillow or cover sections together.

The seams of the pillow provide another possibility for decorating. Use cording made from a contrasting color to accent a pillow. Various types of fringe or edging can also be sewn into the seam. For a special effect, try adding a ruffle in the seam of the pillow. Make the ruffle from matching or contrasting fabric or make it by gathering a ribbon. Button-tufting adds a special look to pillows and seat cushions. Use either self-covered buttons or any shank-type button. Plan the button arrangement on a paper pattern and transfer the markings to the right side of the cover pieces. To attach the buttons, use a darning needle threaded with strong cord. Start from the underside of the cushion and push the needle through to the topside and through the button shank. About ⅛ inch from that point, pass the needle back through the cushion to the underside and through the shank of the second button. Pull up the cord ends tightly, tie securely under the button, and clip the ends. Tassels add the finishing touches to the corners of pillows or to the center of the gathered end of a bolster. The method for making tassels is the same for all types of yarn. The size and fullness of the tassel should be proportional to the size of the pillow or cushion on which it will be used.

To make a 4-inch tassel, cut a piece of cardboard 4 inches long and 3 inches wide. Wrap the yarn even around the cardboard lengthwise, starting and stopping at the bottom edge. Take a length of yarn, draw it under the loops at the top edge of the cardboard,

and tie it up securely. Hold the cardboard in one hand and cut through the loops at the bottom edge of the tassel. Tightly wrap another length of yarn around the tassel strands about 1 inch from the tied end of the tassel. Tie a knot and bury it among the tassel strands.

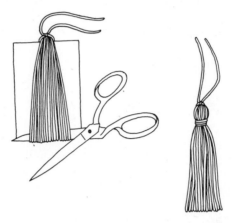

Attach the tassels to the cushion by the lengths of yarn extending from the tassel top by one of two methods. Twist the lengths and include the ends in the seam allowance before joining the corner sections, or sew the tassels by hand to the completed cushion, threading the yarn ends through a darning needle.

Create one-of-a-kind pillows with machine-appliqued felt designs. Brightly colored tassels finish the corners of each pillow.

Chapter 7

Slipcovers for Chairs and Sofas

Slipcovers have long been considered problem-solvers in home decorating. A bright new slipcover can give new life to a worn and faded piece of furniture; likewise, it can protect your fine furniture from a child's sticky fingers or rambunctious activities. When you cover odd pieces of furniture with matching slipcovers, you will add a coordinated look to any room's decor. Or, use slipcovers to add an accent color or a dramatic design to a dull room. Because making slipcovers costs much less than reupholstering furniture, you can try new ideas on a small scale—before you go ahead with an adventurous decorating scheme.

Also, you can easily change your slipcovers with the seasons. For example, use pastel colors in the summer to give your home a cool, refreshing look.

With the wide range of fabrics available, it's not hard to create a complete wardrobe of slipcovers for every room in your home. New fibers and finishes—in prints or solid colors—have made possible easy-care, soil-resistant fabrics.

Slipcovers are not difficult to make, so don't be afraid to start—even if you are a beginning seamstress. They take time, however, so follow each step carefully and accurately. The instructions on the following pages will take you through each step.

The love seat pictured at the left is covered with a Toile print. This neat, tailored, snug-fitting slipcover is a welcome addition to this traditional setting. The same print has been carried over to the draperies to produce a unified look throughout the room.

Slipcover Basics

Start by taking a good look at the piece of furniture you want to cover; is the frame sturdy and the padding firm? Disregard worn, frayed, and faded upholstery or stuffing that has flattened out. If your chair or sofa is solid and comfortable and has good design lines, it's well worth your time and effort to cover it.

Types of fabrics suitable for slipcovers run the whole gamut of natural and synthetic blends. One of the advantages of slipcovers is being able to take them off and home-launder them when they get soiled; select washable fabrics instead of those that need to be dry-cleaned.

Sturdy cottons and cotton blends (including heavier wash-and-wear or permanent-press fabrics) are ideal for slipcovers. Corduroy, twill, and denim are also good choices. And don't overlook the possibility of using stretch fabrics for your covers; special double-knit fabrics are designed especially for slipcovers and upholstery use. Although these fabrics may cost a little more to buy, the stretching properties will ensure a snug, neat fit on your chair or sofa. Or, you might try an unusual type of fabric, such as a lightweight fake fur or pile fabric (many of these can be washed and tumble dried). You also can use patterned sheets for making slipcovers. They are particularly pretty for bedroom chairs or chaise lounges.

Making a muslin pattern first is a good idea if you're not an expert. The procedure is the same as for the finished slipcover, and you have the advantage of working out any mistakes on the muslin. Use this muslin as a pattern for your actual cover.

To make a slipcover—without first making a muslin pattern—follow the same procedure, using your fabric when cutting the sections and pin fitting. If your chair or sofa already has a slipcover, you can take it apart and use the pieces for the pattern. Don't forget to add accurate seam allowances.

Welting or cording usually is used in the major seams of the slipcover to form a sharp, crisp line. Make the welting to match the slipcover, or use a contrasting color. If you wish to make your slipcover with a contrasting welting, either purchase ready-made welting or cover your own. If you cover your own with a contrasting color, make sure the fabric you use has the same care characteristics as your slipcover fabric. Sometimes, covers are made without welting in the seams; this can be quite attractive if the slipcover is well fitted.

Heavy-duty zippers or snap tape strips are used to make removal of the slipcover easy. Heavy-duty zippers—specially made for slipcovers—are available in 24-, 27-, 30-, and 36-inch lengths. Snap tape can be cut to any length desired. Plan to have a zipper or a snap tape closing along one side of the outside back of a chair. For a sofa, the opening can either run down the center back or on each side of the outside back sections. Each cushion also requires an opening. The zipper or snap tape should extend across the back and around at least one corner.

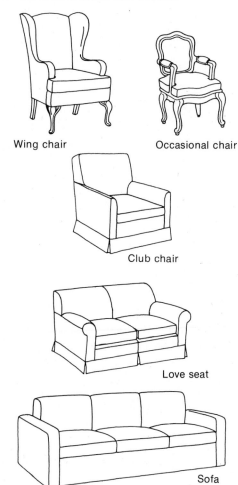

Wing chair   Occasional chair

Club chair

Love seat

Sofa

This illustration shows types of furniture most often slipcovered. The estimated yardages for these are given on the next page.

Identifying the parts of the chair will help you to follow the directions for constructing your slipcover. The illustrations in this chapter show chairs; however, sofas have the same basic parts and are slipcovered following the same procedures. The following illustration shows all the different parts of the basic chair and identifies them by name.

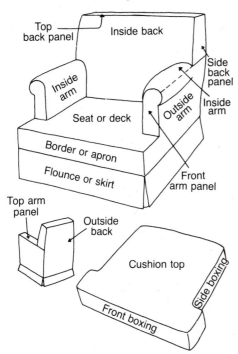

Estimating yardage can be done in two ways. You can follow a fabric guide such as the one given here, or you can measure all sections of your chair or sofa and add two inches at every seam line. You'll also need to add allowances to be tucked in between the chair frame and the seat deck (ten inches at the back and five inches at each side). Allow one extra yard for covering welting for a chair, and 1½ yards for a sofa. Also make allowance for the skirt, if you plan to use one on the slipcover.

While this type of yardage measurement is accurate, it helps to know where specific pieces will be used and how they will be sewn together. If you're a beginner at slipcovering, use these figures as a starting point, and take the overall dimensions of your chair with you when you go shopping for a fabric. An experienced salesperson can help you figure the exact yardage that you'll need for your project.

The following yardage is figured for 48-inch fabric, without pattern or repeat:

Wing chair	6½ to 7½ yards
Occasional chair	4½ to 5 yards
Club chair	6½ to 7½ yards
Cushion	1½ yards
Love seat	8½ to 10½ yards
Sofa (6 to 7 feet)	10 to 14 yards

For 54-inch material, reduce this yardage by 10 percent. You'll need to allow more yardage if the fabric has a pattern with repeats.

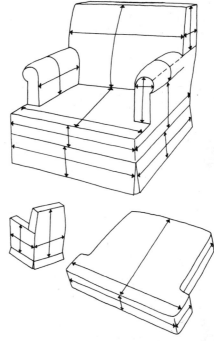

The illustration above shows the areas to measure to determine the yardage. Total all the lengthwise measurements plus seam and tuck-in allowances. Remember to make an allowance for the skirt, if you plan to use one. This will give you the number of inches you'll need; divide this by 36 to determine the number of yards you'll need. If the fabric you select is very wide, it may be possible for you to cut some of the pieces, such as the arm section, side-by-side.

Fabrics with a definite pattern or design repeat require special planning. If this is your first attempt at making a slipcover, you will find that a solid color or an allover design is easiest to work with. Large prints, one-directional designs, plaids, and stripes require more time in planning, cutting, and construction—as well as more fabric.

Matching the fabric on the chair or sofa is an important consideration. The designs on large patterns should be centered on the inside back of the chair, as well as on both sides of the cushion. On a sofa, center the design on each of the back sections and cushions. Match the inside arm pieces and center the design on the outside back also. It is not necessary that the two outside arm panels match, as they will not be seen at the same time.

A striped pattern must be matched from the top of the back to the seat, across the seat cushion, and down the front to the floor. You must also match stripes to form a continuous stripe across each arm from the seat to the floor. With a picture type of design all figures must be right side up on every section. Hold the fabric with the right side to you when placing it against the chair. In this way, you can see the pattern and decide how it will look best; it will also be easier to match stripes, plaids, or any other patterns.

Preparing the furniture is a necessary preliminary to fitting slipcovers. Be sure the old upholstery is clean, and repair any sagging springs. Mend any rips or tears in the old covering, too. If the stuffing has flattened or hollowed out, fill in with new padding. Cover the padded places with heavyweight muslin, and sew the muslin to the original cover.

When making the slipcover, follow the seams of the original upholstery. Watch the grain to make sure the piece is shaped correctly. And determine the type of skirt to use and where it will start. The top of the skirt is usually above the floor. To finish a slipcover that does not have a skirt, extend the lower section deep enough so that you can fold under the chair.

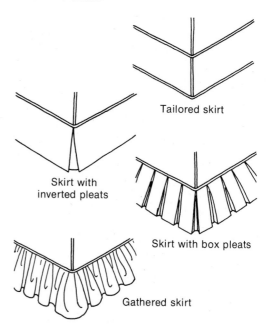

Tailored skirt

Skirt with inverted pleats

Skirt with box pleats

Gathered skirt

If the chair has a spring seat, the corners of the upholstery will be boxed, so the fabric won't tear as the springs contract.

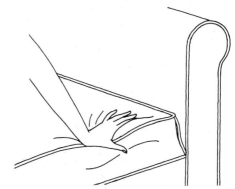

The same fitting is necessary on the seat cover; this will be shown as the chair is fitted. As a rule, both T-cushions and square cushions have spring-action seats.

Slipcover Construction

You can construct a slipcover for any chair or sofa by following the instructions below.

Start by fitting the muslin. Always work with the straight grain of the fabric. The grain should run vertically from the floor, even if the panel you're cutting is on a slant. Never stretch or pull fabric while pinning or cutting.

Cut the muslin lengths for the basic sections first. Start with the inside back of the chair. Fold the fabric in half lengthwise, and rest it on the back of the chair so it drapes down the back and onto the seat. Remove the cushion so you can work on the chair-seat deck, which will be slipcovered with body of chair. Cover cushion separately.

With your fabric resting on the chair, pull the fabric back so the cut edge extends 2 inches past the far back edge of the chair. Bring the fabric down along the inside chair back, across the seat deck, and down the front edge. Make a mark 6 inches from the floor. To this mark in the fabric, add 12 inches (2 inches for the welting seam at the front edge of the chair back and 10 inches for the tuck-in allowance where the deck joins the back). Cut straight across the fabric at this measurement.

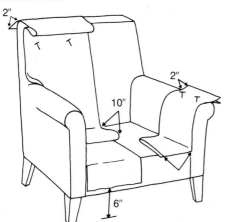

Next, lay the folded fabric across the top of the chair arm (with the cut edge extending 2 inches past the far outside top edge and the fabric running over the top of the arm and down the inside surface of the arm).

Make a mark where the arm meets the deck. To this mark add 5 inches for tuck-in allowance between the seat deck and the arm. Cut the fabric at this measurement. Do the same with the opposite arm of the chair.

To cut the lengths of muslin for the outside back of the chair, start with the cut edge of the muslin 2 inches above the top of the chair. Measure from this point to 6 inches

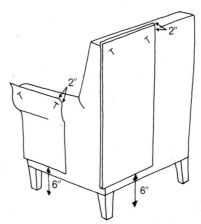

from the floor, and cut the muslin straight across at this measurement.

For the outside of the chair arms, start with the cut edge of the muslin extending 2 inches beyond the outside top edge of the arm, and measure to a point 6 inches from the floor. Be sure the muslin conforms to the curvature of the outside of the arm.

The arm front panel, the pieces of the slipcover on the very front surface of the chair arms, and the side back panels are cut separately while you're fitting pieces together.

Pinning the muslin in position is the next step. After the fitting and the pinning, the sewing is easy. Start by pinning the first panel to the top back panel of the chair with T-pins. The top edge should extend exactly 1 inch beyond the back of the chair. At the front edge of the top, pin a double 1-inch fold.

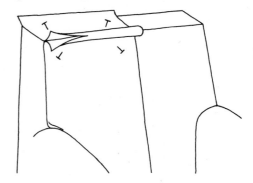

Moss green welting accents the seams on this natural linen slipcover and repeats the green-and-white treatment used for the windows.

The deep, tailored skirt with the mock corner pleats conceals the chair's legs. Wash-and-wear finishes make this fabric easy to handle.

Cut through the center of the fold. Now, you have two pieces with a regular 1-inch seam allowance in which you can sew the welting. If your chair is curved across the top, it will be easier to cut this top back panel and the side back panels in separate pieces. However, they can be cut in one continuous strip. Let the upholstery seams be your guide.

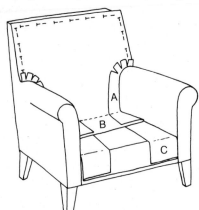

Starting from the center top of the chair, smooth the muslin down toward the seat of the chair, pinning seam lines as you go. Shape around the arm, and clip in on the seam allowances. Allow a 3-inch tuck-in at **(A)**, and a 5-inch tuck-in at the back crevice on both the inside back and seat **(B)**. Fold 3 inches for the tuck-in at the seat sides **(C)**.

If your chair has rounded edges, you will have to ease the fabric around the curves. Do this by forming small pleats or basting the seam line and easing the fullness.

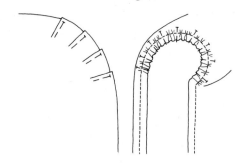

Fit the outside back piece of the muslin to the back of the chair. Pin the center of the muslin to the center of the top of the chair. Pin and shape down each side of the chair to 6 inches from the floor.

If you cut the top back panel and the side back panels in a continuous strip, start at the center of the top on the chair and pin the muslin to the inside back and outside back of the chair. If necessary, shape with a seam at top corners of the chair. Remember to use 1-inch seams throughout the construction of the slipcover.

Shape the muslin over the inside arm. At the back of the arm, shape the muslin to follow the shape of the tuck-in on the inside back—where the arm joins. Only one arm needs to be fitted in the muslin. Pin the arm side section to the outside back muslin.

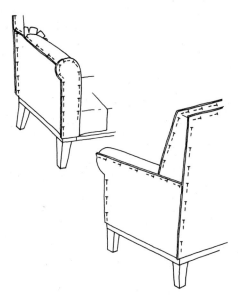

Next pin the outside arm section to the inside arm section. Measure the length and the width of the front arm panel. Cut a length of muslin; pin and shape the muslin to fit the arm panel. Pin this piece to the inside and outside arm pieces. Allow 1-inch seams. The arm panel is pinned just to the platform on the inside front, but to the full length on the outer arm.

To make a pattern for the cushion cover, measure the top of the cushion and the depth of the boxing. Using these measurements plus the seam allowances, cut 2 pieces of muslin for the top and the bottom of the cushion. Cut three bands this length, plus 4 inches. Add seam allowances to the depth measurement. Fold two of the boxing strips in half lengthwise; the zipper will be inserted between these folds. Pin the muslin sections over the cushion, then trim and notch the seams. If you are making a cover for a sofa with cushions of different sizes, you need to fit covers for each size cushions.

When all sections are pinned together, trim the seams to an even 1-inch allowance. Notch the seams every so often so that you will have a guide when fitting the pieces together.

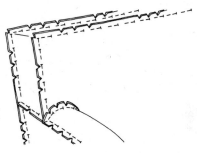

Mark all seam lines with pencil or chalk before unpinning the muslin from the chair.

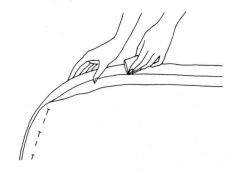

Fold the back, inside back, and seat pieces in half and make sure they're even. Cut duplicates of the arm pieces from muslin.

To determine the exact yardage, mark the fabric width on the floor or table. Lay the muslin pieces within the width measurement. Add an additional yard for cutting the bias strips to cover the welting for a chair; 1½ yards for a sofa. If you're using a print, be sure to allow extra fabric for centering the motifs. You'll also need extra fabric for matching stripes or plaids.

Cut out the pieces, using the muslin as a pattern, and cut the bias strips to cover the welting. The average chair requires 18 yards of bias; 36 yards are needed for a sofa.

Sewing the slipcover is easiest when done one section at a time. Start with the cushion cover. Make covered cording or welting (follow the directions in (Chapter 2), using 1-inch seam allowances.

Sew the welting to the right side of the top and bottom sections of the cushion, with the seam allowance of the welting along the cushion edge. Clip the welting seam allowance at the corners before turning. Leave several inches of the cording free at either end so it can be joined in a continuous line **(A)**. Overlap the two ends of the welting about 1½ inches and cut off the extra welting. Along one end, remove the stitches that hold the bias over the cord. **(B)**. Cut the exposed cord off so that the two ends of the cord just meet. Folding under the end of the bias strip, wrap the free end around the other welting and stitch in place **(C)**.

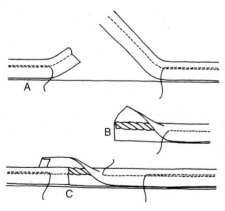

For cushion boxing, press two of the three bands in half lengthwise. Sew the zipper between the folded edges. Follow the zipper package directions for a centered seam application. Turn under 2 inches on the ends of the remaining band. Lap it over ends of zippered band, and stitch 1½ inches in from folds.

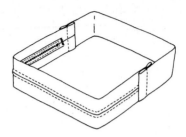

Be sure the zipper is open, then sew the upper and lower cushion pieces to the boxing, using inside seams. Then, turn to the right side, through the zippered opening.

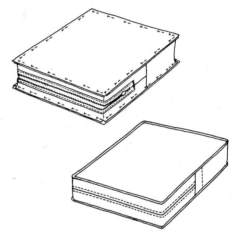

Next, make the back section of the chair. Sew welting around three sides of the back piece (top and two sides). Join top and side back panels, and sew welting around the front edge only.

Sew the back to the top panel, leaving seam allowances free at the lower band where it joins the arm. Sew the inside back piece to the top band, leaving the same seam allowance free. Now, fit this section to the chair.

Next, sew the cording around the arm plate. Clip the cording seam allowance so it follows the curve of the arm.

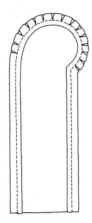

Join the inside and outside arm pieces. If you cord this seam, first sew the welting to the right side of either piece. Pin the pieces to be joined together. Stitch just inside the original stitching line of the piece that you previously corded.

Mark the depth of the chair seat on the front arm plate. Sew the arm plate to the arm sections from this point to the end of the outside arm piece. Check the fit of this section of the chair before continuing.

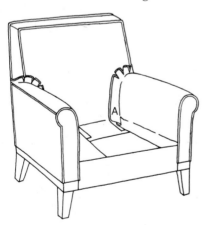

Sew the back section of the outside arm to the lower edge of the top band. Sew around the seam where the arm joins the inside back piece. This seam continues to the end of (A), the arm tuck-in allowance.

Fit the seat or the deck piece in the chair. Here, the boxing allows for the spring action at the front of the chair. Sew the back and side edges to the inside back and inside arm

pieces, forming the tuck-in. Fold front piece down over apron of the chair, and pin the corner to form a boxing. Clip seam allowance at base of this pinned boxing seam.

Turn the pinned corner to the inside and sew with an inside seam. Turn to the right side. Sew the seam allowance below the clip to the front arm panel.

On the T cushion, the spring action is at point (A) at the base of the arm. The seat is cut with a 3-inch tuck-in at the sides, but is shaped to the front of the chair with only seam allowances added.

The apron band is cut separately. At section (A), the boxing is made by inserting a square gusset piece that sews to front arm panel, inside of T, and seat inside the tuck-in.

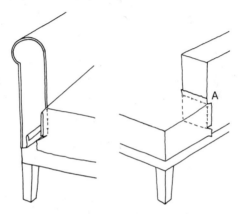

Slipcover skirts are optional. However, if you decide to make one, remember that the length of the skirt or flounce may vary, but it is usually 7 to 8 inches. Measure from the floor to the point where the skirt will be attached to slipcover; mark it with a row of pins around cover. Cut skirt desired length plus 1½ inches for hem and 1 inch for seam allowance.

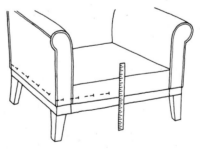

Cut skirt pieces across the fabric on the same grain as the slipcover. The number of lengths necessary depends on the style. Cut strips lengthwise only when a stripe is used.

You may choose from four types of skirts for your chair or sofa. Each skirt is described below and is pictured on page 138.

Make straight or tailored skirts by cutting 4 strips the length of the chair sides plus seam allowances at ends. Sew skirt along marked line with a welted seam.

Inverted pleats are attractive at the corners of the slipcover. Determine the depth of pleat at each corner. Add 4 times this amount to the distance around the chair. Cut strips to this length. Join strips so that the seams are hidden by the pleat.

Box pleats also can be used. Pleat the fabric strip to determine size and depth of the pleats. Space pleats evenly, with the center of a pleat at center front. Multiply the number of pleats by the number of inches in each pleat. Cut the necessary number of strips. Do any piecing under the pleats.

Gathered skirts usually are made by cutting the fabric 2 to 3 times the distance around the chair. Fabric weight and fullness determine the number of strips you will need.

Instead of hemming skirts, you can make them double. For the yardage, figure twice the skirt length plus seam allowances. For a lined skirt, the lining is cut 2 inches shorter than the skirt. Sew the lower edge of the lining and the skirt together. Press back the hem. Sew the lining and skirt together at the top, and you'll have a perfectly hemmed skirt.

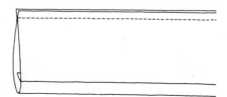

Sew pieces of twill tape or ½-inch elastic to the slipcover at each corner on either side of the legs. Tie tapes under the legs of the chair to keep the slipcover from riding up.

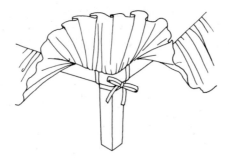

Slipcover closures can be made on either side of the back of chair. Use a zipper or gripper tape for closure.

Sew one side of the zipper to the arm side of the back opening. Lap the corded edge of the backpiece over the zipper and topstitch. (This usually can be done close to the welting so the stitching hardly shows.) Sew the zipper right into the skirt of the slipcover; sew gripper snap tape in the same manner.

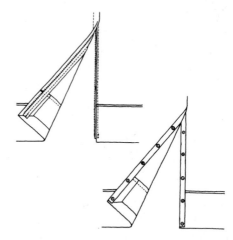

You may also want to make armguards to protect areas that get the most wear and tear. Cut them from the arm patterns, and use slipcover fabric. Tuck in at seat, and snap or pin under the arm.

If you want your slipcover to fit like upholstery, omit the skirt. Make the slipcover to the point of putting on the skirt. Put slipcover on chair. Chalk a line around bottom of chair apron. Trim 3 inches below this line.

Trim cover around chair leg, leaving a ½-inch seam allowance (**A**). Sew welting to this edge (**B**). Clip in on seam, turn to inside, and whipstitch the seam allowance back.

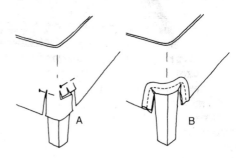

There are a number of ways to finish the lower edge of this slipcover. For a completely covered underside, cut a piece of heavy muslin to fit over the bottom of the chair, inside the 3 inches turned back on the cover. Fit the cover over the chair and attach the muslin to the cover with separating zippers. A quicker method is to turn under ½ inch along the lower edges of the slipcover and edgestitch. Then, place the cover on the chair and stretch the cover to the underside. Firmly tack the slipcover to the chair frame.

Furniture with exposed wooden frames, like the occasional chair illustrated on page 136, can be slipcovered also. These usually are fitted with separate sections for the back, seat, and arms.

The seat must be fitted around the posts for the back and the arms. Pin the fabric to the seat and fit it tightly against the wooden posts. Mark the seam line and then stitch welting to the seam line at each of these posts. Turn the raw edges of the welting and the fabric to the underside and overcast or cover with bias tape. The seat cover is secured with tapes tied under the chair. Make separate covers for the upholstered sections on the arms by cutting a section for the top and then stitching welting to both side edges. The ends may need darts to shape. Add sections on either side to reach under the arm and overlap. Hem the bottom edges and sew welting across both ends. Fasten with snap tape or Velcro.

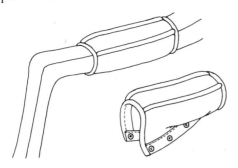

Knit Slipcovers

New polyester double-knit fabrics specially made for home decorating help you to fit a slipcover more snugly. A knit cover will retain its shape better than other fabrics.

If you're a novice at slipcovering, polyester double knits will make learning easier and more enjoyable. Just make sure the fabric you choose is designed to be used for slipcovers and upholstery.

Since polyester double knits are usually 60 inches wide, you'll need fewer yards than you would with ordinary fabric. Also, you don't need to cut the strips to cover the welting on the bias, which saves fabric.

In figuring yardage for knit slipcovers, remember that all pieces should have loops running up and down in the same direction. To determine the direction of the knit, find the end that doesn't ravel and use that for the bottom of each slipcover piece.

To cut knits, use long, even strokes and a sharp, rigid pair of scissors. Avoid raveling on all pieces by stay-stitching each piece with a straight machine stitch ¼ inch from the cut edge.

Use polyester or nylon thread. For machine sewing, use a size 14 ball-point needle.

Double-knit upholstery fabrics are ideal for slipcovers. The one shown here uses white welting to accent the design lines of the chair.

Ball-point pins are helpful in pinning because they force the knit fibers apart instead of piercing them.

Use 12 stitches per inch for lengthwise seams and 15 stitches per inch around curves. If possible, use a stretch stitch. Make welting for knits from the same fabric or a contrasting knit in the color or pattern of your choice. Contrasting fabric should have the same construction, wearability, and laundering properties as the slipcover.

The following instructions are for a wing chair without a skirt. They can be adapted to any style chair or sofa.

To estimate the yardage needed, measure the piece of furniture as illustrated below.

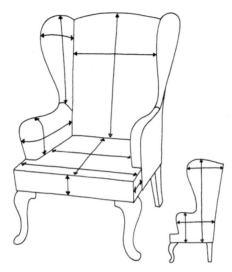

Add 1-inch seam allowances to all sides. Total the lengthwise measurements, including a 10-inch tuck-in between inside back and platform. Also, if you wish to have a skirt on your slipcover, determine the type and add the necessary length measurement. This total is the approximate number of inches you'll need; divide by 36 to determine the number of yards you'll need. If fabric is very wide, cut some sections side-by-side.

Cut and pin-fit the sections of the chair, using the actual slipcover fabric.

Inside back (piece 1): Remove the cushion, and lay the fabric right side up on the chair inside back. Using T-pins, pin the fabric to the chair. Make a chalk mark along the seam line of the top edge of the chair. Allow a 1-inch seam allowance and cut.

The seam where the inside back of the slipcover joins the inside wing pieces re-

quires a fabric allowance for tucking in to ensure a smooth fit. To do this, taper the cut from the 1-inch regular seam allowance at the top edge to a 3-inch tuck-in allowance, where back and seat platform meet. At this point, fold over 10 inches of the fabric to be used for tucking between chair back and platform. Continue with the fabric across the seat platform, allowing 3 inches on each side to tuck in between chair arms and sides.

To keep the fabric from moving, pin it to the chair with T-pins. Where the arm front meets the chair seat, discontinue the tuck-in allowance; cut the fabric with a 1-inch seam allowance beyond the seam line that joins the seat platform cover to arm fronts **(D)**. Allow 1 inch for seams, and cut the fabric along the outside edges of the deck side and front **(E)**.

Inside wing (piece 2): Pin the fabric right side up to the top inside wing surface. Mark with chalk along the seam edge on the outside curve of the wing **(F)**. Allow a 1-inch seam allowance beyond chalk marks and cut the fabric. Cut the seam where the wing joins the back, with the same tapering tuck-in allowance as on the back pieces. Pin the seam together as illustrated in the drawing below. Be sure that each piece of fabric is smooth and snugly fitted.

Inside arm (piece 3): Pin on fabric and mark with chalk along the seam line for joining the wing and arm **(A)** and along outside edge of the arm **(H)**. Allow a 1-inch seam allowance and cut the fabric for these two seams. With chalk, mark the seam joining deck to front

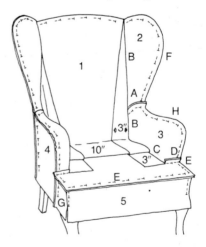

edge of arm **(D)**. Allow a 1-inch seam allowance and cut. Continue the cutting line for

3 inches to provide tuck-in allowance, as on the chair deck piece. Cut the back edge of arm piece to correspond with tuck-in allowance on side seam of back piece.

Outside back: Pin the fabric to the chair with T-pins. With chalk, mark along top seam line, and cut a 1-inch seam allowance beyond this mark. Chalk-mark side seams and cut with a 1-inch seam allowance. Allow 1 inch of fabric below the bottom edge of the chair and cut. Pin along the seam lines.

Outside wings and arm (piece 4): Pin the fabric to the chair. Make a chalk mark along the seam line where outside back and sides join. Allow a 1-inch seam allowance and trim off extra fabric. Later, snap tape or Velcro will be inserted in this seam. Pin seams together.

Mark along the seam line that will join the outside piece (4) to the inside wing and arm pieces (2, 3). Allow a 1-inch seam allowance and cut. Continue the cutting line straight down from the front edge of the chair arm to the bottom of the chair to form seam G. Cut the fabric 1 inch below the bottom of the chair. Pin seams together.

Front edge piece (piece 5): Pin the fabric to the front apron on the chair and around the sides where seam G will be sewn. Mark the fabric at this seam line and at the top and bottom edge of the chair front and sides. Allow a 1-inch seam allowance on all marked lines and cut. Pin along seam lines.

To construct the knit slipcover, join inside wing pieces (2) and the inside arm piece (3) to form seam A. Next, join this piece (2, 3) to the inside backpiece (1), starting at the top and working down to where the deck joins the sides and back. Then, reverse the work and sew seam, joining the arm front to the deck. Continue sewing these pieces together (seam C to meet seam B). Ease in any excess tuck-in allowance fullness where all pieces join: Trim, if necessary.

Sew in snap tape or Velcro. On pattern piece 4, stitch one side of the tape to the seam allowance. Place the tape right side up on the right side of the fabric. Make sure the tape is positioned close enough to what would have been the seam line so that when the tape is shaped, the side- and backpieces will fit together as snugly as if they had been sewn together in a regular seam.

Sew welting to side seam allowances of the outside back pieces. (Use uncorded welting about 1 inch wide, and cut on the fabric's crosswise grain.) Next, join this welted outside backpiece to the outside arm pieces, starting at the top and continuing until you reach the snap tape stitched onto the side-piece. At this point, pin the back- and side-pieces onto the chair again. Position the second half of the snap tape on inside of the backpiece so it will line up with the tape sewn into sidepiece. Pin it in place so you have a good smooth fit, and sew it down.

Join the front edge piece (5) to the deck edges at seam E. Use welting in this seam.

Pin the welting onto the piece that will cover the outside back and sides. When welting is sewn, pin this piece to the assembled frontpieces and sew together. Ease fullness around curves of wings and arm edges. This welted seam will extend down the outside front arm edge (seam G) to the bottom of the chair in one long continuous seam.

Finish the bottom edge with welting on all sides. On each of the four sides, attach a 1½-inch strip of fabric to the bottom edge of the slipcover in the space between the chair's legs. Turn under the raw edge and stitch close to the edge. To the underside of this strip, sew the soft, fleecy part of the Velcro. Glue the other portion of the Velcro to the underside of the chair.

To cover a T-cushion, lay the fabric on the cushion and mark around the edges with chalk. Cut 1-inch seam allowances. Cut one piece for the top and the other for the bottom. For the width of the boxing strip, measure the cushion from top to bottom and allow 2 extra inches. For the zippered section of the boxing strip, measure the width of the cushion across the back, and add 17 inches. Cut two strips the length and width you decided on for the boxing strip.

Measure from a point 8 inches forward of the cushion's back corner, around the front of the cushion, and to a point 8 inches from the opposite back corner. Add 2 inches to this figure for seam allowances; cut one strip this long and the proper width for the boxing strip. Fold the two back boxing strips in half lengthwise. Place folded edges together and insert zipper. Attach zippered back strip to front strip, using a 1-inch seam allowance.

Sew welting to both the top and bottom cushion pieces. Then sew the top and bottom cushion pieces to the boxing strip with 1-inch seams. Press slipcover's wrong side with a steam iron, and press the right side.

Chapter 8

Room Dividers and Wall Hangings

Use fabrics to divide or accent the living areas of your home. Partition an existing room to make a dining area into a separate nook, divide a bedroom shared by sisters so each has her own private area, or section off work space to create a den without walls.

Design a room divider to suit your needs. Depending on its purpose, it can be positioned permanently, designed to open and close, or made completely portable for use in several locations. Set a casual mood with transparent or flowing fabric strips, openwork weaving, or lengths of yarn attached to rods. For a more permanent divider, try a bold print attached to a giant frame or folding screen. Get the home handyman into the act; he can build the frame or the screen and mount accessory hardware on ceilings and walls.

Use fabrics to make instant artwork, too. Cut a section of a favorite print or textured fabric and hang it on a rod or mount it over a wooden frame. A large, fabric-covered panel is an easy way for you to cope with that empty stretch of wall space in the foyer.

The first step with either project is to analyze your home. Where could fabric help extend space, increase privacy, or contribute contemporary design interest? You can be a designer or an artist with elegant, inexpensive fabric as your decorating tool.

Bold, bright fabric panels with geometric appliques create a separate dining area. For an open, informal effect, this room divider is suspended from a hanging rod; weights help stabilize the fabric. Coordinated panels may also be used for draperies.

Living and dining space can be divided in style and at little cost, using a single layer of fabric that's handsome on both sides—or a reversible curtain. Locate ceiling joist, attach a traverse rod to ceiling, then mount divider.

Room Dividers

Almost any fabric and hanging combination can be used to make room dividers. Each combination of fabric and technique produces a divider that guarantees you privacy, suggests separated space, or adds beauty to any room.

How to design your room divider: Set the design for your divider by answering the following questions: Will the divider be positioned permanently or moved from one area to another? Must it open and close? Should the divider actually partition space, or can it be transparent and hint at a separation? Will the divider be seen from both sides, or will one side face a wall or closet? Will the divider be the central design interest in the room, or will it blend with other artwork and furniture pieces in the room?

How to select fabric: Medium- to heavyweight fabrics such as broadcloth, sailcloth, chintz, denim, mattress ticking, and seersucker are suitable for most room dividers. Transparent sheers must be firmly woven to ensure a neat, crisp appearance. To add extra body to a soft fabric, spray the fabric with sizing, bond two layers together, or iron on a backing using a bonding web.

If your divider will be exposed to sunlight, select a fade-resistant fabric. If you plan to clean your divider, test wash or dry-clean a sample of the fabric and the trimmings before you start. Inspect them for fading, shrinkage, distorted grain, and fraying seams. If you have a problem with the fabric sample, simply try another fabric.

Felt is an ideal choice for loose panels or covered screens because it doesn't require seam finishing. However, it fades quickly in sunlight and cannot be laundered. To preserve the good looks of a structured room divider, coat it with clear-drying varnish. Use a spray or brush variety.

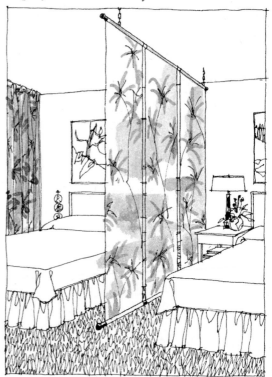

To provide privacy in a shared bedroom, hem lengths of fabric and stretch them between two wooden poles. Attach the top pole to the ceiling with chains. Select a sheer, firmly woven fabric that matches or coordinates with the draperies. The fabric gives the occupants the illusion of privacy, but it still maintains an open feeling in the room.

Permanently positioned partitions can be made in a number of ways. For a very stable divider, attach narrow boards along the ceiling and the floor. Tack panels of fabric to the upper board. Stretch the fabric until it is taut and tack it to the lower board. If you are using the full width of the fabric, you may not need to finish the edges. However, if the selvages are woven tighter than the fabric, trim them off and finish the edges. Make narrow hems along the sides or fold the raw edges over the front about ½ inch and cover with decorative braid. To conceal the tacks along the top and bottom of the partition, cover them with molding strips or color-coordinated braid.

Another method uses brass rods or wooden poles suspended from short chains attached to the ceiling with fabric panels hung from them. Hem the edges of each panel or make them reversible—like a pillowcase—with seams enclosed. Insert rods or weights in the hem of each panel to stabilize the divider.

For a casual look, attach rods or rings to the ceiling and floor and prepare fabric panels similar to a shower curtain—with eyelets along the top and bottom. Use drapery cord or some narrow rope to lace the panels firmly to the fastenings.

To create an open effect, lace the cording or rope between the ceiling and the floor. Use braids, ribbons, yarns, glass beads, spools, or tassels to add color.

Flexible dividers are made to open and close as needed. One method involves mounting a traverse rod on the ceiling and hanging a ceiling-to-floor curtain from it. Open and close the divider as you would draperies. Panels of fabric can also be hung from loops or rings—similar to a floor-length cafe curtain—on a suspended rod. Either select a fabric that will appear the same on both sides or make the curtain reversible.

Portable dividers are handy in several different places. One method mounts a panel of fabric between tension poles. Place the poles far enough apart so that the fabric is tightly stretched and smooth.

Folding screens make ideal portable room dividers. Cover the screen with fabric, using wallpaper paste or staples. Cut the lengths of fabric about 3 inches longer than the area to be covered. Spread the wallpaper paste, which has been mixed to the consistency of whipped cream, evenly on the screen. Place the fabric on the screen and smooth with a damp sponge to eliminate wrinkles or bumps. If screens are wider than fabric, overlap selvages and match designs. When paste is dry, trim away excess fabric with a single-edge razor blade. The fabric can also be attached with a staple gun. On most fabrics, staples will not show so you can position the fabric and staple it in place. If staples show, cover them with braid or trim glued in position with wallpaper paste or fabric glue.

The drawnwork divider below combines color and texture. Remove all the burlap threads before reweaving the panel with slats and yarns.

Use your favorite fabric to create art by the yard (above). Cut a length of designer print and staple it over a narrow wooden frame.

Decorator towels make easy and economical wall hangings (below). Narrow brass rods are held by short hems at the top and the bottom.

Wall Hangings

Turn fabrics with a stunning printed or woven design into wall decorations. To give your fabric the look of a modern painting, build a simple frame with 2x2-inch boards. Stretch the fabric over the frame and staple or tack it to the underside of the frame, mitering the corners. A section of heavy corrugated cardboard or lightweight plywood can also be used as the base.

Attach the fabric with wallpaper paste or staples. Use a standard picture frame—or an old one repainted—to enclose a panel of fabric, as you would a photograph. Fabric can also be hung flat against the wall. Make hems at the top and the bottom and insert rods or poles through the hems.

← *Sun scenes, easily appliqued on fabric panels by machine or with press-on bonding, are stapled or glued to this folding screen.*

Chapter 9

Table Linens

Tabletop magic requires no secret formula. Even the simplest meal will be received with enthusiasm if the table appointments are creative and colorful. And there's no easier way to accomplish this than by sewing your own table linens. No matter what type of dinnerware, flatware, cutlery, and serving pieces you own, you can enhance their beauty with a variety of attractive table linens.

When designing table fashions, take into consideration your family's dining style and the type of entertaining that you do most often. You can achieve whatever degree of formality you want when you take the time to sew your own table linens.

Start with a basic supply of linens—tablecloths, place mats, runners, and napkins—in the colors and fabrics of your choice. As you become more skilled, become more inventive, too—experiment with patchwork, ruffles, applique, novelty trims, and embroidery. Be sure to use easy-care or permanent-press fabrics because these fabrics will reduce your workload when washday rolls around.

Be sure to take all the necessary measurements before you start shopping for fabric. Then, make a tour through the fashion fabric, drapery fabric, and needlework departments. Try bedding departments for colorful designer sheets and towels and specialty shops for unusual handwoven scarves and throws. You may find just what you want at the remnant counter, or even in the budget shop.

This one-fabric look begins with the checked gingham floor-length tablecloth covered with a smaller embroidered cloth. Add the matching draperies, white casement curtains, and velvet cushions with checked bows—all are home sewing projects.

Tablecloths to Fit Every Table

You can have a complete change of scenery for your table as often as you wish if you sew your own tablecloths. With the wide variety of colors, patterns, and textures of materials in both natural and synthetic fibers, you have unlimited opportunities for creating a wardrobe of tablecloths that harmonizes with your decor and fits your table exactly.

How to Measure for Tablecloths

Be sure to measure your table accurately before you shop for fabric. To avoid any errors, make a drawing of your tabletop with the exact measurements of the length and the width of the table. Then, add the width and the length of the drop to each side and to each end.

If you're planning to make a formal tablecloth, add 16 to 24 inches to both the length and width of the tabletop. For an informal tablecloth, you won't need quite as much drop—10 to 14 inches will do. Never have less than 10 inches of overhang, or your tablecloth will look skimpy. On the other hand, don't let the tablecloth drag on the floor; the only types of tablecloths that should just barely touch the floor are the banquet cloth and the circular tablecloth.

How to Select and Prepare Fabric

Your choice of fabrics for tablecloths is nearly limitless. You can find just what you are looking for, whether your tastes lean toward solid color or patterned fabrics, vivid or muted tones, or smooth or textured surfaces.

And you don't need to be concerned with tablecloths that will require hours of tedious ironing. Even the most lustrous linen, the sheerest organdy or dotted swiss, and the finest cotton have the permanent-press finish that endears them to today's homemakers.

To ensure a truly coordinated look, take a piece of your dinnerware with you when you shop for fabric so you can tell if the two are compatible in color, texture, and pattern.

After making your selection, you'll need to prepare the fabric for sewing. Whatever type of cotton fabric you buy, be sure to find out

if it has been preshrunk; imported cottons very often are not preshrunk. To shrink, leave the cotton folded up as it comes off the bolt. Roll it up, forming loose folds. Fill a tub or basin with lukewarm water. Let the cotton soak until it is fully saturated. Squeeze gently to remove as much water as possible.

Hang the fabric over a shower bar or a clothesline to dry. Smooth it with your hands as it hangs. Iron the fabric while it is still slightly damp.

Before you cut your fabric, be certain it is on-grain. To get the straight grain, clip the selvage at the short edge and tear across the fabric. If the fabric will not tear easily, pull a thread across the fabric and cut carefully along the pulled thread.

Never have a seam running down the middle of your tablecloth. Regardless of whether your table is round, square, rectangular, or oval, you'll use the same technique. Use one length of fabric down the middle of the table, and join strips of equal width at either side.

Allow ¾ inch for hems and ½ inch for the seams, wherever the fabric will be joined.

Fabrics come in several widths. The most common widths are 36 inches, 39 inches, 42 inches, 45 inches, 48 inches, 54 inches, and 60 inches. If you want to avoid having any seams in your tablecloths, use bed sheets. You will find an array of solid colors and patterns in 72x104-inch, 81x104-inch, 90x115-inch, and 108x115-inch sizes.

Types of Tablecloths

The most popular types of tablecloths—square, rectangular, banquet, oval, and round—are discussed below.

Square and rectangular tablecloths: These are the simplest table covers to make; just follow this example:

If you have a square table that measures 42 inches across and you want the cloth to have a 14-inch drop, the finished cloth should measure 14 plus 42 plus 14 inches, or 70 inches square. If you choose fabric that is 39 inches wide, cut the center strip 70 inches long plus the ¾-inch hem allowance at each end, for a total of 71½ inches. Cut two strips the same length and 17¼ inches wide for the side strips. Join the center and side strips with ½-inch seams, and hem the edges either by machine or by hand, using the ¾-inch hem allowance. The finished table cover will measure 70 inches square.

If you have a rectangular-shaped table, use the same method, but alter the measurements according to the tabletop dimensions.

Whatever the size of your table and the width of your fabric, you can have a perfect fit if you measure accurately, and then add the seam and hem allowance.

Banquet cloths: If you wish to make a banquet cloth that will reach nearly to the floor for a square or rectangular table, measure the table, and cut and seam the fabric so that it reaches exactly to the floor on all sides when you place it on the table. Weight the cloth with books to hold it in place, and mark with pins on one corner exactly where it reaches the floor. Cut off the excess material on the curved, pinned line. Check the fit, fold it in quarters, and then cut the remain-

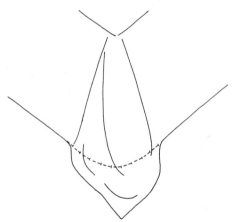

ing three corners to match. Finish the edge with a narrow hem, and the tablecloth will clear the floor by approximately ½ inch.

Oval tablecloths: To make an oval tablecloth, measure the length and width of your tabletop. Then, make a rectangle, plus the drop and hem. Join the fabric strips, following the instructions for the rectangular cloth. Place the cloth on the table, making sure it is centered, and weight it with books to hold it in position. Then, mark the hem as you would for a dress, using a yardstick to measure up from the floor. Pin-mark the cutting line one-half way around, from one side center to the other side center. Then, fold the

cloth in half, making sure the pins are in a smoothly curved line. Cut off the excess fabric. It will help you to mark the yardstick with a piece of colored tape at the point where

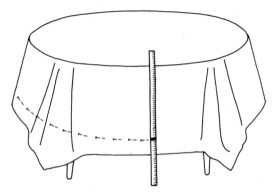

the pins are to be placed. Finish the edge with a narrow hem.

Round tablecloths: To make a round tablecloth, measure the diameter of the tabletop and add to this the number of inches of drop to either side. For example, if you have a table with a diameter of 48 inches and you want a 30-inch drop, add 30 inches plus 48 inches plus 30 inches. Use one width of material for the center of the table and full or split widths of fabric, depending on the width of the fabric, for each side to make a 108-inch square. Stitch the three strips together (if your fabric is patterned, be sure the patterns match) and press the seams open. Spread the fabric out on the floor and find the center of the cloth by folding it in quarters. Tie a string to a pencil, and cut the string to 54 inches. Use a thumbtack to hold the end of the string in place, and draw a quarter circle arc. Cut through the fabric adding the hem allowance. Finish with a hem

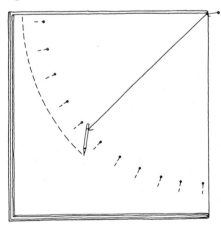

In the photo above, a colorful handmade table cover gives an old kitchen table a new personality. The heavy striped cotton picks up colors found elsewhere in the room. To make a table cover like this, simply cut and seam fabric to the proper dimensions and hem the edges.

If you are making an oval or round table cover with a sheer fabric such as organdy or dotted swiss, you may prefer to finish it with a narrow rolled hem. To do this, first run a row of machine stitching ¼ inch from the edge all the way around. Then, trim the edge close to this stitching line. You'll find that it is not only much easier to roll the fabric over this row of machine stitching, but the roll will be smoother, too. Roll the edge of the fabric just a few inches at a time between the thumb and the forefinger.

Use a slip stitch to catch and hold the roll in place. Take a single thread of the fabric for each stitch. Continue rolling the fabric a few inches at a time. The machine stitch is too tight if you find a point that seems to resist smooth rolling. Correct this by clipping the stitch before you continue on to the next stitch. (This procedure will smooth out the fabric and make it roll correctly.) Continue rolling and stitching. Make all of the stitches small and uniform.

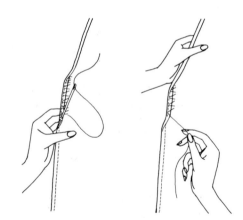

Trimming Tablecloths

Adding trim to either handmade or ready-made tablecloths is a great way to give table linens that extra spark of individuality. Don't hesitate to duplicate or to adapt any of the suggestions for trimmings that are mentioned on the next page. Or, if you wish to do so, create your own novel and exciting trims.

Lace, braid, and ribbons offer countless opportunities for trimming tablecloths. Use them to edge table covers, as inserts between strips of fabric, or over seams where you have pieced fabric. Be sure that both fabric and trim are preshrunk, or shrink them before stitching.

You also can use a heat-sensitive bonding web to attach ribbon or braid. Simply place a strip of the bonding web between the fabric and the trim and iron it on, following the directions on the package.

Bands of contrasting fabric or strips of patchwork also make interesting trims for table covers. Choose colors and patterns that complement your furnishings and tableware. Iron-on tape is easy to apply. In addition, you can cut it into whatever designs you choose. Experiment with the placement of your motifs before you apply the heat that bonds them permanently to the fabric.

Ruffles and ruffled edgings add a nostalgic touch to contemporary linens. You can add a ruffled edging to table covers of any size or shape. For a circular tablecloth, you can have tiers of ruffles cascading down the sides. Either make your own ruffling or purchase it ready-made.

Painted tablecloths will appeal to the artist in the family. On table covers stamped for embroidery, use fabric paints that come equipped with their own easy-to-use dispensers. Or, create your own designs. If you have patterned dinnerware, you can repeat the same pattern on the table cover.

Applique is an effective way of adding a personal touch to tablecloths. Use solid-color fabrics in contrasting colors for applique, or cut designs from patterned fabrics. Follow the instructions for appliqueing that are given in Chapter 5.

Embroidery is another handsome type of decoration for table covers. Choose from floral, geometric, or abstract designs. Or, for a truly personal look, embroider monograms or your family's coat of arms on your linens.

The layered look is especially appropriate for round tables. Simply place a smaller size or round decorative table cover over a floor-length circular tablecloth.

To add decorative interest, the green circular tablecloth below was edged with braid. The black-and-white square cover—tasseled at the corners—introduces another pattern and texture. This is an example of how you can achieve a total look when you sew for your home.

Other Tabletop Linens to Sew

Just as you replenish, expand, and accessorize your own wardrobe to give it new vitality, give the same consideration to assembling a collection of tabletop linens of your own creation. It doesn't take a lot of time, money, or sewing talent to produce distinctive table covers with truly original designs.

Instead of apologizing for your card tables that show the ravages of use, dress them up with new fitted covers that will draw rave notices from your bridge group. Or, surprise your family at Sunday breakfast by setting the table with colorful new place mats, or table runners and harmonizing napkins.

Game Table Covers

Don't discard card tables whose tops show heavy use. Instead, make new covers of wipeable vinyl and give the tables a lively look.

To make the one below at the left, cut white vinyl the size of the tabletop plus a ⅝-inch seam allowance. Cut the side strips as long as the table width, plus a 7-inch allowance for the corner tabs. Cut the strips 4¾ inches wide, each one a different color. Hem the side drops, then stitch them to the top section. Cover the buttons with vinyl, and stitch them to the tabs.

The bridge table cover below at the right is made of checkered vinyl. To make one like it, cut the vinyl the size of the tabletop, leaving a ⅝-inch seam allowance on each side. For the inverted scallop pattern on each side, draw a rectangle the width of the side of the table, plus the ⅝-inch seam allowance, and 6½ inches deep. Mark off a 2½-inch depth exactly in the center and then draw an inverted scallop from each side of the rectangular bottom to the center spot. Using this pattern, cut the fabric and lining to this size for each side of the table cover.

Topstitch the side fabric pieces to the top of the table cover. Sew the lining pieces together at the corners. Baste the lining to the table cover. Bind the bottom edges with bias tape; fold under and slip-stitch the top edges of the lining to the table cover. Make large tassels for each corner (see instructions for making tassels on page 133) from rug yarn. Tie the tassels together with the yarn ends and pin them in place in the four corners.

Place Mats

Place mats are so simple to make and so compatible with today's life-style that there's no reason why you can't have a generous supply.

Easy-to-follow instructions are given above for making this spill-shrugging vinyl table cover to protect or disguise the top of your card table.

Follow the simple directions above to make this tailored, checked card table cover that fits as snugly as a custom-made slipcover.

Pictured above is a sampling of place mat designs that will inspire you to test your own creative ability and design mats that harmonize *with your furnishings and your tableware. You can make a whole wardrobe of place mats to suit all of your mealtime needs.*

Place mats range in size from 12 to 14 inches deep and 16 to 18 inches long. When you cut them, be sure to allow for the hem. The size is important because you may find that eight small place mats will fit on your tabletop comfortably, while a larger size will necessitate cutting down to six place settings. Measure your tabletop to see what size mats are best for you. Keep in mind that mats should be large enough to hold a complete place setting without crowding it.

In most cases, just hem rectangles of fabric and add trim if you wish. Or for reversible place mats, use a double thickness of material. If you use a different fabric on each side, you can mix or match them.

Many fabrics are suitable for making place mats. You can make them of drapery fabric, gingham, calico, denim, organdy, dotted swiss, striped mattress ticking, sailcloth, or handloomed fabrics. And while you're making place mats, why not make a set of napkins of matching or contrasting fabric. Combine checked gingham place mats with polka dot napkins, floral mats with striped napkins, or for a dainty and elegant look, embroidered organdy place mats with lace-edged napkins. The only guidelines are to combine fabrics that are comparable in weight and texture.

Search for pieces of fabric left over from other sewing projects. You may be pleasantly surprised to find you have scraps that can be combined to make a set of patchwork place mats. Line them with denim or calico print, and edge them with a suitable binding. You might even like to make a set of napkins from the lining fabric.

Denim, striped mattress ticking, and sailcloth are especially durable for place mats. Make red or blue bandana-print napkins, or to accent them, buy bandana-print handkerchiefs.

For the ultimate in easy-to-make, easy-care place mats, simply buy fingertip towels fringed at the ends, and stitch decorative braid at both ends to give them a custom look. Be sure to shrink the trim if it isn't preshrunk. Use these velvety-looking mats for both indoor or outdoor meals. Add matching or contrasting washcloths to replace napkins, and visions of tedious ironing fade away.

The layered look in table runners adds a special touch to this table. Wider yellow runners provide a background for the paisley-print runners, *which are pointed at the ends. Add to this dark blue napkins that repeat the wall color, and you have a delightful color combination.*

Table Runners

Create tabletop drama with bold and colorful table runners. Because of their flexibility, they're becoming increasingly important as table covers. For those who are new to sewing for the home, table runners are good to start with because they are easy to make.

You can make runners from any of the fabrics that you would ordinarily use for tablecloths or place mats. Or, if you wish, there is a specially woven runner fabric that you can purchase by the yard in table linens departments. With this runner fabric all you have to do is buy the length you need and hem or fringe the ends. There are many colors and designs in this runner fabric; many are handmade, so you can add an expensive look to your dining or serving area.

Runners are usually placed on both sides of a rectangular dining table and hold several place settings. For a square or circular table, you can crisscross two runners in the center of the table. If you wish to combine runners with place mats, use a runner down the center of the table and matching or harmonizing place mats at the ends of the runners.

Table runners should be approximately 12 inches wide; the length will depend on the dimensions of your dining table. You can make them to fit the top exactly, or you can have a drop of 8 to 10 inches at either end.

You can make runners from a single length of material by simply hemming around the edges, or you can make them from a double thickness of fabric, which makes them reversible. You can hem the ends along the straight edge, scallop the ends, or taper them to a point. You can hem single-layer runners by hand or by machine, using a neat narrow hem. For the double-thickness runners, allow for a ½-inch seam when you are cutting. Place right sides together and machine-stitch around the edges, leaving an opening long enough to turn runner right side out. Use a whipstitch to close this opening.

The place mats and runners above are reversible — one side in stripes, the other in diminutive checks. Alternate the mats and the settings, too, *combining rich chocolate brown stoneware with abstract patterned porcelain. Make a set of brown napkins to complement both fabrics.*

Napkins

There's nothing quite like cloth napkins to give a table setting an elegant, finished look. With cloth napkins, you can turn even the simplest meal into a gala event. Now that most cotton and even the finest imported linen fabrics have a permanent-press finish, cloth napkins have regained the popularity and wide usage they once had. They are easy to launder, require little or no ironing, and are so nice to use.

Naturally, you will want to choose fabrics that are soft, smooth, and have a high degree of absorbency. After choosing a suitable fabric, let your imagination be your guide. Mix and match colors and patterns to complement your tablecloths, table runners, place mats, and dinnerware.

The most important consideration when you are making napkins is the size. The finished size for dinner napkins may be 18, 20, 22, or 24 inches square; luncheon and break-

fast napkins should be 17 inches square; tea napkins 12 inches square; and cocktail napkins 4x6 or 6x8 inches. For use at buffet dinners, you might like to use 12x18-inch rectangular napkins. This size is a special favorite with men because they can spread a large napkin across their knees without having to worry about it falling off while they are eating a meal.

When you are measuring and cutting fabric for napkins, be sure to include the hem allowance. For example, if you are sewing luncheon napkins that will measure 17 inches square when they are finished, remember that you must cut the fabric 18 inches square and sew a ½-inch hem.

If you are making formal dinner napkins, it is almost essential that you hem the material by hand. For all other sizes of napkins, neat machine stitching is acceptable and will produce professional-looking results. For an elegant trim, you might like to add a dainty lace edge to either tea or luncheon napkins.

Chapter 10

Bath and Closet Accessories

Bring your bathroom into the world of high fashion with colorful—and functional—bathroom accessories. When carefully planned, these items will transform the stark room you once hid behind a closed door into an attractive and practical room you'll be proud of. Start by designing matching shower and window curtains; to save money, use printed sheets or bedspreads. Then add other accessories to complement the decor of your bathroom: covers for the tank and seat of the toilet, a bath mat, and a contour rug. Finally, trim your bath and hand towels with decorative braid, ribbons, or appliques.

Clever closet storage accessories—custom-made to fit your special needs—will help relieve that 'cluttered' look in your home. And, these bright closet accessories will add sparkle to an otherwise dull closet.

Garment bags will keep your out-of season clothing clean and will help prevent fading. Fabric-covered storage boxes will neatly hold your hats, gloves, and scarves. Store your shoes in a shoe bag mounted on the inside of your closet door. Shoulder covers will protect clothing you wear frequently from dust.

Don't hesitate to try any of these ideas. The directions for all of these accessories are on the following pages; you'll be surprised at how easy they are to make.

Rich colors and soft textures give a small bathroom a feeling of elegance. Velvet shower curtain, seat cover, and chair cushion were made from a washable bedspread and trimmed with washable ribbons. "Unreal" silver fox carpet completes the mood.

This striped awning is made from a shower curtain held in place with two spring tension rods. The colors are repeated in the accessories.

Colorful shower curtains are easy to make from printed bed sheets—you needn't worry about seams. A plastic liner provides a water barrier.

Bathroom Accessories

Break away from an ordinary bathroom decor. Create a special effect with unusual fabrics and intriguing ideas.

Shower Curtains and Liners

These can hang together on one rod with two sets of hooks, or can hang separately on a regular rod used in combination with a spring-tension rod. Be sure that the rod you choose is rustproof.

To make the curtain, measure the distance from the rod to where the bottom will end. Then measure the width to be covered by the curtain. Add 5½ inches to the length for the top and bottom hems, and 3 inches to the width for the side hems.

Follow these directions to make a single curtain 72 inches square. If you need a larger curtain, adjust the measurements. For a double curtain—opening in the center and pulled back to either side—make two curtains.

For a standard shower curtain you'll need one double bed sheet (or 4½ yards of 44- to 48-inch fabric) and one plastic shower curtain liner. If you are using a sheet, cut it 75 inches wide and 77½ inches long. Or cut two pieces of fabric 38 by 77½ inches and seam them together in a ½-inch seam. Use a French or flat-fell seam to enclose all raw edges. Across the bottom edge, turn ½ inch to the wrong side, turn up a 3-inch hem, and stitch. Across the top edge turn 1 inch to the wrong side, turn 1 inch again to form a double 1-inch hem, and stitch. Turn ½ inch to the

Coordinated linens for bed and bath provide →
endless decorating opportunities for you, the seamstress. In the colorful bathroom pictured at the right, the impressive-looking ceiling to floor shower curtain was sewn from a sheet matching the bath and hand towels.

Grommets, or large eyelets, make neat, durable holes for shower curtain hooks. Hammer the grommets in place using an attaching tool.

wrong side down each side, turn a 1-inch hem, and stitch. Place the liner on the wrong side with the top edges even, and mark through the holes in the liner for positions of the holes on the curtain. Make a ⅜-inch buttonhole or place grommets at each mark. Add trim if desired.

Place the hooks through the holes in the curtain and then through the holes in the liner. Hang curtain on rod with liner on inside and curtain on outside of the tub.

To make a tieback, cut fabric into a 7x41-inch strip. For a double tieback you'll need two pieces. Cut a piece of stiffening 3x40 inches for each tieback. Place stiffening 1 inch from the edge of the fabric strip—with ½ inch of the fabric extending beyond each end—and pin in place. Turn this ½ inch at each end over the stiffening and press. Turn the 3-inch side of the fabric up over the stiffening and press. Next, fold ½ inch down along the remaining side and press. Fold this doubled ½ inch down over the stiffening and overlap the raw edge. Press and pin in place. Stitch around all four sides of the tieback ¼ inch from the edge. Make a buttonhole or loop at the center of each end of the tieback to hook to the wall. Trim the tieback with ribbons, braid, or fringe.

Toilet Tank and Seat Covers

To make the tank cover, measure the tank lid. Measure from the lower edge of the lid, across the top, and down to the lower edge of the opposite side for both the length and width. Add 2 inches to each of these measurements, and cut the rectangle of fabric. Place the rectangle over the tank lid—wrong side out—and pin the corners as shown below. Clip the excess fabric ½ inch from the pins.

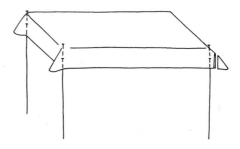

Stitch along the pins, and backstitch at both ends. To make the casing, stitch one edge of bias tape around the lower edge of the lid cover and turn it to the underside. Stitch the other edge of the bias to the cover, forming a casing. Leave an opening to insert elastic. Insert ¼-inch-wide elastic in casing, place cover over lid, and adjust elastic to hold cover. Overlap ends of elastic and stitch. Then stitch open section of casing.

To fit the tank cover, measure the distance around the front and both sides of the tank; add 6 inches to allow the cover to wrap around the back of the tank. Measure the height of the tank and add 2 inches. Cut the fabric. Bind the two ends with bias tape, or turn under and stitch a narrow hem. Stitch one edge of the bias tape across the top of the tank cover. Fold the tape to the underside and stitch to form a casing. Insert the elastic

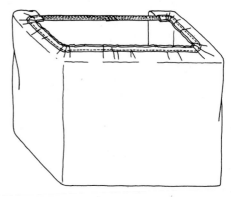

in the casing and fit the cover over the tank. Adjust the elastic and join the ends together. Remove, then cut a piece of elastic approximately 10 inches long and attach to one side of the cover at the lower edge. Again, fit the cover over the tank and adjust the elastic. Attach the other end of the elastic to the opposite side of the cover with a metal hook. Finish the lower edge with decorative braid, using binding or a narrow hem. Place the cover over the tank and mark the location of handle. Make a small buttonhole at mark, just large enough for handle to slip through.

To make the seat cover, make a paper pattern the size of the toilet seat lid. Add 1 inch all the way around the pattern and cut the fabric. Applique or trim if desired. Stitch bias tape around the outer edge, to form a casing similar to that of the tank lid cover. Insert ¼-inch elastic into the casing. Place the cover over the seat and adjust the elastic for a snug fit. Stitch ends of elastic together and cut off excess. Close opening in casing.

How to Make Bath Rugs

Make them from fake fur fabrics, heavy terry cloth, or terry velour. A small bathroom may require specially-sized rugs, so—to get the exact size that you need—make your own. First decide on the desired size and shape. If you want a contour rug, cut a paper pattern and fit it around the base of the stool until you get an exact fit. Cut out the rug.

On regular shapes—oval, rectangle, or square—finish by attaching 2-inch washable fringe around edges. Pin straight edge of fringe ½ inch over raw edge of rug. Turn under ½ inch at end of fringe and overlap beginning. Be careful not to stretch fringe because this will cause rug to curl. Ease in excess fullness at the corners and around the curved edges. Sew the fringe to the rug with two rows of machine stitching.

For contour rugs, finish the shaped edge with bias tape. Open out one edge of the bias tape and pin along the shaped edge of the rug with right sides together and raw edges even. Ease the tape around the curves. Turn under ends of tape and stitch ¼ inch from edge. Clip curves and turn tape to underside and press. Pin and then stitch tape to rug.

To prevent rugs from slipping, attach rubber backing to the underside. On contour rugs, trim off ¼ inch along the contoured edge. Place the backing against the wrong side of the rug with edges even. Using carpet thread and a large needle, hand stitch the backing to the rug along all edges.

How to Trim Bath and Hand Towels

Do this with decorative braid, ribbons, or appliques to give your bathroom a coordinated look. Select the trimmings to match or complement the window curtains, shower curtain, or other decorative features in the room. Stitch rows of decorative braid or ribbons along ends of towels. Be sure to select machine washable braids and ribbons.

Pin the trimmings to the towels, folding under ½ inch at each end. Topstitch or use a small zigzag stitch around all edges. Be careful not to stretch the towels or trimmings. Try combining different colors and textures for special effects. Towels can also be decorated with motifs cut from scraps of curtain fabric. Follow the directions for machine applique on page 108.

Practice on old towels to determine the proper stitch width. Fold the raw edges under ½ inch and press. Pin the fabric to the towels and topstitch around all edges. Accent the edges of the fabric with rickrack, using the jumbo width on bath towels and the regular width on hand towels.

Appliques turn white towels into decorative masterpieces. Machine-appliqued mushroom was cut from brown, white, and black fabric.

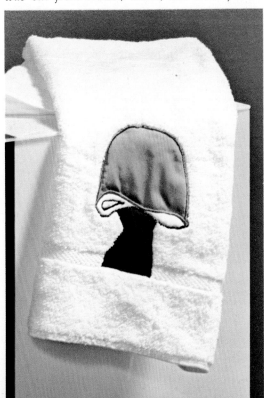

Storage Accessories

"A place for everything and everything in its place," can make your home a more pleasant place in which to live. For there's nothing more aggravating early in the morning than hunting in the closet for a clean garment or a new pair of shoes. With careful planning and a few hand-sewn items you can quickly turn a muddled bedroom closet into an organized place in which to store your clothes—and for little money.

For example, in the closet across the page all the items have used the same plain and colored sheets—garment bags, jumbo garment bag, padded coat hangers, shoe bag, and even the covered boxes above the hanger rail.

You won't have to spend enormous sums of money to make these bright, handy accessories for your own closet—the only necessities are a few yards of fabric, a knowledge of sewing basics, and some imagination. In a few short hours you'll have added interest to a dull closet with these quick, easy projects.

However, before you dash off to the local department store to select fabric for use in your closet, keep your total decorating scheme in mind. A bold purple, green, and blue print may go well in your closet and speak highly of your sewing skill and creativity, but will not say much about your decorating knowledge if the closet opens out into a room using a delicate rose red patterned wallpaper.

Covered Storage Boxes

Making gay and useful storage boxes like those in this closet couldn't be easier—no sewing is required and the only materials you need are a heavy white cardboard box, a length of material, and a roll of vinyl tape or a bottle of glue.

Cover the bottom half of the box first: cut a piece of fabric to equal the circumference of the box plus 2 inches by the height of the box plus 6 inches. Wrap the fabric around the box and glue or tape the fabric together at the back. You'll have an extra three inches at the top and bottom of the box. Miter the corners of this excess fabric and tape or glue it to the inside of the box and the bottom of the box. Repeat with the top half of the box.

Padded Coat Hanger

Make a padded coat hanger by wrapping cotton or polyester batting around the arms of the hanger to a depth of ¾ inch. Anchor the ends with hand stitches. Place the hanger on the covering fabric's bias grain and trace around one arm. Allow 1 inch around all sides; cut four pieces on the bias grain. With right sides together, stitch two arm cases, leaving the center edges open. Trim seams and turn the cases right side out.

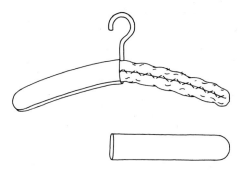

Slip the cases over arms of the hanger overlapping at the center and turn raw edges under. Blindstitch together around the center of the hanger. Trim with ribbon at the center.

Shoulder Covers

These fit over standard hangers. Add ½-inch seam allowance along curved edge. Cut two pieces for each cover. Mark a 2-inch opening at the top for the hanger. With right sides together, stitch along the curved edge, leav-

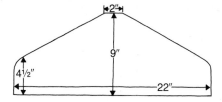

Printed and solid color sheets were sewn to make →
the garment bags, the jumbo garment bag, shoe bag, shoulder covers, padded hangers, and covered storage box in the closet at right.

ing the seam open between the top marks. Backstitch on both sides of the opening. Clip the seam allowance along the curve; press the seam open. Topstitch on both sides of the opening to hold the seams in place. Bind the lower edge with double-fold bias tape, or finish with a narrow hem.

Garment Bags

Using the shoulder cover pattern, measure from the hanger opening to the desired length. Standard lengths: 36 inches for blouses or jackets, 45 inches for dresses, and 60 inches for floor-length gowns. With a ½-inch seam allowance on all sides, cut two sidepieces for the garment bag. These hold two garments.

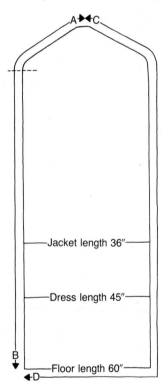

Measure the distance from A to B. Add 1½ inches to this and cut a strip of fabric this length by 7 inches wide. Boxing strip will contain the zipper. Cut this strip in half lengthwise, making two strips 3½ inches wide. Place right sides together and stitch a 1-inch seam from top down 15 inches—backstitch to reinforce the end. Baste remainder of seam. Press seam open and insert zipper in basted area. Close seam below zipper. Measure C to D and add 1½ inches. Cut a

boxing strip this length by 5 inches wide; piece strip if necessary. With right sides together, join two boxing strips with ½-inch seam at point B-D. Press seam open. Fold 1 inch to underside at point A of boxing strip, and topstitch close to folded edge. Starting at A, pin boxing strip to one side section, right sides together. At top center, fold under end of boxing strip, C, to meet A. Press and stitch close to fold. Join strip and bag with ½-inch seam. Open zipper and pin and stitch to other side section in same way. Press seams open; turn bag right side out.

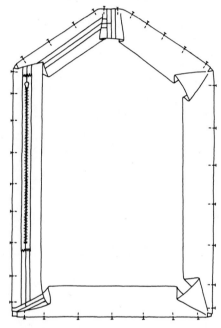

Jumbo garment bags hold several garments at one time. You'll need a frame for the top; use one from an old bag or buy an inexpensive plastic bag and remove the frame. Cut rectangles for top and bottom using frame as a pattern, and allow ¼ inch beyond frame on all sides for seams. To establish measurements for sidepieces, determine length desired and add 1 inch for seams.

For the width, measure half the distance around the frame and add 1½ inches for seams. Cut two pieces by these measurements. With right sides together, baste the sidepieces together lengthwise in a 1-inch seam. Press the seam open and insert the zipper in this seam. Close the remainder of the seam below the zipper. With right sides facing, stitch the remaining lengthwise edges together in a ½-inch seam. Place the frame

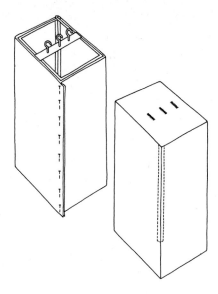

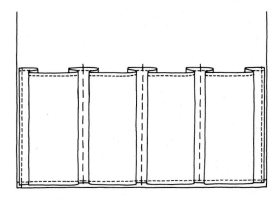

Working from the bottom up, pin the first strip of pleated pockets across full width of the backing, with the lower edges even. Baste along bottom, sides, and between pleats.

over the top piece and mark the openings needed for hangers. Make buttonholes at each mark. Open the zipper and pin the top and bottom pieces in place, aligning the corners. Stitch ½-inch seams. Turn the bag right side out and press the bag, forming creases down from each corner. Insert the frame at the top, passing the hangers through the buttonholes. If desired, cut a piece of cardboard the same size as the frame and insert the cardboard in the bottom of the bag for additional sturdiness.

Shoe Bags

To make a shoe bag, you'll need 1¼ yards of 48-inch fabric, 5 yards of narrow bias tape, 5½ yards of wide bias tape, and metal grommets. Cut one backing piece 20x40 inches and three strips for the pockets. Make the strips 14½ inches deep and 24 inches wide. Bind

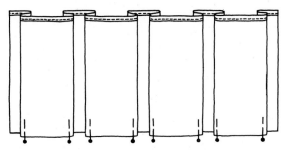

the top edge of each of these strips with bias tape. Form four 4-inch box pleats with each strip and baste along the lower edge to hold the pleats securely in place.

Repeat until the three pocket strips are attached in horizontal rows approximately 3 inches apart. Stitch narrow bias tape over basting stitches at the base of each row. Stitch narrow bias tape over the three inner basted pocket seams, stitching along both edges.

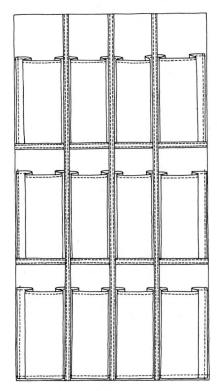

Fold under a double 2-inch hem at the top, press, and stitch. Bind outer edges with wide bias tape. Mount five metal grommets along top hem, following the package directions.

Chapter 11

Children's Rooms Are Special

Discover the true joys of sewing by creating special fashion for your child's room. Design bright, colorful surroundings that express your child's personality and reflect his or her life-style. Use sturdy, easy-care fabrics that will take the rough-and-tumble life day after day—and make washday easier for you.

Use your child's multicolored toys as a part of the overall design theme; create a unified look by repeating one print or color in the curtains, spreads, pillows, and wall hangings. Gingham checks, calicos, or prints used for curtains and bedspreads will combine especially well with wall accessories and playthings.

Sew comical quilts—playmates by day, and warm friends at night. Or make a larger-than-life pillow, a take-along sleeping bag that doubles as a coverlet when fully opened, a wall hanging with pockets (for fun and function), a rug that becomes a railroad landscape, or even a tent that folds out of the way when not in use.

As your child grows, his interests and activities will change, so you'll want to start with ideas that can grow with him. For example, you can add a dust ruffle to a crib quilt to make a coverlet for a youth bed. Or you can decorate a youth-sized bedspread with trim and appliques and use it to perk up a bunk bed.

Delight your daughter with this bright, Mexican-style bedroom. Roller shade plus floor-length cafes team up to create the effect of a long window; and the bouncy ball-fringe trim repeats the tones of the bright red painted furniture.

Personalizing Ready-Mades

If you're hesitant about making a quilt for a child's room because you think it takes too long, there's a way you can do it in half the normal time. A ready-made spread with a simple, bold design can be outline-stitched for a new "quilt" look. The Children of all Nations spread, shown below, is a good example of the type of design to select. Other ideas can use clowns, dolls, or trains.

Outline-quilting by machine will bring the design to life by making it stand out from the background. You will be stitching around the edge of the motif, so choose a large, simple design that doesn't have too many curves and corners.

Also give ready-made curtains a personal touch by adding trimming. Select plain, well-constructed curtains, add matching braid or other trim along the hem lines, and you'll find that they can easily be made to coordinate with the rest of the room.

A hanging headboard and coordinated stuffed toys add a personal touch to the room below. But keep in mind that you'll need to buy two bedspreads if you wish to make the hanging headboard and the stuffed toys.

It's easy to add a custom touch to a ready-made spread and curtains. Outline-quilt the figures on the spread, insert contrasting corners, and add decorative trim. The headboard is part of another spread that covers a cushion form and hangs from a wall-mounted cafe rod.

Pin trim on curtains near the edges and miter the corners before stitching. Stitch both sides of the trim in the same direction.

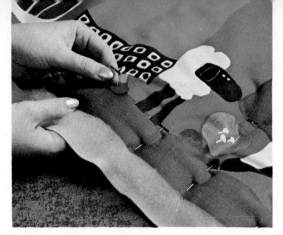

Before you start quilting, hold the spread, polyester batting, and sheet together with T-pins placed from three to four inches apart.

To make a twin-size quilted spread, you'll need a twin-size printed bedspread, a king-size sheet, a large roll of polyester batting, 3-inch-wide braid equal to the distance around the spread, the same amount of 3-inch-wide bias tape, and a coordinated solid color fabric for the corner pieces. First, trim off hems and finish the edges of the bedspread and sheet. Place the sheet on a large flat surface, and cover it with a 96x108-inch sheet of polyester. Smooth out wrinkles, being careful not to stretch the batting. Place the spread over the batting right side up. Pin the three layers together with T-pins, starting at the center on one side and working toward both ends. Pins should be placed at right angles to the edge, 3 to 4 inches apart. Place a second row of pins 5 to 6 inches from the edge. Continue pinning in rows from one side to the other, making sure that there are no wrinkles.

As you work, roll or fold pinned portion of spread toward the center. After pinning, trim away excess sheet and any batting that extends beyond the bedspread. All edges should be even. Stitch ½ inch from cut edges to prevent layers from slipping.

Quilt a small area at a time, working from center of spread to the edges. Plan quilting so bulk of spread is not under the sewing machine arm.

To make the doll, cut out design, allowing ½ inch all around. Stitch to backing, right sides together, leaving opening. Turn to right side, and stuff.

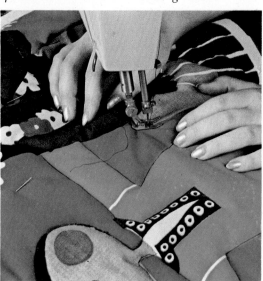

To outline-quilt the design, release the presser foot tension on the machine and set stitch length for a medium-long stitch. If this is your first attempt at machine quilting, first practice on fabric and batting scraps. Make sure the machine pressure is set properly, so all layers will move along at the same time. Start quilting around a figure near the center of the spread and work toward the outside edges, planning lines of quilting so the bulk of spread isn't under machine arm. Add more T-pins to hold layers together, removing them as you sew. Stitch around designs, carefully outlining one section at a time.

To make contrasting corner inserts, place the spread on the bed and mark the corners. Starting at the point of the corner (at the edge of the bed), pin side- and foot-drop sections of the spread together so the pins form a straight line to the floor. Measure 6 inches from this line toward the center fold, and mark with a pin on each side. Also mark the corner point.

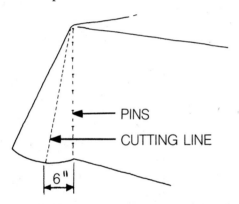

PINS

CUTTING LINE

6"

Remove pins holding corners together and lay the corners out flat. Draw a triangle connecting the three pins. Allow ½ inch on the spread for seams, and cut out this piece to use as a guide for the insert. Machine-baste the cut edges to hold the batting in place.

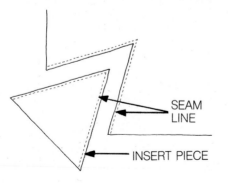

SEAM LINE

INSERT PIECE

Remove the curve from the bottom of the cutout section by cutting a straight line between the lower points. Cut two triangles from this pattern, adding 1-inch seam allowance to the sides. Sew the inserts to the spread, slashing the spread at the points to prevent puckering.

To trim the edges with braid, pin the braid to the outside edges of the spread and the corner inserts, overlapping the finished edge of trim over the spread about ½ inch. Topstitch in place. Pin 3-inch-wide bias tape to the underside of the braid, and stitch the two edges together on the lower edge. Baste bias tape to the underside of the spread, covering the seam allowance; stitch in place, stitching from the right side of the spread.

Make a hanging headboard that coordinates with the bedspread by covering a thin foam rubber cushion with the same spread fabric. Use a foam pad 1½ to 2 inches thick, about 24 inches high, and as long as the bed is wide. Cut a section of the second spread, polyester batting, muslin, and solid color backing the size of the cushion plus a ½-inch seam allowance around all edges. Place the batting over the muslin and cover it with the spread section. Pin and quilt around the design the same as for the bedspread.

Cut boxing strips from the solid color fabric. The strips should be 1 inch wider than the depth and 1 inch longer than the perimeter of the cushion. Join the strips into one long strip and pin to the padded section, overlapping and turning under raw ends. Stitch a ½-inch seam. To form the loops for hanging the headboard, cut three strips of braid 8 inches long. Fold the strips in half and pin the ends to the seam allowance along the right side of the top edge of the backing. Baste along the seam line. Pin the backing to the boxing strip with right sides together, aligning the corners. Stitch a ½-inch seam around the top and the two ends, leaving the bottom open. Trim the seams, clip the corners, and turn right side out. Insert the foam pad, fold in the seam allowance along the bottom, and slip-stitch the edges closed. Hang headboard from a wall-mounted curtain rod.

Trimmed curtains complete the picture. Add coordinated braid to a pair of curtains. The braid can be applied in several rows across the bottom and up the center. When turning square corners, be sure to miter the braid before stitching. (To miter, see page 26.)

Nurseries call for special attention. The ruffled canopy crib gives this nursery a very special soft look. The ruffle is repeated in the valance; *the sheer draperies can be closed to diffuse strong sunlight. An opaque roller shade can be lowered to block out the light at nap time.*

Quilts for all Ages

There's a quilt for every age group: a delicate little gingham crib or carriage comforter, or an appliqued quilt for the toddler; a comical cartoon quilt for an older child; and a quilted sleeping bag for a teen-ager. Each can be the focal point of the room.

Quilts or comforters for the carriage, crib, and youth beds are good projects for the beginning quilter. Their small size is easy to handle, and an entire quilt can be completed in just a few short hours.

Quilts for babies should be made of soft and delicate fabrics. Select tiny prints in light colors, pale checked ginghams, or pastel solids. Use only washable fabrics. Soft finish permanent press fabrics are a good choice, because they will look like new even after many washings. A dainty, pieced quilt is as practical in a baby carriage as it is pretty in a nursery. The finished size for a baby's quilt should be about 36x54 inches. To make a regular pieced quilt for a crib, follow the general quilting directions given in Chapter 5.

Reversible comforters can also work well in babies' cribs. Try a combination of gingham on one side with a matching pastel on the other side. To assemble, lay the backing on a flat surface. Place the quilt top face down over the backing. Lay a layer of polyester batting over the quilt top.

Pin and baste the three layers together, keeping the edges even. Stitch a ½-inch seam on three sides and all four corners, leaving one end open to turn. Trim batting out of the seam allowances. Clip the corners. Turn the quilt right side out. Carefully pull out the corners. Fold seam allowances in along the opening, pin and slip-stitch the edges together.

Again, lay the quilt out on a flat surface and smooth out all layers. Baste the three layers together, working from the center to each corner—being careful to keep all layers smooth and even. Also, baste through the center crosswise and lengthwise. Chalk-mark a simple line design on the top and machine quilt—or hand tuft with soft yarn or pearl cotton. (See tufting, page 112.)

Pink tulips bloom everywhere in the bedroom pictured above. The one-pattern look, achieved by using matching wallpaper and fabric, creates a room-widening effect. The laminated roller shades match the draperies. The wallpaper conceals the built-in storage next to the bed.

A ruffled pillowcase makes an attractive companion for the comforter. Measure the baby's pillow; cut the top and bottom pieces, following the directions for a lapped-back pillow on page 127. Next, cut 5-inch-wide bias strips to equal twice the distance around the pillow. Join the bias strips into one long strip. Stitch the ends together so that you end up with a circle.

Press the seams open, fold the strip in half lengthwise, and press. To gather, machine baste (the longest stitch on the machine) ½ inch and ¼ inch from the raw edges. Pull up the threads, gathering the ruffle to fit the pillow top. Pin the ruffle around all four edges of the top so the ruffle is to the center of the pillow; cut edges even. Stitch a scant ½-inch seam. Complete the pillow, following the direction for lapped-back pillows.

Appliqued quilts are a good choice for toddlers. Let your child's interests be the guide in selecting applique designs. A very young child will love identifying baby animals. Airplanes, boats, and trucks would delight a little boy, while dolls, flowers, and butterflies would charm your little girl. Choose a different design for each block, or use the same design on all blocks and vary the fabrics. If you're not good at drawing designs freehand, trace shapes from coloring books or some other source. Limit yourself to very simple shapes—they will work best for the appliques.

Choose gay washable printed fabrics for the appliques; all-cotton or cotton and polyester blends are best. Applique each block separately by hand or machine. Use embroidery floss to outline the features or details on each block. Follow the directions in Chapter 5 for setting the quilt top together and assembling the quilt. Then, either quilt by hand or machine, or tie with tufts.

*Red and white checks adorn the walls, bedspread, →
and curtains to provide the perfect setting for the combination of new and heirloom pieces featured in this little girl's room. The quilt-spread is a simple pattern of pieced blocks, hand quilted.*

Comical quilts turn a youngster's bedtime from hassle to heyday! Lion and elephant comforters are one-of-a-kind originals that will last for many years to come. Approximately 44x58 inches in size, they can be made of 45-inch no-iron sailcloth or a similar sturdy, washable fabric.

The elephant comforter requires 1⅞ yards of light blue material for the top—all the other colors are appliqued to this piece— and the same amount of matching or contrasting fabric for the back. For the appliqued parts, you'll need ⅞ yard dark purple, 1⅜ yards light purple, ¼ yard dark blue, ⅛ yard bright green, and ⅛ yard white.

The lion requires 1⅞ yards of orange for the top of the comforter and the same amount of identical or contrasting fabric for the back. For the appliqued parts, you'll need the following amounts of fabric: 1⅛ yards yellow, 1⅛ yards magenta (the magenta section of the lion's tail is the only piece that is cut on the bias), ½ yard blue, and ⅛ yard each of purple, white, red, and pink fabric.

Each animal also requires a 45x59-inch sheet of polyester batting, plus embroidery floss in various colors for embroidering the features and tying. Enlarge the pattern on brown paper, using this scale: one square equals four inches. Cut out the pattern. Pin the pattern to the fabric for the top and back sections. Allow ½ inch beyond the edge of the pattern on all sides, and cut it out. Then, cut the pattern apart for the various appliqued sections. Pin appliqued patterns to proper colored fabrics. Cut out appliques, adding a ½-inch seam allowance around outer edges.

Machine-stitch around outer edges of all the applique pieces ½ inch from edge, using matching thread. Fold under on stitching line, clip where needed, baste, and press.

Pin the applique pieces to the comforter top and applique in the following order: elephant—head, ears, tusk, white eyes, blue eyes, and toes; lion—mane, face, ears, tongue and chin, cheeks, white eyes, blue eyes, nose, two tail sections, and bow. Stitch the applique in place with a straight stitch close to

The diagrams below are for the elephant and lion quilts. Enlarge each diagram, using the scale one square equals 4 inches. The quilt top and back

pieces are cut to the shape of the outline. Ears, tusks, eyes, and other pieces are cut from bright colors and are machine-appliqued to the quilt top.

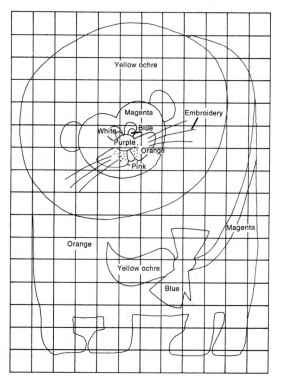

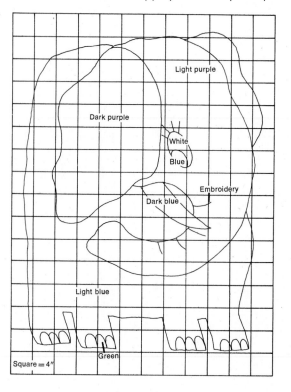

Comical lion and elephant quilt shapes are sure to delight a child because they're not like any quilt he's ever seen before. Made from bright, *durable sailcloth, and filled with lightweight batting, they combine three quilt-making techniques: appliqueing, embroidering, and tufting.*

the edge or with a zigzag stitch. Use thread to match applique piece. Embroider whiskers and eyelash with embroidery floss.

Roll out the batting on a large, flat surface and baste the backing section to it. Trim away the excess batting. Place the comforter top over the back section with the right sides together. Pin the three layers together, making sure all layers are smooth and all edges are even. Baste around the outer edges. Machine-stitch around the outside, leaving a

large opening to turn the comforter right side out. Trim the batting out of the seam allowance. Clip seam allowance at the corners and around the curves. Turn right side out. Pull out corners and curved areas.

Fold in the seam allowance along the opening and slip-stitch closed. With embroidery floss, tack around all appliqued areas one to two inches apart, tying tacking thread off individually at the back. Tack the large areas at random, using matching embroidery floss.

184

Slumber bags provide cozy sleeping accommodations for overnight guests. A matching tote makes the slumber bag easy to store.

This slumber bag/comforter requires 4 yards of 36-inch fabric for the outside and the same amount for the lining. Fabrics for both the outside and the lining should be washable. Select a sturdy, brightly colored fabric such as sailcloth, sport denim, or ticking to make the bag suitable for sleeping outdoors on warm summer evenings. Use lighter weight fabrics for bags that will stay indoors. Cotton flannel makes a warm, cozy lining. A flat twin-bed sheet may also be used for the lining, eliminating the middle seam.

You'll also need 90 inches of ¾-inch-wide Velcro closure tape, 2½ yards of ¾-inch-wide grosgrain ribbon, two sheets of 68x70-inch polyester batting, and yarn for tying.

Cut two pieces of fabric 35x70 inches from both the outer and lining fabrics, or cut the sheet to 68x70 inches. To assemble the slumber bag, join the two pieces of outer fabric—right sides together—with a 1-inch seam, forming a 68x70-inch piece. Join the

Girls will be snug and sound all night long at pajama parties with their own take-along slumber bags. Opened up, bags double as comforters.

two pieces for the lining in the same way. Press seams open. Place lining fabric face down on the floor, and place the two layers of batting over it.

Cover with outer fabric, right side up. Pin the four layers together, making sure the layers are smooth and the edges are even. Baste 1 inch from the edge and through the center lengthwise and crosswise. Machine-stitch 1 inch from the outer edge. Trim the batting out of the seam allowances. Trim the lining seam allowance to ½ inch.

Place slumber bag on floor with the lining side up. Fold the seam allowances of the outer section toward the lining side on the stitching line. Starting from the center seam, bottom left-hand side, pin hook side of Velcro over the cut edges of seam allowances with tape ½ inch from the fold. Clip the tape at the corner and continue pinning up the side of the bag, ending 10 inches from the top. Pin the loop side of the Velcro to the other side in the same way.

Carefully baste the tapes in place. Machine-stitch along both edges of Velcro. Above the closure tape and across top of bag, cover seam edges with grosgrain ribbon, mitering the corners. Stitch along both edges of ribbon.

Place the opened slumber bag on the floor, smoothing out all layers. With a long needle threaded with yarn, take a small stitch through all layers (needle should go straight down and straight up) and tie knot on top. Clip ends about ½ inch from knot. Make ties over entire slumber bag 6 to 8 inches apart.

Slumber bag tote requires 1⅜ yards of fabric to match or coordinate with the slumber bag. Cut a rectangle 27 inches wide and 46 inches long from the outer fabric. Fold in half crosswise with right sides together and mark along the fold. Sew a ½-inch seam on one side; press open. To shape the corner, fold the bag so that the side seam is directly on top of the marked line. Stitch across corner 3½ inches from the point. The line of stitching will be at right angles to seam. Repeat with other side seam. Fold a double ½-inch hem around top edge, press, and stitch.

Turn the bag right side out and press. For handles, cut two pieces 4½x10 inches. Fold in half lengthwise, turn in the raw edges, and topstitch close to the edges. Pin one handle on each side of the tote, placing the ends 2½ inches below the top edge; stitch in place, and backstitch for reinforcement.

Patchwork takes many forms to delight a child. Below, a larger-than-life-size floor pillow is made from oversized patches of bright prints. At the right, patchwork pieces form acrobats on this child's exercise mat.

To make the floor pillow, sew prints together with a double zigzag stitch, forming a piece about 5x6 feet. Cut out the doll shape and applique the face, using two large covered buttons for the eyes and six small ones for the lashes. Back the pillow with heavy cotton fabric and insert a zipper down the center. Make a muslin pillow form the same shape as the doll, and stuff with shredded foam. Insert the pillow through the zipper opening.

The exercise mat measures 44x60 inches and is assembled like a regular quilt. Select fabrics that are washable so the mat can be machine laundered. Make the quilt top from six blocks, piecing each with assorted fabric squares and triangles. Applique the acrobats' heads over the adjoining pieces. Frame the blocks with a band of dark navy and finish the quilt with a wide, printed border. Attach plastic drapery rings to one end. Now when the mat is not being used for exercising or relaxing, you can use it as an attractive wall decoration.

A child-sized quilted mat is ideal for limbering-up exercises or just relaxing. Plastic rings are sewn to one end to facilitate wall hanging.

This colorful, larger-than-life-size floor pillow (5x6 feet) is a pre-teenager's delight. Not only is it a pillow for general relaxation, it also *doubles as a bed for overnight guests. Make it as colorful as possible using bright, bold prints. To keep it clean, use washable fabrics.*

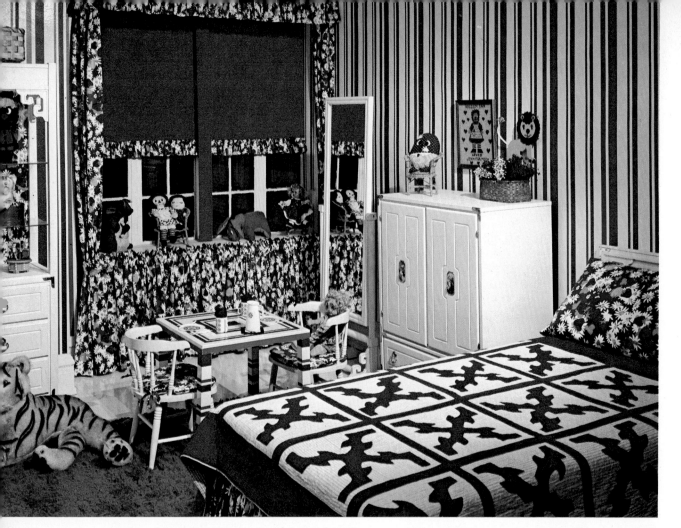

Bright, clear colors set a cheerful mood in the bedroom above. One fabric — an easy-care strawberry and wild-flower print — was used for the window treatment, the dust ruffle on the bed, the pillow cover, tie-on cushions for the child-sized chairs, and as a backing in the toy shelves.

Window Wizardry

The windows of a child's room are the frames through which he views the world. To a child, they're a very important part of his room, so treat them importantly. Cafe curtains are a natural choice because they're casual and easy to make. (For how-to, see page 38.) You may wish to line them to keep out as much light as possible during nap times. Combine unlined cafe curtains with fabric shades or shades you've appliqued yourself.

To applique window shades, cut motifs from closely woven fabrics, such as polished cotton, chintz, or percale. To keep raw edges from raveling, paint the cutting line on the back with clear nail polish before cutting. If large areas are to be done, use an iron-on interfacing. (Test nail polish on scraps; some fibers, such as acetate, will dissolve.) Cut designs out carefully and arrange them on the shade. Then apply one cutout at a time with fabric glue. Smooth it out carefully, checking that all edges are attached securely. To make fabric shades, see page 60.

An awning canopy can turn a child's room into a circus tent, a street vendor's flower cart, or an ice-cream parlor. Awnings combined with shades or shutters can block out light completely, or they can let in plenty of sunshine.

Awnings are hung on two regular curtain rods. The top rod has a 2-inch return and is placed at the top of a window. The bottom rod will need an 8-inch return and should be placed 10 inches down from the first rod. Measure a piece of fabric the width of the area to be covered and 16 inches deep; add ½ inch for seams at each end and 2 inches for the casing at the top. Then, measure the sides of the awning, as illustrated below.

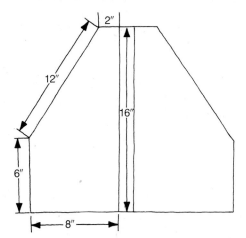

To these pieces add seam allowances of 1½ inches for side hems and 2 inches at the top for the casing. Cut two sidepieces, reversing one so you have both a left and a right side. Stitch the shaped sidepieces to the center piece. Cut a piece of lining or facing fabric 8 inches deep (6 inches for lining and 2 inches for the casing into which the bottom curtain rod fits). Pin this facing piece to the bottom of the awning, right sides together. If you plan to shape the bottom with scallops or points, draw the pattern on the facing and stitch along the guidelines. Then press and stitch the side hems. Trim and clip the seams. Press the facing to the back side of the awning. Make the lower casing with 2 inches of the facing fabric as shown.

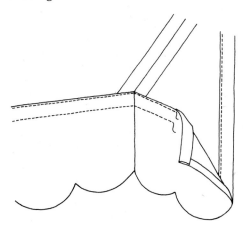

Turn under 2 inches of fabric at the top of the awning and make a casing for the top rod.

Pullman sleeping cars from the railroads have a special charm—creating a private little world for a youngster to dream of long trips.

Use curtains at other places in the room, too. In the bedroom pictured above, cafe curtains have changed ordinary bunk beds into private pullman sleeping cars. When the curtains are drawn, each child has a completely separate sleeping area; this is ideal for bedrooms shared by children with different bedtimes. In the picture at left, simple cafe curtains conceal the radiator under window.

To change your bunk beds into a pullman car, make cafe curtains from bright fabric. Curtain the 'lower berth' by attaching a plain cafe rod to the underside of the frame of the upper bunk. For the "top berth," the rod is attached to the ceiling or the walls. If the beds are open at the ends, also hang curtains at the head and foot. Make the cafe curtains with a casing for the rod, or hang them with cafe rings for easier opening and closing. Line the curtains for maximum privacy.

To conceal a radiator with curtains, first extend the windowsill to cover the radiator. This also provides a handy shelf for dolls and stuffed animals. Mount a plain cafe rod on the front of the sill. Make simple cafe curtains with a casing for the rod and a heading that will extend slightly over the sill shelf. Construct the curtains with an opening in the center so they can be pushed to the sides for maximum heat circulation.

A young sailboat fan lives and dreams here. A real sail is hung from the ceiling and attached to the bed frame, turning it into a boat. Waves *painted on the walls, rope ladders hanging from the ceiling, a deck chair, and other marine equipment carry out the boating theme.*

Wall Things

Decorate the walls of your child's room with interesting—and useful—items. Select decorations according to your child's age and interests: mount a paper kite on the wall and add felt flowers and butterflies to complete the picture, drape a wall with fishing net and enclose beach souvenirs, or hang a sail and turn a bed into a boat. Wall pockets are attractive, and they encourage a tidy room.

A multi-pocket organizer can be made from bath towels or any sturdy fabric. Cut the fabric about 25x39 inches. Stitch a ½-inch hem on the sides. Turn under 1½ inches at the top and bottom for casings and stitch. Attach various-sized pockets in a patchwork scheme. Insert brass rods at the top and the bottom, and hang on the wall (low enough for your child to reach) near a play area.

A snake of pockets, made from brightly printed fabrics, can be any length. Make the backing from a solid color and attach the pockets by topstitching. Then, embroider a smile on the snake's face and give it button eyes. Attach plastic rings along the top and hang it above your child's crib.

To make the supersize pocket hamper, cut plywood into a pocket shape—about 20x28 inches. Cut denim 6 inches larger than the wood backing. Make a narrow hem along the top. Fit the denim over the board; allow the pocket to bow out at the top, tapering to fit at the bottom. Mark and embroider the two lines of decorative stitching. Staple the raw edges of the pocket to the underside of the backing. Cut the flap about 10 inches deep. Hem raw edges along the bottom and sides. Add embroidery and the button. Staple top of flap to backing; mount on closet door.

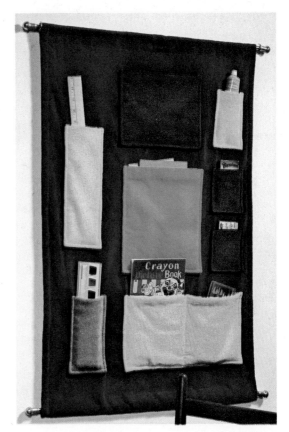

A gigantic denim pocket is an easy-to-make laundry bag. Mount this offbeat hamper on the closet door or in another convenient location.

Hanging pockets provide handy storage for toys and craft items. Hang them near the play area, low enough for your child to reach easily.

A snake of pockets filled with interesting toys and playthings makes a perfect crib-time companion for the very young child. However, it

works just as well as a grab bag in bedrooms of teen-agers or those not so young. Make this handy item from scraps of bright fabric.

Colorful Rugs

Forget what you've heard about those long hours needed to make a rug. All you need is a pair of scissors or shears and a sewing machine to sew a colorful felt rug in next to no time.

Be your own designer and make the rug any size or shape to fit your need. Select a heavyweight felt for the background color (50 percent wool is best). Cut the designs from brightly colored felt and applique the separate designs directly onto the background. Set the machine for a full-width satin stitch and use heavy-duty mercerized thread to match the felt. With felt, there is no need to turn under any edges.

If appliqueing by hand, use embroidery floss to match the felt motifs and sew with a blanket stitch or a buttonhole stitch. Trim the outer edge with 4- to 6-inch-wide cotton or wool fringe. Place the fringe on top of the felt, overlapping the edge of the rug by ½ inch, and attach by machine with two rows of stitching ¼ inch apart. Do not stretch fringe because this will cause the rug to pucker.

A landscape rug, as pictured below, provides a base for a train track. A young engineer will have many hours of pleasure running trains around the lake and through the various settings. The background of the rug is heavy dark green felt, and the lake and roads are cut from blue and brown felt and are machine-appliqued to the base. Let the size of your child's train set be your guide in designing this rug. Add roads, rivers, and paths to accommodate various train settings —stations, water tanks, and villages.

Cut out the various areas and arrange them on the backing. Baste in place and then applique by machine with a wide satin stitch, being careful to keep the backing and appliques smooth and flat.

Fake fur fabrics also make quick and easy rugs to brighten children's rooms. Fur fabrics can be cut into giant foot prints, animal-skin shapes, or traditional shapes such as squares, rectangles, or ovals. For realistic-looking animal-skin rugs, mount the fur fabric on a felt backing and allow the backing to show as a border. Finish fur rugs with fringe or fold-over braid.

A "landscape rug" will delight the small boy who loves to play with model trains. Make the rug any size that you want. (The extent of the railroad system will determine the size.) Use heavy dark green felt for the base of the rug and machine-applique felt cutouts for lakes and roads.

Felt rugs are fun to make and are an easy way to brighten a child's room. Cut animals and other motifs from felt and applique to a felt base.

Little braves will have many happy hours in this corner tepee. Select a sturdy fabric with an Indian motif and follow the directions below.

Abstract storybook motifs in wake-up colors make a rug especially appropriate for young children. To make the rug as pictured above, cut animals, birds, trees, flowers, letters, and numbers from felt and applique them to a 45-inch-diameter white felt circle. Stitch heavy-duty ball fringe around the outer edge.

A rubber rug mat or carpet pad used under any of these rugs makes them skidproof. Or, paint the underside with a liquid designed for this purpose. Spray the rug with soil-resistant liquid when finished. Dry-clean a felt rug that becomes soiled.

Playhouses

All children love playhouses of any shape or size. And many are easy to sew.

A tepee playhouse, pictured above right, requires two six-foot 2x2's and about 2½ yards of 45-inch-wide sturdy fabric; try sport denim, sailcloth, upholstery, or drapery fabric. Cut the fabric in half lengthwise and make a 1½-inch hem along the lengthwise and bottom edges. Staple the hemmed edge to the two 2x2's. Lean the boards into a corner in an inverted V shape, placing the bottom of the boards approximately 20 inches from the wall. Fasten the fabric to the walls, folding excess fabric inside of tepee.

Make a portable playhouse by using a card table as the base. Fabric covers the top of the card table and extends to the floor on all four sides, forming the ceiling and walls. Cutouts in the "walls" are windows, and the front door opens with zippers.

You'll need approximately 5 yards of durable fabric for the walls and ceiling, two 28- to 30-inch zippers and clear plastic for each of the windows. Use different colored felt scraps for applique trimmings.

Cut the fabric to fit the top of the card table, allowing ½-inch seams on all sides. Cut walls of the house for three sides of the card table, allowing ½-inch seams at the top and sides and 1½ inches at the bottom for the hem. For the front of the house, cut the wall into three sections; allow ½-inch seams at the corners and one-inch seams on each side of the door (center section).

Cut out the windows and stitch plastic over the openings. Decorate the outer walls with felt appliques of flowers, trees, shutters, and window boxes. Stitch the walls together and hem the lower edge of the walls and door. Insert the zippers on either side of the door, with the open end of the zipper at the hemmed edge. Stitch the walls to the top sections. Place house over card table. Then, put a "For Rent" sign in front of the house and your new neighbors will move in.

Chapter 12

Outdoor and Casual Furniture

More leisure time means more time to spend outdoors at the patio, deck, poolside, or in the backyard. Use your indoor skills to perk up your outdoor living areas. Whether your outdoor areas are used for active sports, gala barbecues, intimate patio dinners, family picnics, sunbathing, or just quiet moments of relaxation, you can do many things to make the setting attractive.

You can easily turn a hodgepodge of unmatched, faded, or worn outdoor furniture into a coordinated living area by making new covers and cushions. Update director's chairs, butterfly chairs, and circle chairs with new covers. Make your own, or add a personal touch to ready-made replacement covers with machine-stitched appliques. The bright, clear summer colors are ideal for appliqueing simple shapes such as sunbursts, stylized flowers, mushrooms, and apples.

Or you can decorate outdoor furniture for indoor use. Soft or deep-pile fabrics make outdoor chairs ideal for family rooms, recreation rooms, and dens.

Family picnics will become special events with bold new picnic cloths and table mats. Make coordinated mats and pillows to perk up your poolside areas. Step-by-step directions for all of these ideas and many more—including a hammock slipcover and a sports equipment organizer—are included in this chapter.

Butterfly chairs and circle chairs are great favorites for outdoor relaxation. A bright appliqued bird keeps watch over the garden pool from its special seat on the circle chair. A handsome Victorian design decorates the butterfly chair.

Casual Chairs

Butterfly chairs, circle chairs, and director's chairs all invite relaxation on the terrace or patio, along the side of the pool, or in the family room. Help promote a gay, light-hearted mood with covers with bold designs.

Give butterfly chairs a new life with stunning, appliqued covers. Buy a replacement cover or make your own. If you make the cover, take the old cover apart and use it for a pattern. For a new cover, use canvas, duck, or denim. Fake fur, velour, and other medium-weight fabrics also can be used; but these fabrics must be backed with canvas, duck, or denim for durability. Also include wide bias tape for binding the outer edges and twill tape to reinforce the center seam.

Cut out the chair cover pieces, allowing for the center seam. Also cut small reinforcement pieces for each corner and the corner pockets. Cut the pocket pieces on the fold. Apply the applique before joining the top and bottom pieces.

To make an applique similar to the one shown on page 192, draw a freehand design—one for the top half, and one for the bottom half. Both sides will be cut on the fold, so you need only half a design. The top design should measure approximately 18 inches at the fold and be 15 inches across (for half of the design). The chair seat design should measure 15½ inches on the fold line and measure 13½ inches across (for half of the design).

Pin the pattern on folded canvas and draw around the design. Cut. Unfold the canvas and pin it to the chair top and seat. Machine-stitch, using the full width of the satin stitch. Next, pin the reinforcement pieces to each corner and stitch around the edges. If you decide to use backing, attach the reinforcement pieces to the backing sections. Pin the pocket pieces over the reinforcements and baste along the outer edges.

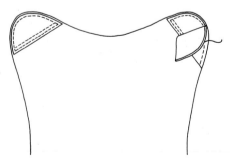

Join the top and bottom sections and bind the seam with twill tape. If backing is used, stitch the center seam and bind. Then pin the cover and backing together—wrong sides together—and baste around the outer edges. Bind the outer edge with wide bias tape. Press applique, and place cover on chair.

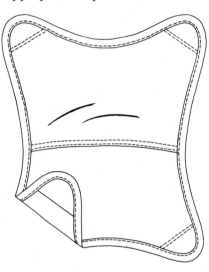

Circle chairs are also a great place for appliqued covers. To duplicate the bird design shown on page 192, make a paper pattern. The bird's body is approximately 13 inches long and 8½ inches deep. Draw on five tail feathers, a scalloped wing, eye, beak, and legs. Then draw separate pattern pieces, using your first drawing as a guide. Pin your first pattern on the center top half of the cover. Cut out pieces from canvas. Replace the paper pattern with canvas pieces. Baste and then machine-stitch with a satin stitch around each piece.

Spark new life into director's chairs with new covers and matching paint. For each chair, you'll need canvas for the seat and back, ½ yard of 50-inch fabric or ⅔ yard of 30-inch fabric, scraps of assorted colors of canvas for appliques, and two pieces of 16-inch-long ¼-inch dowel to hold the covers in the side grooves.

For the seat and the back, measure and cut the canvas, using the old cover as a pattern. Be sure to allow for hems along the edges. Do not make the seams until the applique is finished. Cut the selected designs from scraps of fabric and applique to new seat and back sections, using the satin stitch set at the full width. Hem the edges of the back and seat

Director's chairs and a campstool take on new colors to perk up a patio. The canvas covers and matching enamel finishes are keyed to summer fun. As folding chairs, they are convenient for indoor use, too. The motifs, cut from canvas scraps, are machine-appliqued to the covers.

sections. Form the casing for the seat dowels and the back posts; stitch in place, carefully turning all of the raw edges.

To make the applique designs as shown, draw the shape on paper and cut it out. Then trace around paper patterns on the canvas.

For the mushrooms, draw seven mushroom shapes varying in height from 4¾ to 10½ inches. Cut tops and stems separately. Pin six mushrooms to the chair back and one to the seat, with the mushroom tops overlapping the stems. Baste and stitch.

For the apple motif, draw a pattern on paper for three 4½-inch apples and one 3-inch apple and the leaves. Draw a cross section in one large apple (to be cut from white). Cut from the canvas; position the three apples on the chair back and the small apple on the seat. Baste in place. Applique, using thread to match the pieces.

For the floral design, draw a pattern for four 5½-inch-long flower shapes. Draw one flower for the seat 13 inches long. Pin the patterns on the canvas scraps and cut out.

Position the four smaller flowers on the canvas back. Do not allow the designs to overlap the side seams of the back. Pin and baste. Do the same positioning, pinning, and basting for the large flower on the seat. Using thread to match each piece of applique, machine-stitch.

Campstools or folding stools provide additional seating anywhere. And they are lightweight and easy to store.

To cover a campstool like the one pictured above, you'll need two pieces of 15-inch canvas: one layer for the seat and a second layer for the reinforcement. You'll also need upholstery tacks and scraps for the applique. Remove the old seat and use it as a pattern. Cut canvas for the seat cover and reinforcement, allowing ample fabric for turning under at the ends. Draw a paper pattern of an 11-inch circle separated into six triangular spokes. Cut design from the bright canvas and applique to seat cover. Join seat cover and reinforcement with a hem on the long edges. Turn under ends and tack in place.

Recycle lawn chairs by replacing the worn webbing with bright new canvas. A pocket hidden on the back of the chair holds accessories.

Recycle folding lawn chairs or chaise lounges with bright new canvas or sailcloth covers. Cut crosswise and lengthwise pieces of fabric for the seat and back, the width of the old plastic webbing and long enough to wrap around the frame. Encase the raw edges with bias tape. To duplicate the chair above, cut large arrows from white canvas and applique by machine, using a heavy-duty needle and heavy-duty thread. Attach the cover with the old screws, adding washers to prevent the fabrics from ripping. If you choose duck or sailcloth, double the fabric for strength and treat it as one piece when sewing.

Lawn chairs also can be covered with heavy-duty woven-back vinyl. Cut both the lengthwise and crosswise sections almost as wide as the chair (the straight part of the frame). Turn under the edges ½ inch and topstitch ¼ inch from the fold. Then applique vinyl designs to the lengthwise piece, using large zigzag stitches. At the ends of each piece, turn under the vinyl 1 inch—just beyond the rows of screws on the frame—and topstitch ¼ inch from the fold. In each of these folds, insert a wire the thickness of a coat hanger to prevent ripping. Attach crosspieces first. Add washers beneath screws.

Refurbish casual furniture and separate cushions with a fresh coat of paint and new covers for the cushions. If your chairs have odd-sized cushions or you plan on using a specific color or design, make the covers.

Start by taking a good look at the condition of the cushion; is it firm and well-shaped or is it flat and lumpy? If the cushion is not in good shape, replace it. Purchase precut cushions or cut your own from foam rubber.

For the cover, there is a wide range of fabrics from which to choose. Vinyl fabrics will shed water and are easy to wipe clean; the knit-back vinyls work best, because they have the most 'give.' Canvas covers will withstand rugged use. Duck, denim, and sailcloth are also sturdy fabric selections. Heavyweight chintz, poplin, velour, terry cloth, and upholstery fabrics also can be used. Whatever fabric you choose, make sure it won't fade in sunlight. Also, look for fabrics treated to repel water and soil.

You can use either the old cover or the cushion measurements for the pattern. Follow the general directions in chapter 6 for constructing the covers. Zippers, snap tape, or Velcro closings make covers easy to remove.

Protective covers for outdoor furniture will help keep the cushions clean and extend the life of a chair or chaise lounge. Make protective covers from vinyl, plastic, or canvas.

Determine the widest point of the chair, usually the outermost point of the arms. This measurement will give you the width of the main piece; add 1 inch for seam allowances. To find the length, measure from the floor at the front of the chair to the top of the back, over the back, and down to the floor again. Add 2 inches for hems, and cut one piece on the lengthwise grain. For the side sections, measure from the top of the back to floor and from the top of the seat to the floor.

For the length of the base, measure from the front of the chair to the back. Mark the base length plus a 1-inch seam allowance along the lengthwise grain. Then mark the front and back depths, allowing 1 inch for the hem at the lower edge. For the upper edge, connect the two depth measurements with a straight line. Add ½ inch beyond the line for the seam allowances and cut the two side sections. Pin-fit and stitch ½-inch seams. Turn a 1-inch hem around the lower edge, leaving a short opening at the back. Insert a drawstring into the hem.

Summer is yours to enjoy in this relaxed setting. The sunny patchwork hammock is really an old faded one with a bright new cover made from patches of colorful canvas. The casual chair sports bright cushion covers made to coordinate with the hammock.

Hammocks are a great place to relax in on lazy afternoons. Give your hammock a new look with a patchwork cover. You'll need canvas in various colors for the patches; 5 or 6 packages of black, single-fold bias tape; two packages of black cotton hem facing; heavy-duty thread; and 6-inch black fringe.

This patchwork design is intended only as a cover for an old canvas hammock—not a replacement. Attach the patchwork to the old cover and stitch the two covers together.

Start by removing the fringe on the old hammock cover and open the seams holding the rods at either end. Measure width and length of old hammock cover and divide area evenly to determine the size of the squares. The ones shown above are 7-inch squares.

Cut squares from the canvas, allowing ½-inch seams on all sides. Arrange the squares in lengthwise strips, according to your design; stitch together, using a heavy-duty machine needle. Press seams open and stitch down the seam allowance on both sides, close to the seam line.

Sew the strips together side by side. Press and stitch down all seams. Baste the single-fold bias tape over all seam lines. If you want to add padding between old and new covers, cut polyester batting to fit over the old cover.

Place the patchwork cover on the old cover and baste the covers together along the bias tape and outer edges. Stitch the covers together along both sides of the bias tape starting at the center seam. Stitch all tapes lengthwise then stitch crosswise. Bind the outer edges with bias hem facing. Restitch the casing for the rods. Stitch fringe to the edges. Insert rods in casings and mount hammock.

If you prefer a solid color hammock with an appliqued design, measure the length of your hammock and cut a canvas panel to that size. Seam the panels together lengthwise, until the proper width is reached. Applique the designs on the cover. Place the new cover over the old, adding padding if desired. Baste the two covers together along seams; stitch along seam lines. Complete the cover, following directions for the patchwork cover.

Patio and Beach Accessories

To prevent burned, bare toes, spread out cheerful sunning mats on a sun-drenched deck. They're ideal to stretch out on for tanning or for drying off after a swim. Make your own in a rainbow of bright colors, using your appliqued designs. Make mats from canvas or sturdy fabrics such as duck, sailcloth, or terry cloth.

The yellow mat below requires 2½ yards of fabric, 2 yards of 6-inch-deep cotton fringe, scraps for the applique, and 6 yards of bias tape for binding the edges.

Cut the fabric 31 inches wide, and bind the two long edges with the bias tape. Draw the design for applique and cut from fabric scraps. No seam allowance is needed. Arrange the design on the mat and pin it in place. Baste. Machine-applique using a satin stitch; be sure to encase all raw edges. Cut fringe, allowing 1 inch to turn under at each end. Sew fringe to each end of mat, with two rows of machine-stitching across each end.

For the child's mat, you'll need a piece of fabric 22x45 inches, 1⅓ yards of 4-inch-deep cotton fringe, scraps for the applique, and 2½ yards of bias tape. Draw a pattern for the applique design, using the photograph as a guide. Finish the mat as described above.

Pillows invite relaxation on a sunny deck or patio. The ones shown below are made by covering polyfoam forms with canvas. You may wish to make sets—mats and pillows appliqued to match. Start by making the basic pillow forms or purchase ready-made forms. Then sew brightly colored covers, decorated with sunny appliqued designs. For directions on making the pillows and covers, refer to Chapter 6.

Cheerful sunning mats invite sunbathing at water's edge. Make the canvas mats long for adults, and short for children. Applique the mats with summertime motifs and trim with fringe. Sunny pillows with machine-appliqued designs provide additional comfort.

Bold geometric designs adorn these generous-sized pillows that are ideal for relaxing on a grassy knoll or at poolside. The shiny vinyl fabric gives them a dramatic appearance—and prevents any moisture problems. Shredded foam filling makes them comfortably soft.

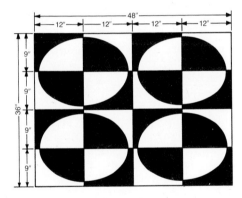

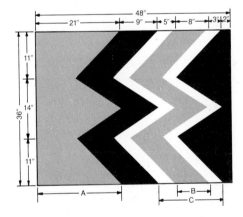

Giant-size pillows make great loungers for lawn or poolside. The ones pictured above are covered with waterproof vinyl. You can also use canvas, duck, or another sturdy fabric. The covers are removable.

For each pillow you'll need two pieces of unbleached muslin 36x48 inches, eight one-pound bags of shredded foam rubber, one 36-inch zipper, 2 pieces of 36x48-inch vinyl or covering material, and additional fabric for the applique design pieces.

The black-and-white pillow requires two pieces of white (36x48 inches) and one piece of black fabric (42x54 inches). The tricolored pillow requires 1 piece of white (36x26 inches), one piece of black (36x48 inches), and two pieces of brown fabric (one 36x48 inches and one 36x29 inches).

Sew the muslin inner cover together, leaving approximately 10 inches unstitched. Turn the cover right side out and stuff with the shredded foam rubber. If possible, stuff outdoors. Open one end of a bag of foam and insert it in the muslin cover. Shake out the foam and continue adding stuffing until the muslin cover is full. Stitch the opening closed and brush off any foam clinging to the muslin case. Cut out applique pattern pieces, following the sketches above.

Cut a ½-inch allowance on all edges. Before sewing, check your machine stitches on a scrap of fabric. For vinyls, the stitches should be fairly long. Special needles and presser feet are available for sewing plastics.

Turn under the ¼-inch hem allowance on all edges of the applique pieces, except those that will be sewn into the seams. (On plastic, glue this hem allowance down and tape each applique piece to the pillow top before stitching.) Attach applique pieces to the pillow top by stitching close to the hemmed edges. To make the black-and-white pillow, applique the black design pieces onto the white pillow top. The bottom of this pillow is white.

On the brown, black, and white pillow, the bottom is brown. The top is black, and the brown and white pieces are stitched onto it. Stitch the brown area **(B)** to the white area **(C)**; then stitch this completed brown-and-white area to the black pillow top. The brown design area **(A)** is stitched onto the black top.

After the applique is completed, sew the zipper in place at one end of the top and bottom pillow pieces. Open the zipper slightly. With right sides of the top and bottom together, stitch the sides and the end of the case. Trim the corners, open the zipper the rest of the way, and turn pillow cover right side out. Push out corners; smooth seams.

Put the muslin pillow into the case; be sure all corners are in place. Zip the cover closed. With a pillow this size, it's easier to insert the pillow if two people work together.

Picnic and patio table covers call for special attention, too. Bright table covers with matching bench covers and coordinated napkins add to the fun of outdoor meals. Make table covers from terry cloth, bed sheets, burlap, sailcloth, or any other easy-care fabric that strikes your fancy. Try a tablecloth of blue denim and use red bandana print handkerchiefs for napkins. Matching bench covers will be welcomed by your guests, because they will prevent snags on knit slacks.

Keep in mind the problems wind can cause with tablecloths and mats; plan to anchor or weight your table covering in some manner. Weight table runners with wooden dowels at either end. Cut the runner, allowing for a 10- to 12-inch drop at either end. Hem the long edges and then form a casing at each end for the dowel. Dowels will hang over the edge of the table and hold the runner in place. They are easily removed for laundering. Weight

place mats in the same manner, or use heavy metal or wooden drapery rings tied to each corner. A fifth ring attached midway on the left side serves as a napkin holder.

Make picnic cloths with pockets to hold flatware. Measure the tabletop and allow for a 7-inch drop on each side. Stitch on a band of fabric narrower than the drop, leaving the top seam unstitched. Stitch the band vertically to form pockets for flatware and napkins. The flatware will help to hold the cloth in place. Sew drapery weights along the hem of the cloth or attach ties to the underside of the tablecloth to tie around the table legs.

Lightweight folding cots are great for patio, beach, or backyard sunning. With gay covers, like the one at the right, they can become game boards as well. Make the cover of vinyl, canvas, duck, denim, or sport denim. The vinyls will shed water but also become very hot when exposed to strong sunlight.

Measure the length and width of the cot and add 4 inches to all sides. Cut the rectangle for the base. Cut out the areas to match the old cover. Bind these cutouts with the second color. Turn and stitch a narrow hem along the remaining areas of the cover. If you are using vinyl, you don't need to hem.

Place the cover on the cot and mark a line 2 inches in from the frame along the sides and ends. Attach the border along this line; the base material will wrap around the frame and snap to the underside. From the second color, cut border pieces for the two ends and four side sections. Scallop or leave these borders straight. Turn and stitch a narrow hem around all edges of each border piece. (Omit the hems on vinyls.) Pin border pieces along the marked line on the base cover and topstitch in place.

For the game board, cut six strips and two half circles; applique them to the center of the cover, making a 17-inch-square ticktacktoe board. Cut X and O shapes from matching material, or from felt scraps.

Make two small drawstring bags to hold the markers. When not in use, the bags tie onto the ends of the cot. Sew the top half of heavy-duty snaps onto the underside of the old cover; sew the other half of the snap to the underside of the flap to hold the cot cover securely in place.

A sports equipment organizer is a practical and decorative item to keep sports gear in place when not in use. Simply stitch pockets and appliques onto a canvas back and hang the sports organizer on the porch or patio near the play area.

The handy organizer that is pictured at the right requires 2 yards of 29-inch blue canvas, 1 yard red canvas, 1 yard of white canvas, ½-inch grommets, and a 1x28-inch wood dowel.

Encase the raw edges of the blue piece with a large zigzag stitch (using a heavy-duty needle and thread). Turn under 2½-inch hem at top and 3½ Inches at bottom, pin and stitch. From white canvas, cut four 9-inch stars, two pieces 7x18½ inches, and one each 2x8½ inches and 2x16½ inches. From red, cut one of each: 12x23½ inches, 9x29 inches, and 3x17½ inches. Applique the stars to the canvas back and pockets as shown at right. Zigzag the top edge of each of the pockets and press to underside.

To make pockets, pin one side in position, right side up; and zigzag stitch, reinforcing the corners. Pin down the other side so pocket makes a fold in the middle, and stitch. Make a pleat in the pocket so the bottom is flat, and stitch the bottom reinforcing corners. Press folds flat. Finished sizes of pockets: ball holder 8x23, glove holder 12x 13½, bat holder 4½x22½, racket holders 3½x17. Attach five grommets at the top, following the package directions. Slip the dowel into the bottom hem.

This sun-and-fun cot cover-up (below) turns an ordinary cot into a game board. The appliqued vinyl cover snaps on over the original cover.

This all-star organizer (above) stores sports equipment. Custom-fitted pockets hold tennis rackets, balls, a bat, and a glove.

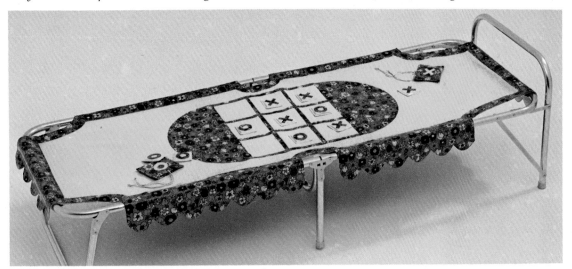

Glossary

Applique — Applying a design or motif cut from separate pieces of fabric to a base fabric by sewing, by bonding with iron-on webbing, or by gluing it to the base.

Apron — The horizontal strip of the window casing underneath the windowsill.

Austrian shade — A decorative window treatment made by vertically gathering lengths of sheer or semisheer fabric, resulting in a swagged effect. The shade is raised by pull cords.

Backstitch — (1) The reverse stitch on a sewing machine used to strengthen a row of stitching at the beginning and end. (2) The most durable of the hand sewing stitches.

Baste — A temporary stitch holding two or more pieces of fabric together before final stitching.

Bias — A diagonal line on fabric that is not on the crosswise or lengthwise grain. The *true bias* is the diagonal line formed by folding lengthwise grain parallel to crosswise grain. The greatest amount of give in a woven fabric is along the *true bias*.

Binding — A strip of fabric used to encase raw edges; it is usually cut on the true bias.

Blend — (1) When two or more fibers are spun or mixed together to form one yarn. (2) To trim or cut seam allowances of a stitched seam to uneven widths.

Bolster — A round or wedge-shaped cushion, usually used for back- or armrests.

Boxing strip — A strip of fabric joining the top and bottom sections of a pillow or cushion. The width depends on the depth of the pillow. Also used on other boxlike forms, such as garment bags.

Box pleat — A pleat made by folding two side pleats in opposite directions to form a plain panel. Used to control fullness, as along drapery headings and slipcover skirts.

Braid — A decorative tape woven the same way on both edges.

Canopy — (1) A piece of fabric fitted over a frame attached to the top of a four-poster bed. (2) A piece of fabric mounted on the wall or suspended from the ceiling, forming a covering over a bed.

Cartridge pleats — A heading used to control the fullness in draperies; stiffening is inserted in the pleats to hold them in a round shape.

Casing — (1) An opening or channel at the top of a curtain through which the rod is run. (2) A hem, channel, or tuck through which cord, a drawstring, ribbon, or elastic is drawn.

Chalk pencil — Special pencils used for marking on fabric.

Clip — To cut into a seam allowance just short of the line of stitching with the point of the scissors; to cut through the selvages or across corners.

Cording — A cotton cord covered with a bias strip of fabric. Also called welting. Used as a seam or edge finish in slipcovers, cushions, and bedspreads.

Cording foot — An adjustable foot that replaces the regular presser foot on a sewing machine and permits sewing close to a raised edge such as along a zipper, welting, or cording.

Coverlet — A short bedspread, usually used in combination with a skirt or dust ruffle.

Crease — A line or mark created by folding the fabric and pressing along the fold.

Dust ruffle — A gathered or pleated skirt that covers the springs and legs of a bed.

Ease — To evenly distribute fullness when one seam is joined to a slightly shorter seam without forming gathers or tucks.

Edgestitch — To stitch close to the edge of a fold after the fabric edge is turned under.

Fabric finishes — The chemical or mechanical treatments applied to fabric to improve their use and care properties.

Fibers — Natural or synthetic filaments from which the yarns for fabrics are made.

Finial — The decorative endpiece of a post or rod, as on a bedpost or curtain rod.

Gathering threads — Two rows of large machine stitching used to control fullness — one row on the seam line, and one row within the seam allowance. Bobbin threads are pulled up until the desired length is reached.

Grade seams — To trim all of the seam allowances within a seam to different widths, thus eliminating excess bulk along the seam lines.

Grain or grain line—The direction of threads in woven material. Lengthwise threads form the *lengthwise grain*, crosswise threads form the *crosswise grain*. When these threads are at right angles, the fabric is on *straight grain*.

Heading—(1) A decorative fabric tuck above the casing. (2) The top edge of a curtain.

Hemmer foot—A special foot that replaces the regular presser foot on the sewing machine; it allows turning and stitching narrow hems without pressing, pinning, or basting.

Jabot—A selection of fabric hung lengthwise, in folds, at a window. It is usually slanted at the bottom and used with a swag. Also called cascade.

Kapok—A fiber filling made from seedpod fiber. Used for stuffing pillows and cushions.

Miter—(1) Used where hems join at the corners as in linens and draperies. It joins two pieces of fabric at a square corner and forms a diagonal line; excess fabric is usually trimmed away. (2) A diagonal line at the center of the corner formed when a band of trimming is applied to a square or pointed shape.

Motif—A single design or decorative pattern.

Napped fabric—Fabrics that have been brushed after weaving to raise the fibers and to create a directional, fuzzy surface.

Notches—V-shaped cutouts along the outer edge of a seam allowance indicating which edges will be sewn together.

Pivot—To turn the fabric on the machine needle, making a square corner along the stitching line.

Plaster screw—A special screw that was designed for use in plaster walls for mounting hardware or accessories.

Pleater tape—Woven tape with equally spaced pockets for pleater hooks. It is used for making pleated headings in curtains and draperies.

Pleats—A method of controlling the fullness in fabrics with regularly spaced fabric folds.

Pressure—The force that the presser foot exerts on the fabric during machine stitching. Regulate the pressure on the presser foot to suit the fabric being used.

Return—On curtains and draperies, the distance from the front of the rod to the wall.

Roller foot—A presser foot specially designed for sewing fabrics which are difficult to handle, such as looped weaves, open weaves, or vinyl.

Roman shade—A window covering made from flat fabric that can be drawn up to form a tailored, horizontally pleated window treatment.

Seam allowance—The amount of fabric allowed for joining sections of fabrics together.

Seam gauge—A 6-inch metal ruler with an adjustable indicator; it is convenient for measuring hem depths and other short distances.

Seam guide—An adjustable aid for sewing straight, even seams. Attached to the bed of the machine by either a screw or a magnet, the seam guide can be adjusted to the exact seam width. The cut edges of the fabric move along the guide as they are being stitched.

Selvages—The two woven lengthwise edges along a piece of woven fabric.

Stiffening—A firm woven or nonwoven fabric used under the main fabric for body, shaping, or support, as in a drapery heading.

Swag—A section of draped fabric above a window; it can be used alone or combined with shades, curtains, or draperies. Also, it can be mounted on a valance board or draped over a rod.

Tailor's chalk—A special chalk used to mark temporary lines on fabric; marks rub off easily.

Tension—The amount of resistance placed against the thread on a sewing machine. When needle and bobbin tension are the same, the two threads are drawn into the fabric to the same degree; this results in a balanced stitch.

Toggle bolt—A special bolt used in hollow wall construction for mounting hardware on the wall.

Tufting—In quilting, taking small hand stitches through all layers and tying the ends to form small bows or tufts on the quilt top.

Valance—A decorative piece of fabric used to conceal curtain rods and fixtures.

Velcro—A nylon hook-and-loop closure tape; the two sides adhere to each other when they are pressed together.

Welting—Cord covered with a bias strip of fabric and inserted into the seams of slipcovers, cushions, pillows, and bedspreads.

Index

A-B

Acetate 12
Acrylic 12
Analogous colors 10
Anchor screw 32
Antique satin 15, 76
Applique 108-109, 202
    hand 108
    machine 108-109
Appliqued quilts 108, 180
Austrian shades 29, 31, 60, 202
    how to make 60-63
Awning canopy 186-187
Backstitch 22, 202
Baste 202
Basting stitch
    even 22
    machine 23
    slip basting 24
Bath and Closet Accessories
    164-173
Bathroom accessories 164-169
    bathroom rugs 169
    shower curtains 13, 165,
        166-168
    toilet tank and seat covers
        165, 168-169
    towel trimmings 169
Bathroom rugs 169
Batiste 82
Bed linens 75, 100-101
    fitted bed linens 100-101
    pillow cases 100
    sheet trimming 100
Bedspreads 12, 13, 14,
    74-93, 175
    basic styles 76
    box spread 75, 78, 79-80
        how to make 79-80
    coverlet 75, 76, 90-91,
        118-119, 202
    dust ruffle 12, 75, 76, 77,
        92-93, 175, 186, 202
    fitted 75, 76, 78-82
        with gathered flounce 80
        with pleated flounce 82

Bedspreads (cont'd.)
    fitted studio couch cover
        84-86
    how to measure for 77
    lining 76, 81, 82
    lining fabrics 82
    personalizing ready-mades
        176-178
    quilted 177-178
    separate pillow covers 83
    throw 76, 86-89
Bedspreads, Canopies, and
    Bed Linens 74-101
Bias 202
    binding 24, 25, 202
    continuous bias 25
    covered cording 25
    strips 24
    true bias 20, 24, 202
Binder foot, machine 19
Binding 202
    bias 24, 25
Blanket stitch 108
Bolsters 15, 83, 123, 124,
    130-131, 202
Boxing strip 202
Box pleat 52, 53, 202
Braid 202
Broadcloth 78
Brocade 14
Bunk beds 175, 187
Burlap 14
Butterfly chair 193, 194
Button tufting 133

C

Cafe curtains 29, 31, 36,
    38-43, 59, 186, 187
    plain 40
    pleated 41
    rings 38
    rods 32
    scalloped 42
Calico 14
Campstools 195
Canopy 13, 75,
    94-99, 202
    arched 96
    awning 186-187

Canopy (cont'd.)
    crib 179
    flat 96-98
    partial 98-99
    rods for 32
Card table covers 160
Carpenter's ruler 18
Cartridge pleats 52, 54, 202
Casement cloth 14
Casing 202
Casual chairs 194-196
Catch stitch 22
Chair cushions 123, 132, 186
Chalk pencil 18, 202
Children's Rooms 174-191
Chintz 14, 20, 76, 82, 84
Circle chairs 193, 194
Clip 202
Closet accessories 165,
    170-173
    covered boxes 170
    garment bags 165, 172
    padded hangers 170
    shoe bag 165, 173
    shoulder covers 165, 170
Color 8-11, 12, 34
    neutral 8, 10
    primary 8, 10
    secondary 8
    terminology 8
    tertiary 8
    vocabulary 9
    wheel 9, 10, 11
Colors and Fabrics 6-15
Color scheme 9-10
    analogous 10
    complementary 10
    monochromatic 10
    planning 10
    triad 10
Comforters 13, 112
    reversible 179
    slumber bag 184
Complementary colors 10
Continuous bias 25
Contour rug 165, 169
Cording 202 (see also welting)
    bias-covered 25
    curved seams 25
    foot 19, 25, 202

206

T-Z

Acknowledgments

*We are happy to acknowledge
our indebtedness and to express
our sincere thanks to the follow-
ing who have been helpful to us
in producing this book:*
Arabesque, Div. of Burwood
Products Co.
Belding Corticelli
Kenneth A. Byrnes
Jan DeBard
The Jack Denst Designs, Inc.
Fieldcrest
C. M. Offray & Son, Inc.
Rug Corporation of America
Sears Roebuck and Co.
Window Shade
Manufacturers Assn.